Experiments and Simulations of Superalloys

Experiments and Simulations of Superalloys

Guest Editors

Ronghai Wu
Xiaoxiang Wu

MDPI

Basel • Beijing • Wuhan • Barcelona • Belgrade • Novi Sad • Cluj • Manchester

Guest Editors
Ronghai Wu
School of Materials Science and Engineering
Northwestern Polytechnical University
Xi'an
China

Xiaoxiang Wu
School of Iron and Steel
Soochow University
Suzhou
China

Editorial Office
MDPI AG
Grosspeteranlage 5
4052 Basel, Switzerland

This is a reprint of the Special Issue, published open access by the journal *Crystals* (ISSN 2073-4352), freely accessible at: https://www.mdpi.com/journal/crystals/special_issues/advances_superalloys.

For citation purposes, cite each article independently as indicated on the article page online and as indicated below:

Lastname, A.A.; Lastname, B.B. Article Title. *Journal Name* **Year**, *Volume Number*, Page Range.

ISBN 978-3-7258-5207-9 (Hbk)
ISBN 978-3-7258-5208-6 (PDF)
https://doi.org/10.3390/books978-3-7258-5208-6

Contents

About the Editors

Ronghai Wu

Ronghai Wu is a professor at the School of Materials Science and Engineering, Northwestern Polytechnical University, Xi'an, China. His research focuses on advanced metallic materials, including superalloys, high-temperature deformation, and creep-fatigue behavior. He has published extensively in these areas and leads several national-level research projects related to high-performance alloys.

Xiaoxiang Wu

Xiaoxiang Wu is a professor at the School of Iron and Steel, Soochow University, China. Her research focuses on nickel-based single-crystal superalloys, especially on the effects of alloying elements and defect behavior on high-temperature mechanical properties. She has made important contributions to understanding rhenium segregation during creep and the role of dislocation–γ' interactions. Her work provides valuable insights into alloy design and microstructural control for advanced superalloys.

Preface

As Guest Editors, we are pleased to present this Special Issue of *Crystals*, titled "Advances in Superalloys", which compiles recent development in the study of nickel-based superalloys, a class of materials critical for high-temperature structural applications.

The articles included in this collection span a wide range of topics—from microstructural control to mechanical property optimization. Notably, several contributions delve into the solidification behavior and post-treatment microstructures of directionally solidified and single-crystal alloys, such as CM247LC and fourth-generation superalloys. These studies shed light on phase morphology, γ' precipitation, carbide evolution, and how these factors govern tensile and creep behavior across temperature regimes.

Particular attention is given to deformation mechanisms under complex loading conditions. Topics include low-cycle fatigue at elevated temperatures, the influence of strain amplitude on dislocation behavior and γ' rafting, as well as the role of stacking faults and dislocation networks in fatigue crack initiation.

Moreover, new insights are provided into the detrimental effects of topologically close-packed (TCP) phases and how alloying strategies can mitigate them. The combination of advanced characterization methods—SEM, TEM, EBSD—and modeling contributes to a better understanding of superalloy design principles.

We extend our sincere gratitude to all authors for their high-quality contributions and to the reviewers for their constructive feedback. We also thank the editorial staff of *Crystals* for their support throughout the publication process.

We hope this collection serves as a valuable reference for both academic researchers and industry professionals engaged in the development and application of advanced superalloys.

Ronghai Wu and Xiaoxiang Wu
Guest Editors

crystals

MDPI

Article

Influence of Strain Amplitude on Low-Cycle Fatigue Behaviors of a Fourth-Generation Ni-Based Single-Crystal Superalloy at 980 °C

Pengfei Wang [1], Xinbao Zhao [1,2,*], Quanzhao Yue [1], Wanshun Xia [1,*], Qingqing Ding [1], Hongbin Bei [1], Yuefeng Gu [1,2,*], Yuefei Zhang [1,2] and Ze Zhang [1,2]

1 Institute of Superalloys Science and Technology, School of Materials Science and Engineering, Zhejiang University, Hangzhou 310027, China

2 State Key Laboratory of Silicon Materials, School of Materials Science and Engineering, Zhejiang University, Hangzhou 310027, China

* Correspondence: superalloys@zju.edu.cn (X.Z.); wanshunxia@zju.edu.cn (W.X.); guyf@zju.edu.cn (Y.G.)

Abstract: Total strain-control, low-cycle fatigue experiments of a fourth-generation Ni-based single-crystal superalloy were performed at 980 °C. Scanning electron microscopy and transmission electron microscopy are employed to determine fracture morphologies and dislocation characteristics of the samples. As the strain amplitude increased from 0.6 to 1.0%, the cyclic stress and plastic strain per cycle increased, the cyclic lifetime decreased, more interfacial dislocation networks were formed, and the formation rate accelerated. Cyclic hardening is associated with the reaction of accumulated dislocations and dislocation networks, which hinder the movement of dislocations. The presence of interfacial dislocations reduces the lattice mismatch between the γ and γ' phases, and the presence of dislocation networks that absorb mobile dislocations results in cyclic softening. At a strain amplitude of 1.0%, the reaction of a high density of dislocations results in initial cyclic hardening, and the dislocation cutting into the γ' phase is one of the reasons for cyclic softening. The crack initiation site changed from a near-surface defect to a surface defect when the strain amplitude increased from 0.6 to 0.8 to 1.0%. The number of secondary cracks initiated from the micropores decreased during the growth stage as the strain amplitude increased.

Keywords: deformation behaviors; low-cycle fatigue; single-crystal superalloys; strain amplitude

1. Introduction

Nickel (Ni)-based single-crystal (SC) superalloys are widely used as high-temperature structural materials in aircraft and advanced gas engines because of their high operating temperatures and excellent mechanical properties [1–3]. The microstructure of SCs comprise two phases: (1) ordered intermetallic γ' phase with an $L1_2$ structure coherently embedded in a disordered solid-solution and (2) γ matrix phase with a face-centered cubic structure. Owing to the reasonable ratio of elements and the heat-treatment process, the γ' phase is composed of cuboidal particles with a volume fraction of up to 70%, and its strength can increase with an increase in temperature, such that the superalloys exhibit excellent mechanical properties and high resistance to fatigue and creep at elevated temperatures [4–6].

Gas turbines operate at high alternating loads for long periods on account of startup and shutdown, resulting in fatigue damage. In recent decades, there has been growing interest in the low-cycle fatigue (LCF) behavior of Ni-based SC superalloys, which has led to extensive research in this area. LCF damage mainly occurs in the lower region of the blade body and blade root, where there is a large stress concentration, with the service temperature ranging from 700 to 1000 °C [7–10]. Due to the complex structure of turbine blades, there are evident strain deformation variances in different areas. Strain amplitude is a crucial factor that dominates the LCF mechanism of a blade. Previous studies have confirmed that with increasing strain amplitude, the responses of cyclic stress, dislocation type, and microscopic deformation behavior change significantly, and the lifetime and design of alloys are affected by the deformation and damage behavior of alloys in different regions [6,11–13]. Cyclic stress responses include cyclic hardening, cyclic softening, and cyclic stabilization, which indicate that, under a constant strain amplitude, the stress amplitude increases, decreases, and basically remains unchanged with an increase in cycles, respectively. Cyclic hardening is mainly related to an increase in dislocation density [14,15], dislocation entanglement [16,17], and the existence of dislocation networks [18] and stacking faults (SFs) [9] reduce the mobility of dislocations in the channels at high temperatures. Cyclic softening is mainly related to the dislocation shearing of γ' phases [18,19], interface mismatch reduction [20], and γ' phase rafting [21,22]. However, dislocation density reduction arises due to dislocation annihilation [18] and dislocation network formation [21] at high temperatures. Cyclic stabilization occurs when the hardening and softening effects are in equilibrium [15,23]. At high-strain amplitudes, cracks mainly originate in the micropores near the surface, whereas, at low-strain amplitudes, oxidation significantly affects crack initiation [24]. Wang [9,12] reported that at a strain amplitude ($\Delta\varepsilon_t/2$) range of 0.5–0.7% at 980 °C, the dislocations are more likely to form dislocation networks at the interface, and, under 1.0% strain, the shearing of the γ' phase by SFs becomes the predominant deformation mechanism. Rafting of the γ' phase occurs under a low-strain amplitude at high temperatures, with dislocation networks tending to be generated at the rafting interface [25]. Previous research [26] has indicated that dislocation climbing is the basic condition for the formation of dislocation networks and is faster under a high-strain amplitude [11], demonstrating that a high-strain amplitude is likely to be more conducive to the formation of dislocation networks. Studies on LCF have primarily focused on first- to third-generation single crystals, with fourth-generation single crystals barely studied, especially the effects of strain amplitude on the cyclic stress response and microstructures at high temperatures.

The addition of rhenium (Re) and ruthenium (Ru) to fourth-generation single-crystal superalloys affects the generation of interface dislocation networks, rafting of the γ' phase, and dislocation shearing of the γ' phase [27–30], which influences the cyclic stress response and fatigue deformation. In this study, a set of LCF tests were performed at 980 °C on a fourth-generation single-crystal superalloy under varying strain amplitudes to understand the effects of strain amplitude on cyclic stress response and deformation mechanisms.

2. Materials and Methods

The material used in this study was a test bar made of a fourth-generation Ni-based monocrystalline superalloy. Its chemical composition is summarized in Table 1.

Table 1. Nominal composition of experimental alloy (wt.%).

Al + Ta	Co + Cr	Mo + W	Re + Ru	Ni
12%	8%	9%	7.5%	Bal.%

The crystal orientations of the cast rods were determined through X-ray diffraction. The loading direction was designed to be parallel to the [001] crystal orientation of the alloy with an angle orientation deviation within 10°. Conventional three-step heat procedures were performed to process the casting material, including a high-temperature solid solution treatment (1340 °C), followed by a two-stage ageing treatment at relatively low temperatures in argon and vacuum (1100 and 870 °C, respectively). Air cooling was performed after each heat treatment. LCF specimens (76 mm in length and 5.5 mm in gauge diameter) were machined and polished from fully heat-treated SC bars.

All LCF tests were conducted using an MTS servo machine (MTS-100kN-10, MTS, Eden Prairie, MN, USA) in the air at 980 °C under fully reversed ($R = -1$) total strain control. The strain amplitudes were 0.6, 0.8, and 1.0%, and a triangular waveform with a constant strain rate of 5×10^{-3} s^{-1} was used. After the fatigue tests, the surface morphologies, crack initiation, and crack propagation of the specimens were observed using a scanning electron microscope (SEM, FEI Quanta 650, FEI, Portland, OR, USA). The chemical compositions of the oxides were determined through energy-dispersive X-ray spectroscopy (EDS, Oxford, UK) under SEM. Microstructural observations of the specimens after fracturing were performed using a transmission electron microscope (TEM; FEI Tecnai F20 S-TWIN, FEI, Portland, OR, USA) operating at 200 kV. The TEM observations were performed on thin {001} foils.

To better observe the morphology of the dislocation, the transmitted sample was cut at the working section 5 mm away from the fracture (perpendicular to the axial), with the thickness of the slice approximately 550 μm. Thereafter, manual grinding was performed below 50 μm and pressed into thin foils of 3 mm in diameter. The thin foils were prepared through double-jet thinning in Tenupol 5 (Struers, Denmark) at 15 V and −30 °C. The electrolyte comprised 70, 23, and 7% vol of methanol, n-butanol, and perchloric acid, respectively. Meanwhile, the evolution of γ and γ' morphologies in the longitudinal sections of 3 mm from the fracture surface was observed via SEM. The sample was mechanically polished and chemically etched in a solution composed of 10 mL HF + 20 mL HNO_3 + 30 mL $C_3H_8O_3$.

3. Results

3.1. Cyclic Stress Response

Figure 1 illustrates the cyclic stress response curves of the alloys tested at 980 °C under different strain amplitudes. As the strain amplitude increased, the cyclic stress of the alloy also increased; hence, the fatigue lifetime gradually decreased. The cyclic stress response also indicates the cyclic hardening/softening of the alloy associated with the structural changes occurring during fatigue. Cyclic hardening/softening curves were constructed by plotting the stress amplitude ($\Delta\sigma_t/2$) vs. the logarithm of the number of cycles to failure (N). For $\Delta\varepsilon_t/2$ values of 0.6 and 0.8%, the alloys exhibited fairly constant stress amplitudes from the beginning of the tests. Thereafter, they exhibited cyclic stability for approximately a few hundred cycles, followed by gradual softening. Finally, near the end of the test, the stress decreased rapidly, resulting in the onset and rapid propagation of fatigue cracks. With an increase of $\Delta\varepsilon_t/2$ to 1.0%, the alloy initially exhibited fast cyclic hardening, followed by cyclic stability. Subsequently, gradual softening and stress reduction occurred, similar to the $\Delta\varepsilon_t/2$ values of 0.6 and 0.8%, respectively.

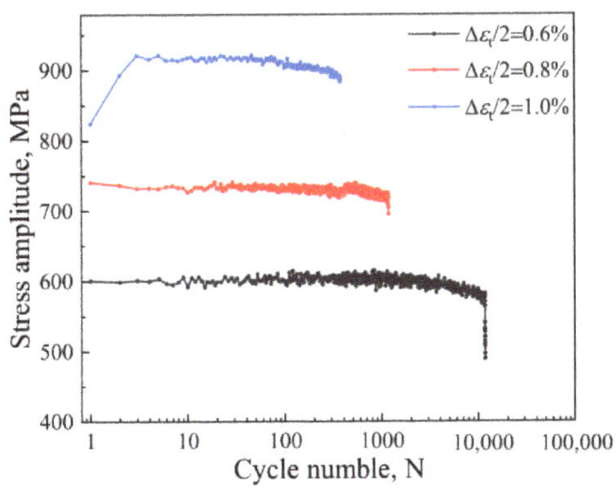

Figure 1. Cyclic stress response curves of experimental alloys at varying strain amplitudes during low-cycle fatigue deformation.

The hysteresis loops at $\Delta\varepsilon_t/2$ values ranging from 0.6 to 1.0% in the first and second half-life cycles are shown in Figure 2a,b, respectively. The central area of the hysteresis loop is wrapped by a yellow curve, as shown in the lower right part of Figure 2. The area of the hysteresis loops indicates the plastic strain energy, and the plastic strain range is characterized by the width of the hysteresis loop [31] when the stress is 0 MPa. The size of the width demonstrates the ability of the alloy to resist plastic deformation during the cyclic fatigue test; the larger the width, the smaller the ability of the alloy to resist plastic deformation [32]. In the first cycle, the obtained plastic strain ranges were 0.016, 0.019, and 0.277% when $\Delta\varepsilon_t/2$ values were 0.6, 0.8, and 1.0%, respectively; in the half-life cycle, the obtained results were 0.006, 0.012, and 0.073%, respectively. Cyclic deformations at half-life are generally considered stable. With the stability of the cyclic deformation, the value decreased, particularly under a strain amplitude of 1.0%. At $\Delta\varepsilon_t/2$ = 0.6%, the plastic strain was negligible. When the strain amplitude increased to 0.8%, the plastic strain increased slightly. Thus, it was demonstrated that, as the strain amplitude increased to 1.0%, the plastic strain increased significantly.

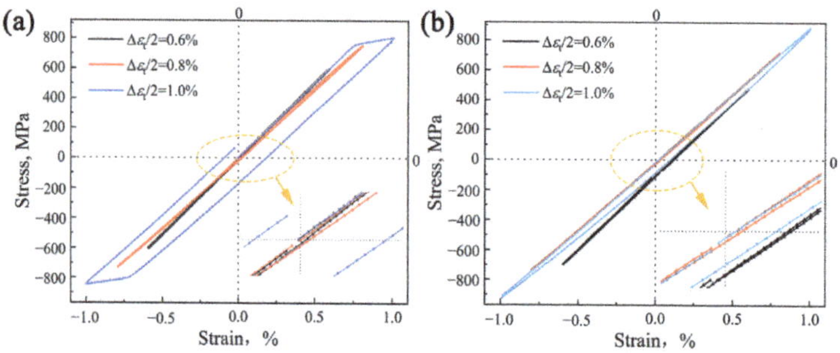

Figure 2. Typical hysteresis loops of the alloy under varying strain amplitudes: (**a**) first cycle and (**b**) stabilized cycle.

3.2. Fatigue Fractography and Fracture Mechanism

As shown in Figure 3, the cracks initiated from or near the surfaces of the specimens, thereafter propagating along the {001} planes; that is, they are perpendicular to the applied stress. The direction of the crack propagation is indicated by the blue arrow. The mechanism of crack initiation and growth results from local stress concentrations in the midplane of the micropore–alloy interfaces, resulting in a circular crack with a relatively featureless surface [24]. When cracking reaches a certain depth, crack propagation translates to the shear mode; that is, it occurs on different {111} planes [20]. Under a strain amplitude of 0.6%, the crack initiated on the surface in a circular morphology with a halo (white arrow) and bright color, as shown in Figure 3a,d. The existence of the halo is linked to the homogenization of slip at high temperatures in the presence of oxidation [33,34]; the oxidation is more pronounced in the bright-colored areas. After crack initiation, the crack propagated along the plane perpendicular to the stress axis, with the propagation speed being low because of the less effective crack growth driver at a lower cyclic amplitude [19]. The stress concentration generated at the defect also formed several secondary cracks (yellow arrows), with a bright halo formed around the pores. As the strain amplitude increased to 0.8%, cracks started to form at the surface defect and exhibited distinct bright regions associated with oxidation, as shown in Figure 3b,e. When the crack propagated in a plane perpendicular to the stress axis, it also produced secondary microcracks with circular halos; however, the number of microcracks were significantly reduced than at the 0.6% strain amplitude. When the strain amplitude was increased to 1.0%, cracks started to form at the surface defect with no evident oxidation trace, and no secondary microcracks with a halo were observed during the crack growth stage, as shown in Figure 3c,f. The oxidation layers formed on the sample surface at strain amplitudes of 0.6, 0.8, and 1.0% are shown in Figure 3g–i, respectively. The oxide layer represented by the dashed box became thinner with increasing strain amplitude, illustrating a decrease in alloy oxidation. The cracks initiated from the oxide layer of the specimen were observed to propagate predominantly perpendicular to the loading axis, similar to the cracks initiated from the subsurface.

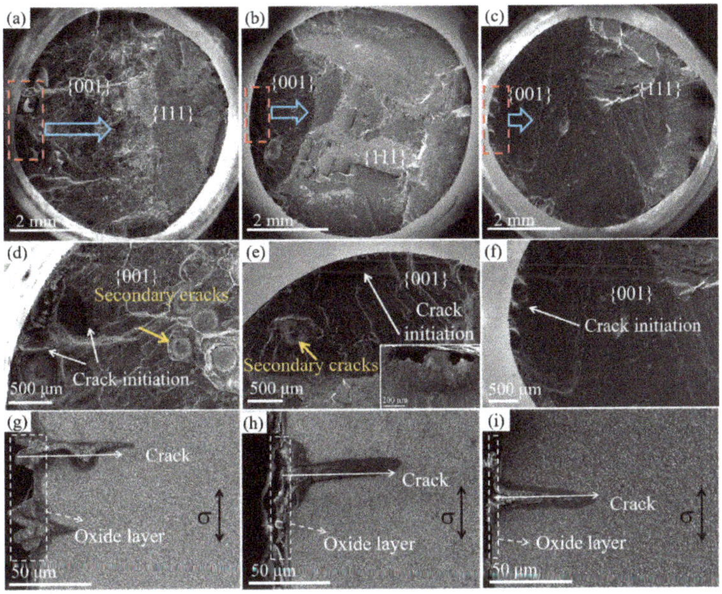

Figure 3. Surface morphologies and oxide layer near the surface of specimens after failure: (**a**,**d**,**g**); $\Delta\varepsilon_t/2 = 0.6\%$, (**b**,**e**,**h**); $\Delta\varepsilon_t/2 = 0.8\%$, and (**c**,**f**,**i**); $\Delta\varepsilon_t/2 = 1.0\%$.

The effect of the strain amplitude on crack initiation and propagation is related to oxidation. At high-strain amplitudes, it is easy to rapidly generate stress concentrations at the surface notches owing to the large cyclic loads, which can initiate cracks. However, at low-strain amplitudes, the cyclic load is small, and it is difficult to rapidly generate stress concentrations that reach the threshold. As time increased, high-temperature oxidation occurred. During the load cycle, the strain mismatch between the plastically deformed metal substrate, and the stiff oxide scale caused repeated cracking and reoxidation, resulting in an oxide plug. The oxide plugs fill the micropores, and the surface micropores (caused by insufficient liquid flow during casting) are passivated after oxidation [34]. This reduced the effective stress concentration of the surface shrinkage cavity by generating a compressive stress in/around the hole. Therefore, the stress concentration at the internal defects reached the threshold faster than that at the surface, and cracks were less likely to be initiated at the surface at low-strain amplitudes.

However, crack propagation along the micropores is an efficient approach for lowering the crack propagation threshold. Micropores can also change the crack direction by modifying the stress intensity factor at the crack tip to form secondary cracks [35]. The crack propagation path is indicated by blue arrows in Figure 4. When the primary crack reaches the micropores, a secondary crack forms, and the direction of the crack propagation changes. Crack propagation occurs at a slow rate under a low-strain amplitude, and the embrittlement effect of oxidation promotes crack propagation due to the sufficient transmission of oxygen (O) along the crack [19]. Consequently, at low-strain amplitudes, more secondary cracks with distinct oxidation signatures appeared during the slow crack propagation stage. The chemical composition of the halo surrounding the micropores was analyzed using EDS, as shown in Figure 4. The analysis demonstrated that the oxide was enriched with Ni, aluminum (Al), tantalum (Ta), Re, molybdenum (Mo), chromium (Cr), and Ru, whereas a decrease in the cobalt (Co) content was observed. One explanation for this phenomenon is that O is transferred during crack propagation, and the partial pressure of O at the crack tip is low, at which point Co is difficult to oxidize [36]. Therefore, the initiation and propagation of secondary cracks are influenced by the oxide composition, particularly at low-strain amplitudes where the oxidation time is longer.

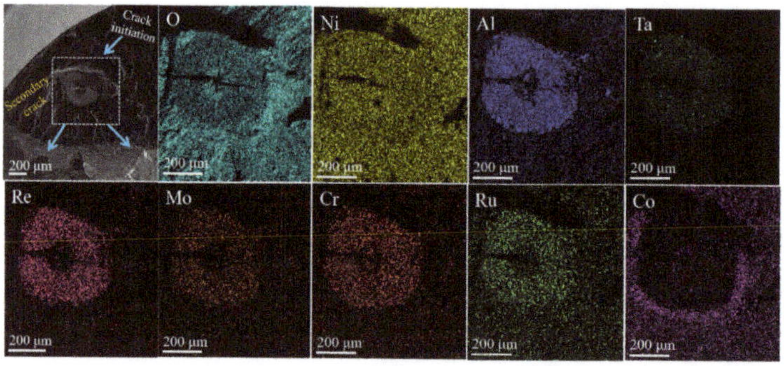

Figure 4. Scanning electron microscope (SEM) energy-dispersive X-ray spectroscopy (EDS),(SEM-EDS), maps of the micropores after fatigue at 980 °C under $\Delta\varepsilon_t/2$ = 0.8%.

A previous study [37] reported that, at 980 °C and low-strain amplitude, the crack initiation occurred from the stripping of the oxide layer on the surface, which is in agreement with the results obtained in another study [38] but different from the results obtained in this study. At similar loading times, the oxide layer thickness and crack length were higher than those obtained in this study, indicating that the alloy was less resistant to oxidation, and cracks were initiated earlier. This may be the main reason for the crack initiation from the oxide layer on the surface at high temperatures and low-strain amplitudes.

3.3. Dislocation Movement and Deformation Mechanisms

Figure 5 illustrates the γ' morphology away from the fracture surface under different strain amplitudes at 980 °C. As shown in Figure 5a, when the strain amplitude is 0.6%, a slight decrease in the degree of γ' cubic was observed. When the strain amplitude is 0.8%, more γ' cubic degree decreased, as shown in Figure 5b. When the strain amplitude was 1.0%, the γ' cubic degree exhibited no evident changes, as shown in Figure 5c. The widths of the transverse channels broadened after fatigue, as shown in Figure 5d. Width broadening was most pronounced at a strain amplitude of 0.8%, followed by 0.6%; however, it was not significant at a strain amplitude of 1.0%.

Microstructural configurations of a fatigued alloy after an LCF test at 980 °C under the strain amplitude of 0.6% were performed, as shown in Figure 6. Figure 6a shows that almost all the dislocations distribute in the γ matrix channels, and a small amount of dislocation networks are generated at the γ/γ' interface. The rafting of the γ' phase is not evident. As shown in Figure 6b, the dislocations bow out through the γ matrix channel, promoting the dislocation slips to the γ/γ' interface. Dislocations piled-up at the γ/γ' interface form a large number of dislocation entanglements. Figure 6c shows that, under cyclic deformation, the dislocation networks are considered to be produced by the reaction of two sets of parallel cross-slip dislocations arising from the misfit interface between the γ matrix and γ' phase [14].

When the strain amplitude increases to 0.8% at 980 °C, typical dislocation configurations and different deformation microstructures are observed, as shown in Figure 7. At this condition, the corners of the cubic γ' phase are appreciably degenerated, and the corresponding width of matrix channels is increased at some deformed regions. Most dislocations distribute along the γ/γ' interfaces and form several dense and regular dislocation networks at the interfaces of the deformed regions (Figure 7a). In comparison with microstructures observed under the strain amplitude of 0.6% (Figure 6), more dislocation networks are observed at the γ/γ' interfaces. Although the cyclic stress increased, almost no dislocations cut into the γ' phases, indicating that dislocation networks have a significant influence on hindering matrix dislocations from cutting into the γ' phases [39,40]. As shown in Figure 7b, bowing and cross-slipping of dislocations in the γ matrix channels piled up at the γ/γ' interfaces, resulting in the generation of dislocation networks rather than dislocation entanglements in the reaction. More small-scale dislocation networks were formed at the interfaces, which were related to greater cyclic stress (Figure 7c).

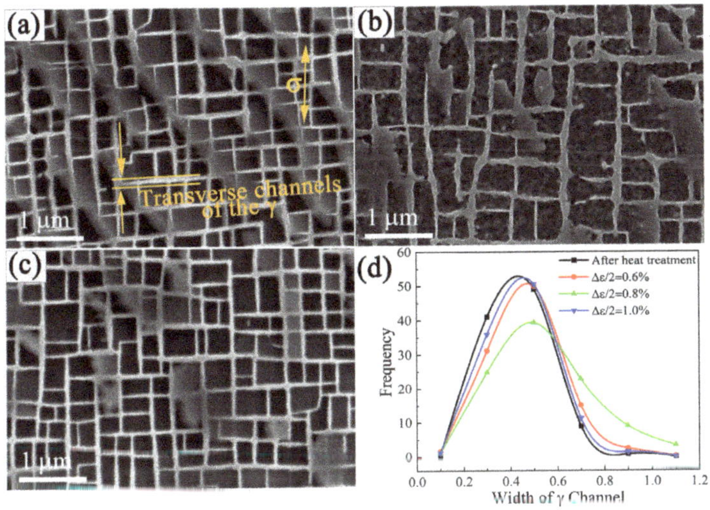

Figure 5. Microstructures of the longitudinal profile: (**a**) $\Delta\varepsilon_t/2$ = 0.6%, (**b**) $\Delta\varepsilon_t/2$ = 0.8%, and (**c**) $\Delta\varepsilon_t/2$ = 1.0%. (**d**) Width of the transverse channels of the γ phase.

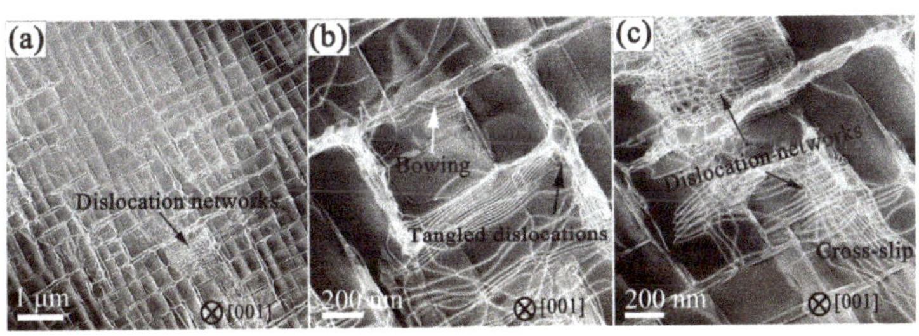

Figure 6. Transmission electron microscope (TEM) bright field (BF) images showing dislocation configurations of an alloy at 980 °C under $\Delta\varepsilon_t/2$ = 0.6%: (**a**) distribution of the dislocations; (**b**) bowing and tangled dislocations; and (**c**) formation of dislocation networks.

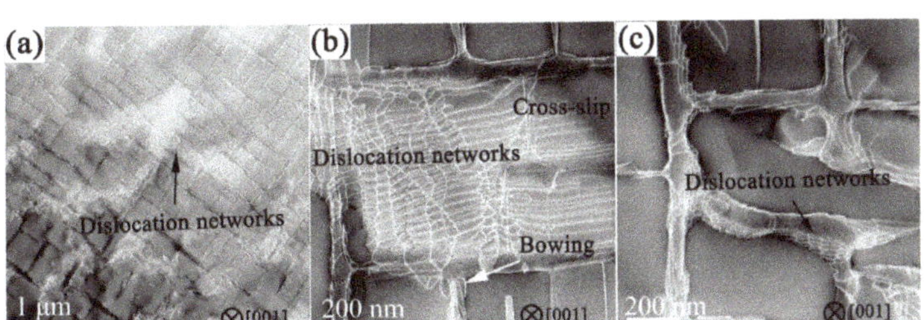

Figure 7. TEM-BF images showing dislocation configurations of an alloy at 980 °C under $\Delta\varepsilon_t/2$ = 0.8%: (**a**) distribution of the dislocations; (**b**) dislocation networks and bowing dislocations; and (**c**) formation of dislocation networks.

Figure 8 shows the typical dislocation configurations of an alloy after a test at 980 °C under a strain amplitude of 1.0%. A large number of regular dislocation networks are observed at the γ/γ' interfaces, which are formed by depositing matrix dislocations, as shown in Figure 8a,b. In addition, a small amount of dislocation shearing into the γ' phases was observed, owing to the accumulation of plastic deformation under high stress, as shown in Figure 8c, which is attributed to the cyclic softening [18,20]. These dislocations are of two main types under the conditions of high-temperature and high-strain amplitude: (1) the γ' phases are sheared by the matrix dislocations, resulting in SF formation within them [9,13,41,42]; (2) the γ' phases are sheared by the superdislocation, which decomposes to form two partial dislocations and superlattice intrinsic SFs [9,12,27,42,43]. The dislocations in the γ' phases exhibit no characteristics of SFs in the samples; thus, it is likely to be a superdislocation.

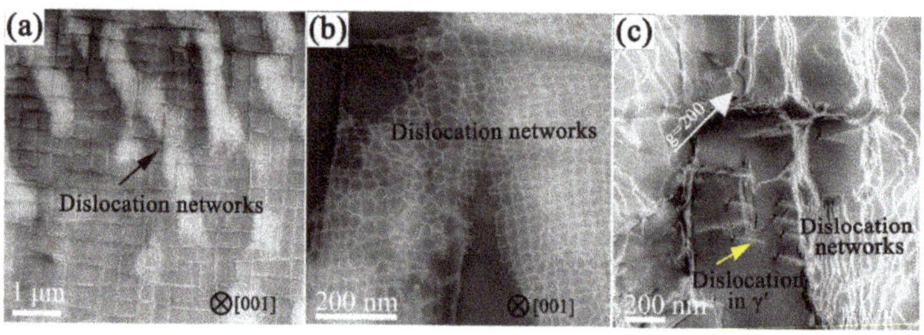

Figure 8. TEM-BF images showing dislocation configurations of an alloy at 980 °C under $\Delta\varepsilon_t/2$ = 1.0%: (**a**) distribution of the dislocations; (**b**) formation of dislocation networks; and (**c**) dislocation in the γ' phase.

Therefore, for the LCF test at 980 °C under a strain of 1.0%, cross-slip and climbing of dislocations are the main forms of deformation, and the shearing of γ' phases by superdislocation also begin to increase.

As shown in Figure 9, there are two main types of dislocation networks at 980 °C: (1) arrangement of transitional dislocation network dominated by slip dislocations (blue segments); and (2) equilibrium dislocation network including hexagonal and rhombic arrangements (red line segment). Transition dislocation networks, which tend to be slightly bowed, consist mostly of slip dislocations and exhibit a relatively irregular arrangement. This transitional arrangement can develop into equilibrium arrangements with hexagonal, rhombic, or octagonal structures [44]. As the strain amplitude increases, the morphology of the interface dislocation network changes.

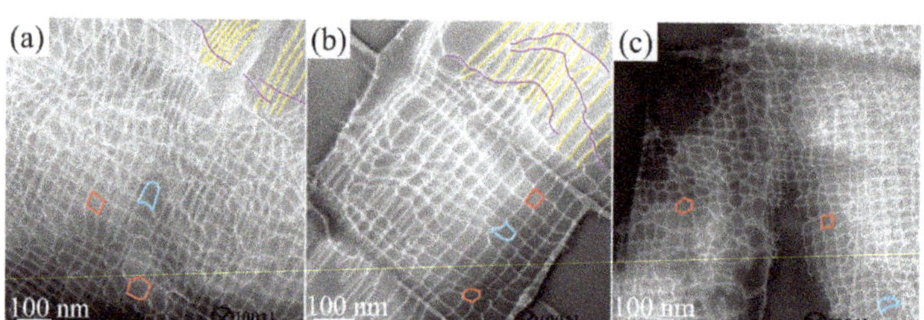

Figure 9. Dislocation networks under different strain amplitudes of an alloy at 980 °C: (**a**) $\Delta\varepsilon_t/2$ = 0.6%, (**b**) $\Delta\varepsilon_t/2$ = 0.8%, and (**c**) $\Delta\varepsilon_t/2$ = 1.0%.

As shown in Figure 9a, under a strain amplitude of 0.6%, two sets of slip dislocations in the upper right corner (yellow and purple lines) and few equilibrium dislocation networks are observed. When the strain amplitude increases to 0.8% (Figure 9b), two sets of slip dislocations intersect. Combined with the analysis illustrated in Figures 6 and 7, we established that the formation of dislocation networks at a strain amplitude of 0.8% may be faster than that at 0.6%, for which the fraction of equilibrium dislocation networks increases significantly. As shown in Figure 9c, when the strain amplitude increased to 1.0%, the fraction of equilibrium dislocation networks further increased, and the slip traces that formed the dislocation networks disappeared. The influence of the strain amplitude on the formation process of the dislocation network may be due to the following two reasons: (1) under a high-strain amplitude, more dislocations accumulate at the interface, which is conducive to the rapid formation of the dislocation network; (2) and under a high-strain amplitude, the dislocation climbs faster, promoting the rapid movement of the dislocation toward the interface.

3.4. Cyclic Hardening/Softening

Owing to the high temperatures, the strength of the γ' phase is relatively high, cyclic deformation is mainly concentrated in the γ matrix channels, and dislocations can move along the {111} planes by bowing out through the γ matrix channels. It is difficult for dislocations to enter the γ' phases and pile up at the γ/γ' interface, which will cause cyclic hardening owing to the interaction of dislocations and the γ' phases [45]. Meanwhile, the appearance of interfacial dislocations reduces the lattice mismatch between the γ' and γ phases, and annihilation occurs when dislocations of opposite signs meet, resulting in a softening effect [46,47]. The formation of dislocation networks through dislocation reactions is an important deformation mechanism at high temperatures. In contrast, the existence of a dislocation network hinders the movement of dislocations and prevent dislocations from cutting into the γ' phase, resulting in the hardening effect [18,41]. However, the dislocation network can absorb the moving dislocations in the γ matrix channels, resulting in a decrease in the dislocation density and cyclic softening [48]. When the dislocation cuts into the γ' phase, resistance to the dislocation movement is reduced, similar to the density of the dislocation that accumulates at the interface, resulting in a softening effect [18]. Remarkably, cyclic stability occurred when cyclic hardening was balanced with cyclic softening.

The cyclic stress response changed from cyclic stability to cyclic hardening when the strain amplitude increased from 0.6 to 0.8 to 1.0% during the initial fatigue stage, as shown in Figure 1. In addition, the area of the hysteresis loop is large under a strain amplitude of 1.0% at the initial stage of fatigue, resulting in significant plastic strain, indicating that the high density of dislocations accumulated and multiplied more than annihilation to adapt to the generation of plastic strain under high-strain amplitude, as illustrated in Figure 2a. As a result, initial cyclic hardening occurred under a strain amplitude of 1.0%. The formation of interfacial dislocation networks is a result of the interaction of the piled-up dislocations, as shown in Figures 8 and 9c. For the samples with strain amplitudes of 0.6 and 0.8%, the area of the hysteresis loop (as shown in Figure 2a,b) is small, illustrating that the dislocation density is low [49]. Therefore, equilibrium between dislocation multiplication and annihilation is easy to achieve, and cyclic stability occurs.

With the increase in the number of cycles, more dislocations are absorbed in the dislocation network, resulting in a decrease in the dislocation density [21]. Thereafter, the formation of interface dislocation networks results in cyclic softening. Under the strain amplitudes of 0.6 and 0.8%, the matrix channel becomes wider, and γ' cubic degree decreases with increasing cycles, as shown in Figure 5, which can reduce the resistance of dislocation movement in the γ channels and result in cyclic softening. At a strain amplitude of 1.0%, dislocations cutting into the γ' phases also contributed to cyclic softening, as shown in Figure 8c.

4. Conclusions

The LCF behaviors of SC superalloys with an [001] orientation at 980 °C under varying strain amplitudes are systematically investigated using SEM and TEM, and variations in their fracture and deformation mechanisms are proposed. In addition, the effects of strain amplitude on the LCF behavior at 980 °C are analyzed in detail. The main conclusions are as follows:

(1) As the strain amplitude increased from 0.6 to 1.0%, the cyclic stress and plastic strain per cycle increased, whereas the cyclic lifetime decreased. Cyclic hardening is associated with the reaction of accumulated dislocations and dislocation networks, which hinder the movement of dislocations. At a strain amplitude of 1.0%, the high densities of dislocations and dislocation reactions resulted in an initial cyclic hardening.

(2) As the strain amplitude increased from 0.6 to 1.0%, more dislocation networks were formed, and the formation rate accelerated. The appearance of interfacial dislocations reduced the lattice mismatch between the γ and γ' phases, and the presence of dislocation networks that absorb mobile dislocations resulted in cyclic softening. The dislocation cutting into the γ' phases is one of the reasons for cyclic softening at a strain amplitude of 1.0%.

(3) The decrease of the γ' cubic degree and the width variation of the matrix channel was pronounced for a strain amplitude of 0.8%. The crack initiation site changed from a near-surface defect to a surface defect when the strain amplitude increased from 0.6 to 0.8 to 1.0%. The number of secondary cracks that were initiated from the micropores during the growth stage decreased as the strain amplitude increased.

Author Contributions: Conceptualization, P.W. and X.Z.; formal analysis, P.W.; investigation, P.W.; data curation, P.W.; writing—original draft, P.W.; writing—review and editing, P.W., X.Z., Q.Y., W.X. and Y.G.; visualization, P.W., W.X. and Y.G.; resources, X.Z.; project administration, Q.D., H.B. and Y.Z.; supervision, Z.Z. All authors have read and agreed to the published version of the manuscript.

Funding: This work was jointly supported by the National Natural Science Foundation of China (91960201 and 52101155), the National Science and Technology Major Project of China (J2019-III-0008-0051), the Key Basic Research Program of Zhejiang Province (2020C01002), the Zhejiang Provincial Natural Science Foundation of China (LR22E010003), and the Fundamental Research Funds for central Universities (226-2022-00050). Thanks to the support of equipment and guidance of experiments of researchers in the Centre of Electron of Microscopy of Zhejiang University.

Data Availability Statement: Not applicable.

Conflicts of Interest: The authors declare that they have no known competing financial interest or personal relationships that could have appeared to influence the work reported in this paper.

References

1. James, C.W.; Edgar., A.S. Progress in structural materials for aerospace systems. *Acta Mater.* **2003**, *51*, 5775–5799. [CrossRef]
2. Cui, L.; Yu, J. The creep deformation mechanisms of a newly designed nickel-base superalloy. *Mater. Sci. Eng. A* **2018**, *710*, 309–317. [CrossRef]
3. Xiong, W.J.; Ai, X.; Wang, J.F. Study of the Creep Behavior of Nickel-Based Single Crystal Superalloy Micro Specimens with Dimensional Effects. *Crystals* **2022**, *12*, 592. [CrossRef]
4. Rouault, H.; Dupeux, M.; Ignat, M. High temperature tensile creep of CMSX-2 Nickel base superalloy single crystals. *Acta Metall. Mater.* **1994**, *42*, 3137–3148. [CrossRef]
5. Ma, X.; Jiang, J.; Zhang, W. Effect of Local Recrystallized Grains on the Low Cycle Fatigue Behavior of a Nickel-Based Single Crystal Superalloy. *Crystals* **2019**, *9*, 312. [CrossRef]
6. Reed, R.C. *The Superalloys: Fundamentals and Applications*, 1st ed.; Cambridge University Press: Cambridge, UK, 2006. [CrossRef]
7. Liu, L.; Meng, J.; Liu, J. Investigation on low cycle fatigue behaviors of the (001) and (011) oriental single crystal superalloy at 760 °C. *Mater. Sci. Eng. A* **2018**, *734*, 1–6. [CrossRef]
8. Jiang, R.; Bull, D.; Evangelou, A. Strain accumulation and fatigue crack initiation at pores and carbides in a SX superalloy at room temperature. *Int. J. Fatigue* **2018**, *114*, 22–33. [CrossRef]
9. Wang, X.G.; Liu, J.L.; Jin, T. Deformation mechanisms of a nickel-based single-crystal superalloy during low-cycle fatigue at different temperatures. *Scr. Mater.* **2015**, *99*, 57–60. [CrossRef]
10. Carter, T.J. Common failures in gas turbine blades. *Eng. Fail. Anal.* **2005**, *12*, 237–247. [CrossRef]
11. Brien, V.; Decamps, B. Low cycle fatigue of a nickel-based superalloy at high temperature: Deformation microstructures. *Mater. Sci. Eng. A* **2001**, *316*, 18–31. [CrossRef]

12. Wang, B.Z.; Liu, D.S.; Wen, Z.X. Tension/compression asymmetry of single-crystal nickel-based superalloy DD6 during low cycle fatigue. *Mater. Sci. Eng. A* **2014**, *593*, 31–37. [CrossRef]
13. Auerswald, J.; Mukherji, D.; Chen, W. Deformation behaviour of the single crystal superalloy SC16 under low cycle fatigue loading. *Z. Metallkd.* **1997**, *88*, 652–658. [CrossRef]
14. Zhang, J.H.; Hu, Z.Q.; Xu, Y.B. Dislocation structure in a single-crystal nickel-base superalloy during low cycle fatigue. *Metall. Mater. Trans. A* **1992**, *23*, 1253–1258. [CrossRef]
15. Huang, E.W.; Barabash, R.I.; Wang, Y.D. Plastic behavior of a nickel-based alloy under monotonic-tension and low-cycle-fatigue loading. *Int. J. Plast.* **2008**, *24*, 1440–1456. [CrossRef]
16. Gabb, T.P.; Welsch, G.; Miner, R.V. The characteristics of γ' dislocation pairs in a nickel-base superalloy. *Scr. Mater.* **1987**, *21*, 987–992. [CrossRef]
17. Gabb, T.P.; Welsch, G. The cyclic stress-strain behavior of a nickel-base superalloy at 650 °C. *Scr. Mater.* **1986**, *20*, 1049–1054. [CrossRef]
18. Huang, M.; Zhao, L.; Tong, J. Discrete dislocation dynamics modelling of mechanical deformation of nickel-based single crystal superalloys. *Int. J. Plast.* **2012**, *28*, 141–158. [CrossRef]
19. Neu, R.W. Crack paths in single-crystal Ni-base superalloys under isothermal and thermomechanical fatigue. *Int. J. Fatigue* **2019**, *123*, 268–278. [CrossRef]
20. Hong, H.U.; Kang, J.G.; Choi, B.G. A comparative study on thermomechanical and low cycle fatigue failures of a single crystal nickel-based superalloy. *Int. J. Fatigue* **2011**, *33*, 1592–1599. [CrossRef]
21. Gabb, T.P.; Welsch, G. The high temperature deformation in cyclic loading of a single crystal nickel-base superalloy. *Acta Metall.* **1989**, *37*, 2507–2516. [CrossRef]
22. Fan, Y.S.; Yang, X.G.; Shi, D.Q. A quantitative role of rafting on low cycle fatigue behaviour of a directionally solidified Ni-based superalloy through a cross-correlated image processing method. *Int. J. Fatigue* **2020**, *131*, 105305. [CrossRef]
23. Fritzemeier, L.; Tien, J. The cyclic stress-strain behavior of nickel-base superalloys—II. Single crystals. *Acta Metall.* **1988**, *36*, 283–290. [CrossRef]
24. Fleury, E.; Remy, L. Low cycle fatigue damage in nickel-base superalloy single crystals at elevated temperature. *Mater. Sci. Eng. A* **1993**, *167*, 23–30. [CrossRef]
25. Hong, H.U.; Choi, B.G.; Kim, I.S. Characterization of deformation mechanisms during low cycle fatigue of a single crystal nickel-based superalloy. *J. Mater. Sci.* **2011**, *46*, 5245–5525. [CrossRef]
26. Shishvan, S.S.; Mcmeeking, R.M.; Pollock, T.M. Discrete dislocation plasticity analysis of the high-temperature cyclic response of composites. *Mater. Sci. Eng. A* **2018**, *712*, 711–719. [CrossRef]
27. Zhou, H.; Ro, Y.; Haradah, H. Deformation microstructures after low-cycle fatigue in a fourth-generation Ni-base SC superalloy TMS-138. *Mater. Sci. Eng. A* **2004**, *381*, 20–27. [CrossRef]
28. Pyczak, F.; Neumeier, S.; Goeken, M. Influence of lattice misfit on the internal stress and strain states before and after creep investigated in nickel-base superalloys containing rhenium and ruthenium. *Mater. Sci. Eng. A* **2009**, *510*, 295–300. [CrossRef]
29. Warren, P.J.; Cerezo, A.; Smith, G. An atom probe study of the distribution of rhenium in a nickel-based superalloy. *Mater. Sci. Eng. A* **1998**, *250*, 88–92. [CrossRef]
30. Khan, T.; Caron, P. Development of a New Single Crystal Superalloy for Industrial Gas Turbines. *Superalloys* **2000**, 729–734. [CrossRef]
31. Pineau, A.; Antolovich, S. *Intergranular Fatigue*; John Wiley & Sons, Inc.: Hoboken, NJ, USA, 2013. [CrossRef]
32. Cui, L.; Yu, J.; Liu, J. Cyclic stress responses of a newly developed nickel-base superalloy at elevated temperatures. *J. Alloys Compd.* **2019**, *773*, 250–263. [CrossRef]
33. Miller, M.D.; Reed, P.A.S.; Joyce, M.R. Effect of environment on notch fatigue behaviour in CMSX4. *Meter. Sci. Tech.-Lond.* **2007**, *23*, 1439–1445. [CrossRef]
34. Reed, P.A.S. Fatigue crack growth mechanisms in superalloys: Overview. *Mater. Sci. Tech.-Lond.* **2009**, *25*, 258–270. [CrossRef]
35. Liu, L.; Meng, J.; Liu, J.L. Effects of Crystal Orientations on the Low-Cycle Fatigue of a Single-Crystal Nickel-Based Superalloy at 980 °C. *Acta Metall. Sin.* **2019**, *32*, 381–390. [CrossRef]
36. Hardy, M.; Huron, E.; Glatzl, U. Oxide Scale Formation in Novel γ-γ' Cobalt-Based Alloys. *Superalloys* **2016**, 991–999. [CrossRef]
37. Fan, Z.D.; Wang, D.; Lou, L.H. Corporate Effects of Temperature and Strain Range on the Low Cycle Fatigue Life of a Single-Crystal Superalloy DD10. *Acta Metall. Sin.* **2015**, *28*, 152–158. [CrossRef]
38. Guo, Y.Y.; Zhao, Y.S.; Zhang, J. Effect of Strain Amplitude on Cyclic Deformation Behavior of Nickel-Based Single Crystal Superalloy DD11 in Low Cycle Fatigue. *Rare Met. Mater. Eng.* **2019**, *48*, 366–374.
39. Zhang, J.X.; Murakumo, T.; Koizumi, Y. Slip geometry of dislocations related to cutting of the γ' phase in a new generation single-crystal superalloy. *Acta Mater.* **2003**, *51*, 5073–5081. [CrossRef]
40. Wang, X.G.; Liu, J.L.; Jin, T. Creep deformation related to dislocations cutting the γ' phase of a Ni-base single crystal superalloy. *Mater. Sci. Eng. A* **2015**, *626*, 406–414. [CrossRef]
41. Decamps, B.; Brien, V.; Moreon, A.J. Deformation microstructures after low-cycle fatigue at 950 °C in Ni-based superalloys: The effect of test conditions. *Scr. Metall. Mater.* **1994**, *31*, 793–798. [CrossRef]
42. Ding, Q.; Bei, H.; Yao, X. Temperature effects on deformation substructures and mechanisms of a Ni-based single crystal superalloy. *Appl. Mater. Today* **2021**, *23*, 101061. [CrossRef]
43. Feller-Kniepmeier, M.; Link, T. Temperature dependence of deformation mechanisms in a single crystal nickel-base alloy with high volume fraction of γ' phase. *Acta Mater.* **1996**, *44*, 2397–2407. [CrossRef]

44. Field, R.D.; Pollock, T.M.; Murphy, W.H. The Development of γ/γ' Interfacial Dislocation Networks During Creep in Ni-Base Superalloys. *Superalloys* **1992**, 557–566. [CrossRef]
45. Lin, B.; Huang, M.; Zhao, L. 3D DDD modelling of dislocation–precipitate interaction in a nickel-based single crystal superalloy under cyclic deformation. *Philos. Mag.* **2018**, *98*, 1550–1575. [CrossRef]
46. Yin, Q.; Lian, Y.; Wen, Z. Atomic simulation of the effect of orientation on tensile/compressive properties in nickel-based single crystal superalloys. *J. Alloys Compd.* **2022**, *893*, 162210. [CrossRef]
47. Li, P.; Li, S.X.; Wang, Z.G.; Zang, Z.F. Fundamental factors on formation mechanism of dislocation arrangements in cyclically deformed fcc single crystals. *Prog. Mater. Sci.* **2010**, *56*, 328–377. [CrossRef]
48. Tian, S.G.; Zhou, H.H.; Zhang, J.H. Formation and role of dislocation networks during high temperature creep of a single crystal nickel–base superalloy. *Mater. Sci. Eng. A* **2000**, *279*, 160–165. [CrossRef]
49. Bin, C.; Wu, W.P. Molecular dynamics study of fatigue mechanical properties and microstructural evolution of Ni-based single crystal superalloys under cyclic loading. *Comput. Mater. Sci.* **2020**, *185*, 109954. [CrossRef]

crystals

MDPI

Article

Microstructural Evolution and Tensile Properties of a Corrosion-Resistant Ni-Based Superalloys Used for Industrial Gas Turbines

Zhenhuan Gao [1,2,*], Shikun Li [3], Gang Liu [3,*], Zhao Shang [3], Dazhuo Song [3], Gongxian Yang [1,2], Juntao Zou [3] and Shuhua Liang [3]

1 State Key Laboratory of Long-Life High Temperature Materials, Deyang 618000, China
2 Dongfang Electric Corporation Dongfang Turbine Co., Ltd., Deyang 618000, China
3 Department of Materials Science and Engineering, Xi'an University of Technology, Xi'an 710048, China
* Correspondence: gaozhenhuan@dongfang.com (Z.G.); liugang@xaut.edu.cn (G.L.)

Abstract: As an important mechanical property, tensile behavior has been regarded as an indicator for the creep and thermal mechanical fatigue properties of Ni-based superalloys. The tensile property of Ni-based superalloys is closely related to the amount, size, and distribution of γ'-phase and carbides. To further clarify the tensile deformation mechanism of the CM247LC alloy, this study investigated its solidification characteristics and directionally-solidified and heat-treated microstructure. The dependence of tensile properties on the varied temperature ranging between 650 and 950 °C is discussed in detail. It was found that the deformation mechanism at 650 °C is dominated by the shearing of dislocations into the γ'-precipitates to form the superlattice stacking faults. At 800 °C, the K-W lock leads to the anomalous yield effects. At 950 °C, the deformation mechanism is dominated by the dislocations bypassing the γ'-precipiates. The results provide a comprehensive understanding of the CM247LC alloy and are beneficial for the development of corrosion-resistant Ni-based superalloys.

Keywords: Ni-based superalloy; solidification characteristic; segregation; tensile properties

1. Introduction

CM247LC (low carbon) is derived from the conventional casting Mar-M 247 superalloy [1–4], which has been used in manufacturing the directionally solidified (DS) turbine blades for power generation applications. By reducing the contents of Zr and Ti combined with the control of Si and S in Mar-M247 alloy (Table 1), the grain boundary cracking during directional solidification was effectively suppressed [1]. Additionally, the carbide stability and intermediate temperature ductility were apparently improved for the CM247LC alloy [3]. According to the application condition of the DS turbine blades, the creep and thermal mechanical fatigue (TMF) properties of the CM247LC alloy have been extensively investigated in the past decades. However, it is worth noting that the tensile property is also an important mechanical property of Ni-based superalloys, which can be used as an indicator for the creep and TMF properties [5,6].

As is well known, the exceptional high-temperature mechanical properties of Ni-based superalloys mainly derive from the strengthening effect of $L1_2$-structured γ'-precipitates embedded in the γ-matrix and the pinning effect of carbides on the grain boundaries [7–12]. It has been proven that the size, volume fraction, morphology, and distribution of γ'-precipitates and carbide has a strong influence on the tensile properties of Ni-based superalloys [13–15]. For example, the extensive cracking of carbide was detected during a tensile test of the DS CM247LC alloy at a lower temperature [16]. Zhang et al. [17] pointed out that the anomalous yield strength with temperature was attributed to the shearing of dislocation into γ'-precipitates to form anti-phase boundary (APB). The microscopic deformation mechanism, derived from the interactions between the gliding dislocations and γ'-precipitates, depends on the temperature and heat-treated microstructural characteristics. Consequently, a comprehensive understanding of the tensile behavior and the internal deformation mechanism of the CM247LC alloy is still needed.

Table 1. Chemical compositions of the CM247LC and Mar-M247 alloys (wt.%) [1].

Alloys	Cr	Co	Mo	W	Al	Ti	Ta	Hf	C	B	Zr	Ni
CM247LC	8.1	9.2	0.5	9.5	5.6	0.7	3.2	1.4	0.07	0.015	0.015	Bal.
Mar-M247	8.4	10.0	0.7	10.0	5.5	1.0	3.0	1.5	0.15	0.015	0.05	Bal.

In this study, the CM247LC alloy was directionally solidified in the Bridgman furnace. The solidification characteristics, directionally-solidified and heat-treated microstructures, and the tensile properties at varied temperatures were investigated. The aim of this work was to reveal the microstructural characteristics of the CM247LC alloy and investigate the dependence of tensile performance on temperature. Additionally, the deformation mechanism with regard to the interaction between dislocation and γ'-precipitate was discussed in detail.

2. Experimental Procedures

The chemical compositions of the CM247LC and Mar-M247 alloys are listed in Table 1. The master alloy of CM247LC was prepared by the vacuum induction furnace, and then directionally solidified in a Bridgeman furnace described elsewhere [18]. The master alloy rod, 14 mm in diameter and 80 mm in length, was cast with a withdrawal rate of 3 mm/min and an approximate thermal gradient of 50 °C/cm. Then, the directionally-solidified samples were subjected to the following heat treatments: (1) 1232 °C/2 h +1257 °C/2 h, A.C. (air cooling) solution heat treatments; (2) 1080 °C/4 h, A.C. first aging treatment; (3) 870 °C/20 h, A.C., secondary aging treatment. The characteristic phase transformation temperature was measured by the differential scanning calorimetry (DSC, NETZSCH STA 449F3) with the heating/cooling rate of 10 °C/min in a flowing stream of Ar. Standard metallographic technique was applied for microstructural observation. The polished specimen was etched with a solution consisting of HNO_3, HF, and $C_3H_8O_3$ (1:2:3), and observed by optical microscopy (OM, OLYMPUS GX71/50), and scanning electron microscopy (SEM, TESCAN-MIRA3). In addition, the constituent phases were characterized using an X-Ray diffractometer (XRD, SHIMADZU XRD-7000) with the scanning rate of 3°/min.

The tensile specimens with the gauge section of $3 \times 3 \times 17$ mm^3 were cut from the directionally solidified specimen by electro-discharge machining (EDM), followed by heat treatment. Tensile tests were conducted on a SUNS CMT 5105 mechanical testing machine with the strain rate of 1×10^{-3} s^{-1} at 650, 800, and 950 °C. Three samples were selected for tensile testing to guarantee the reliability of testing results. To clarify the deformation mechanism, the interrupted tensile test was carried out with the approximate engineering plastic strain of 2~5%. The deformed specimen was observed by transmission electron microscopy (TEM, FEI TECNAI G2 F20). A thin TEM foil perpendicular to the tensile direction was prepared by twin-jet electropolishing in a solution of 10% (volume fraction) $HClO_4$ and 95% C_2H_5OH at −40 °C.

3. Results and Discussion

3.1. Solidification Characteristics and As-Cast Microstructure

The variation of the equilibrium volume fraction of the constituent phases with temperature was calculated by the software JMatPro (Figure 1a). The γ-phase firstly solidifies from the melt as the primary phase, followed with the MC carbide at 1356 °C. With the decreasing temperature, the strengthening γ'-precipitate occurs at 1216 °C. Figure 1b shows the DSC heating and cooling curves of the as-cast specimen. Three endothermic peaks can be clearly observed on the DSC heating curve. The endothermic peaks at 1213, 1347, and 1371 °C on the DSC heating curve should be related to the solution temperature of the γ'-precipitate, melting temperature of the MC carbide, and liquidus, respectively. The freezing range, defined as the temperature range between the solidus and liquidus on the DSC cooling curve, is approximately 67 °C, which has the good consistency with the thermodynamic calculation results.

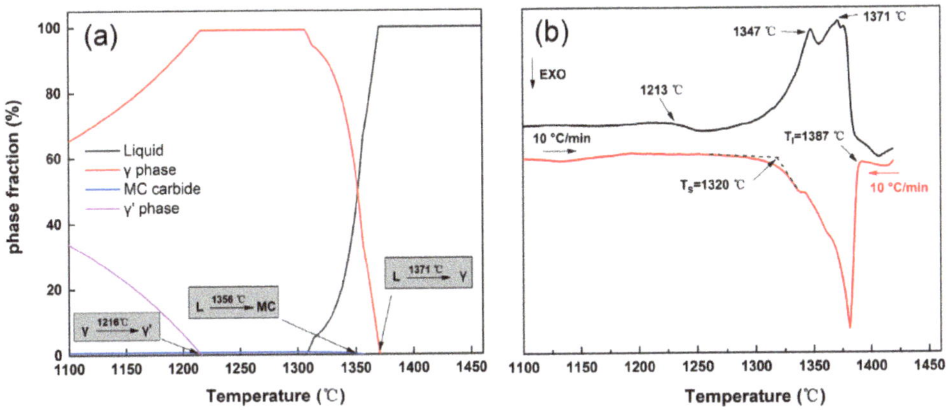

Figure 1. Equilibrium phase diagram and DSC result of CM247LC alloy. (**a**) J-MatPro calculation; (**b**) DSC result.

Figure 2 exhibits the cross-sectional microstructure of the CM247LC alloy after directional solidification. The representative dendritic microstructure with the mean primary dendrite arm spacing of ~165 μm was obtained under the thermal gradient of ~50 °C/cm and withdrawal rate of 50 μm/s (Figure 2a). The dendritic core is composed of the $L1_2$-structured γ'-particles with near-cubic shape embedded in the disordered-FCC γ-matrix (Figure 2b). Meanwhile, the blocky carbides have a strong tendency to distribute in the interdendritic region, and they are preliminarily judged as the MC carbides (Figure 2c). The coarse γ'/γ eutectics also distribute in the interdendritic region with lamellar shape (Figure 2d). Moreover, the solute segregation in the as-cast microstructure was analyzed by the segregation ratio (k), as expressed by:

$$k = C_{DC}/C_{ID} \quad (1)$$

where C_{DC} and C_{ID} denote the chemical compositions of the dendritic core and interdendritic region, respectively. According to the definition of k, values of k greater or lesser than unity indicate the segregation tendency of constituent elements to the dendritic core or to the interdendritic region, respectively. As shown in Table 2, the γ'-forming elements, Ti, Al, Ta, Hf, etc., partition to the interdendric region ($k < 1$), while W and Co preferentially segregate to the dendrite core ($k > 1$). Due to the segregation of the γ'-forming elements during solidification, the size of γ'-precipitates in the interdendritic region (Figure 2c,d) is apparently larger than that in the dendritic core (Figure 2b).

Figure 3 presents the TEM-EDS mapping and the selected electron diffraction (SAED) pattern of the carbide. The SAED patterns definitely indicates that the blocky particle is the MC carbide. Meanwhile, TEM-EDS mapping confirms that the MC carbide is enriched in Ta, Hf, Zr, and Ti, and depleted in Ni, Cr, and B. The solidification temperature of the MC carbide is about 15 °C lower than the liquidus. During directional solidification, Ta, Hf, Ti, etc., segregate to the remaining liquid in the mushy zone, thus promoting the formation of MC carbides. Due to the restriction of the primary dendric arms and the complicated thermosolutal convection in the mushy zone, the MC carbide exhibits an irregular morphology.

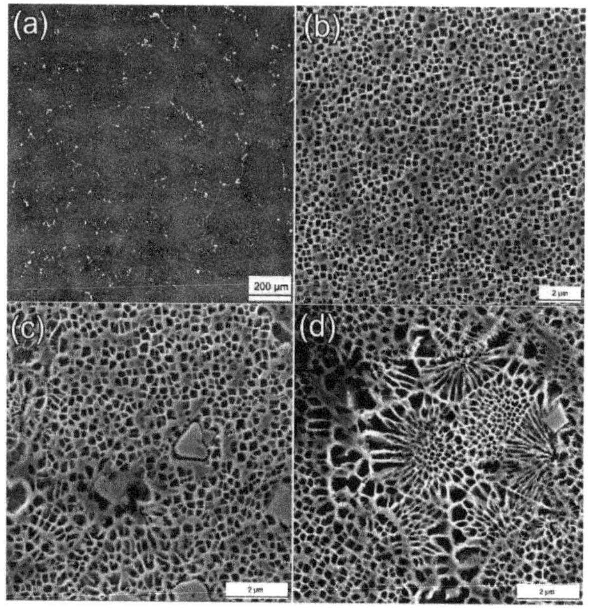

Figure 2. SEM image of the directionally solidified microstructure. (**a**) Cross-sectional microstructure; (**b**) γ'-precipitates in the dendritic core; (**c**) carbide; (**d**) eutectic in the interdendritic region.

Table 2. Chemical compositions at the dendritic core and interdendritic regions (wt.%), and the corresponding segregation ratios.

	Al	Ti	Cr	Co	Ni	Mo	Hf	Ta	W
Dendrite core	3.24	0.42	9.84	11.58	56.91	0.40	0.29	1.49	10.4
Inter-dendrite	3.40	0.46	10.32	10.60	59.36	0.54	0.83	1.55	8.46
Segregation ratios	0.95	0.91	0.95	1.09	0.96	0.74	0.35	0.96	1.23

3.2. Heat-Treated Microstructure

Figure 4 shows the carbide and dendritic core of the CM247LC alloy after solution and two steps aging heat treatment. As shown in Figure 4a, the carbides still locate in the interdendritic region but with the more homogeneous distribution and refined size, compared with the counterpart in the as-cast specimen (Figure 2a). Table 3 shows the chemical composition of the carbide in directionally solidified and heat-treated specimens. According to the SEM-EDS results, the carbide enriched with Ta and Hf is identified as an MC carbide. Figure 4b–d exhibit the γ'-precipitates in the dendritic core after solution and aging heat treatments. In this investigation, a step-wise solution heat treatment up to 1257 °C was applied to dissolve the coarse γ'/γ eutectic and reduce the degree of dendritic segregation. As shown in Figure 4a, the small γ'-particles (0.159 μm) with near-spherical morphology distribute in the dendritic core, which can be attributed to the high nucleation driving force of the supersaturated γ-matrix and the limited growth time during air cooling after solution treatment. Then, the two-steps aging treatments (1080 °C/4 h, A.C. + 870 °C/20 h, A.C.) are used to promote the reprecipitation of the γ'-phase. As shown in Figure 4b–d, the γ'-size significantly increased from 0.159 μm (solution heat treatment) to 0.295 μm (1st aging treatment), and finally to 0.312 μm (2nd aging treatments). After stepwise aging heat treatments, the γ'-volume fraction increased from 40.6% (first aging treatment) to 50.8% (second aging treatments). Meanwhile, the morphology of the γ'-precipitate changed from near-spherical to a cubic shape after aging heat treatments. The cubicity of the γ'-precipitates depends on the competition between the interfacial energy and strain energy [18]. When the γ'-size is small, the interface energy is the dominated factor to determine the near-spherical shape of γ'-precipitates. With the increasing γ'-size, the strain energy derived from the coherent misfit between γ' and γ gradually plays a major role, resulting in the cubic morphology of the γ'-phase.

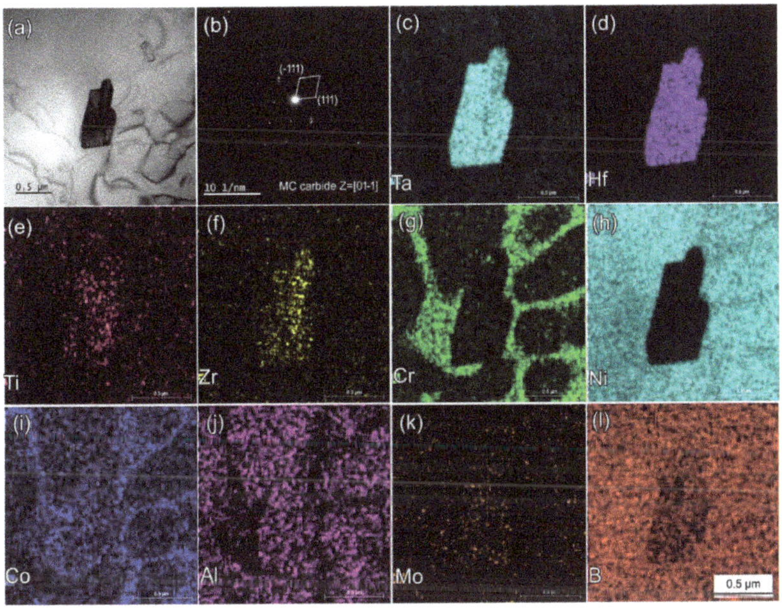

Figure 3. TEM-EDS map and SAED pattern of the carbide in the DS specimen. (**a**) TEM-image; (**b**) SAED pattern of MC carbide; (**c**–**l**) EDS mapping results.

Table 3. Chemical compositions of carbide in as-cast (1232 °C/2 h + 1257 °C/2 h, A.C. solutioning, 1080 °C/4 h A.C. 1st aging and 870 °C/20 h A.C. 2nd aging) and heat-treated specimen (wt.%).

	Al	Ti	Cr	Co	Ni	Mo	Hf	Ta	W
As-cast	0.00	1.64	0.00	0.84	1.93	0.00	47.58	36.96	0.61
Heat-treated	0.06	1.95	0.39	2.16	3.49	0.66	45.27	35.51	0.00

3.3. Tensile Property and Deformation Mechanism

Figure 5 demonstrates the engineering strain–stress curves and the corresponding tensile properties of the CM247LC alloy at different temperatures. As shown in Figure 5a, the σ–ε curves exhibit different characteristics with the increasing temperature. In the temperature range between RT and 650 °C, a significant strain-hardening phenomenon occurs after yield, and lasts to the final fracture. Particularly, the $\sigma - \varepsilon$ curve at 650 °C illustrates the strongest strain-hardening ability, while the flow stress at 800 and 950 °C rapidly rises to the ultimate tensile strength (σ_{UTS}), and then gradually declines until fracture. Figure 5b shows the yield strength (σ_Y), ultimate tensile strength and the fracture strain (ε_f) at different temperatures. From RT to 500 °C, σ_Y, σ_{UTS}, and ε_f decrease slightly. By contrast, σ_Y and σ_{UTS} respectively increase from 764 and 898 MPa at 500 °C to 1021 and 1126 MPa at 800 °C, and then drop to 538 and 693 MPa at 950 °C. An obvious anomalous yield behavior is observed for the CM247LC alloy. Generally, the different between σ_Y and σ_{UTS}, ($\sigma_{UTS} - \sigma_Y$), can be used to characterize the strain-hardening ability. As shown in Figure 5a, $\sigma - \varepsilon$ curve demonstrates the highest value of ($\sigma_{UTS} - \sigma_Y$) at 650 °C, indicating the strongest strain-hardening ability. In addition, the fracture strain decreases first from RT to 500 °C, and then increases continuously from 500 to 950 °C.

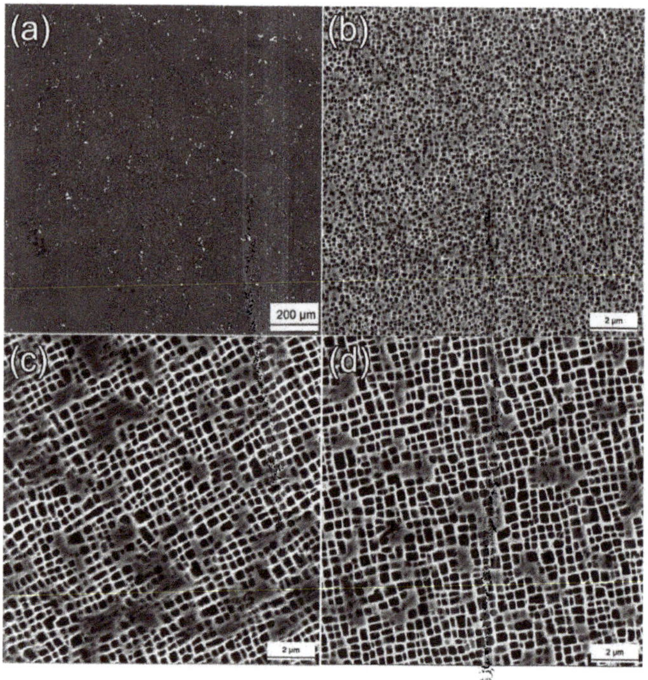

Figure 4. SEM images of carbides and γ'-precipitates after varied heat treatment. (**a**) Carbides after solution and aging treatment; (**b**) γ'-precipitates after solution treatment; (**c**) γ'-precipitates after the 1st aging treatment; (**d**) γ'-precipitates after the 2nd aging treatment.

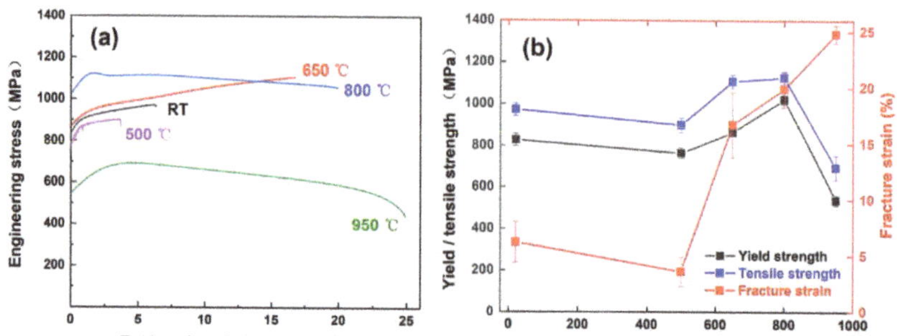

Figure 5. Engineering stress–strain curves and the corresponding tensile properties of CM247LC alloy at varied temperatures: (**a**) $\sigma - \varepsilon$ curves; (**b**) σ_Y, σ_{UTS}, and ε_f.

Figure 6 demonstrates the fracture surface and deformed microstructure after tensile tests at 650, 800, and 950 °C. At 650 °C, the fracture surface inclines about 45° with respect to the stress axis without apparent necking being observed (Figure 6(a1)). Plenty of cleavage steps and river patterns can be clearly seen on the enlarged SEM image of the fracture surface (Figure 6(a2)), indicating that the fracture models to a cleavage fracture. Furthermore, as shown in Figure 7, the crack of the MC carbide is observed near the fracture surface at the tensile temperature of 650 °C. The crack propagation is observed along the interface between carbide and matrix, indicating the detrimental effects of blocky MC carbide on the tensile properties of the CM247LC alloy at 650 °C.

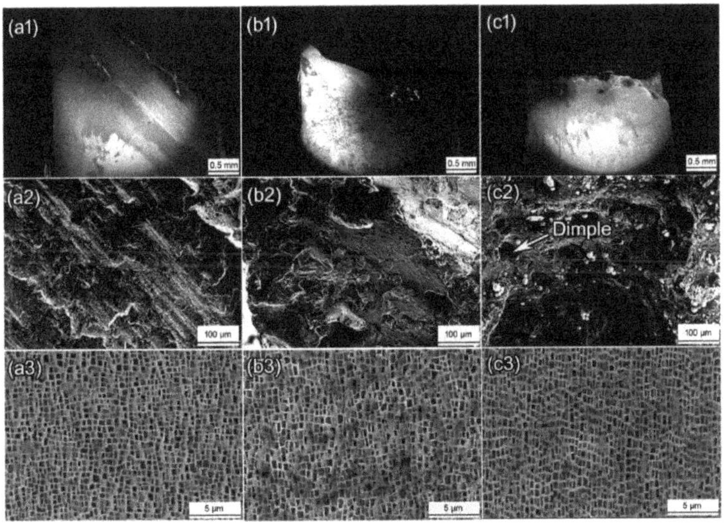

Figure 6. Microstructure characterization of the fracture surface at varied tensile temperatures. (**a1–a3**) 650 °C; (**b1–b3**) 800 °C; (**c1–c3**) 950 °C.

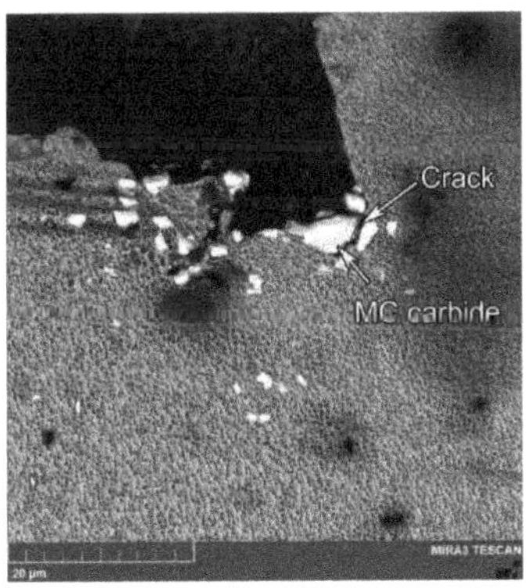

Figure 7. MC carbide near the fracture surface after tensile test at 650 °C.

At 800 °C, the inclined angle between the macroscopical fracture surface and tensile stress axis increases apparently (Figure 6(b1)). Both cleavage steps and dimples can be observed on the fracture surface, demonstrating the mixed facture characteristics at 800 °C (Figure 6(b2)). At 950 °C, the fracture surface is perpendicular to the stress axis with an apparent necking phenomenon near the surface (Figure 6(c1)). Coarse dimples and small oxide particles are observed on the fracture surface, indicating a larger deformation before the fracture at 950 °C (Figure 6(c2)). Figure 6(a3–c3) exhibit the deformed microstructure near the fracture surface. No evident change in the morphology of the γ'-precipitates can be observed at 650 °C. However, the γ'-precipitates were gradually distorted along the tensile direction at the higher temperatures from 800 to 950 °C, which is mainly attributed to the high stress and the increased thermal activation at high temperatures.

For Ni-based superalloys, the fracture mechanism is closely related to the microstructural characteristics and tensile temperatures. Particularly, the size, distribution, and morphology of carbides have a strong influence on the fracture behavior. As an obstacle for dislocation motion, the MC carbide initially provides strengthening effects during tensile deformation. However, the pile-up of dislocations near the large blocky carbide will result in a local stress concentration, thus leading to the initiation and quick propagation of micro-cracks near the interface between carbide and matrix. Therefore, a low fracture strain was observed when the temperature was below 650 °C (Figure 5a). By contrast, as the temperature increases to 950 °C, more slip systems can be activated. Furthermore, when the local stress concentration exceeds the critical value, the partial dislocations can bypass or shear the γ'-precipitates (as shown in the following section) to release the local stress concentration. Therefore, the tensile specimens exhibit a higher fracture strain and plastic deformation with the increasing temperature.

Figure 8 shows the TEM images of the deformed microstructure after interrupted tensile tests with 2–5% plastic strain. At 650 °C, the dislocation tangles in the γ-matrix accompanied with isolated superlattice stacking faults (SSF) in the γ'-precipitates are clearly observed (Figure 8a). The isolated SSFs distribute along the <110> orientations, which can be attributed to the cutting of partial dislocations from the γ-matrix into the γ'-precipitates. When the temperature increases to 800 °C, the dislocation density increases significantly in γ-matrix channels (Figure 8b,c). The dislocations severely tangle in the γ-channels, accompanied with the increased density of SSFs in the γ'-precipitates. It is worth noting that there are some local serrated dislocations along the <010> direction (as marked by the red arrow in Figure 8b), which is generally named the Kear–Wilsdorf (K-W) lock [12]. It has been proven that the cross-slip of dislocations from the {111} to the {100} planes leads to the formation of the K-W lock [12,19], thus resulting in the anomalous yield behavior at 800 °C. With the increasing tensile temperature of 950 °C, the SSFs observed in the interrupted tensile specimens at the lower temperature totally disappeared, while a high density of dislocations presents in the γ channels. According to the TEM observations (Figure 8d), It can be deduced that the tensile behavior of the CM247LC alloy at 950 °C is determined by the cross-slip of dislocations in the γ-matrix with thermal activation.

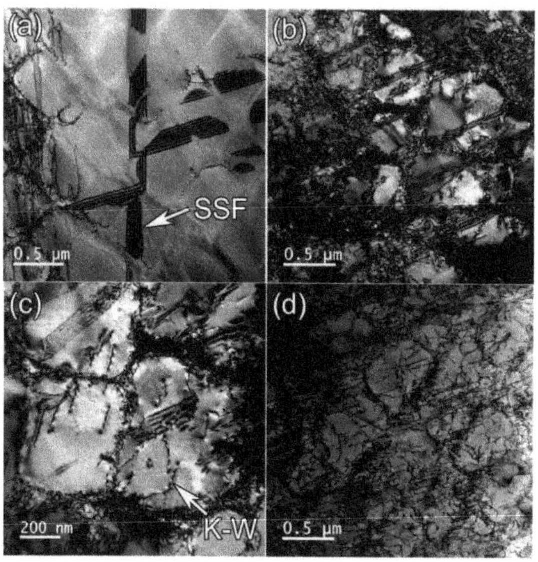

Figure 8. TEM bright image of the deformed specimen at varied tensile temperatures. (**a**) 650 °C; (**b**,**c**) 800 °C; (**d**) 950 °C.

The γ'-phase is the main strengthening phase for the CM247LC alloy. The interactions between γ'-precipitates and gliding dislocations play a critical role in the deformation of the CM247LC alloy at varied temperatures. The Burgers vector of full dislocation in the $L1_2$-structured γ'-phase ($< 110 >$) is twice in magnitude that in the disordered γ-matrix ($\frac{1}{2} < \bar{1}10 >$), which is named as the super-dislocation. The $< 110 >$ super-dislocation tends to dissociate into partial dislocations due to its prohibitively high energy. According to proceeding publications [12,20], the cutting of a partial dislocation into γ'-precipitates will lead to planar defects, including anti-phase boundary (APB) and superlattice stacking faults (SSFs). For example, a $\frac{1}{2} < 1\bar{1}0 >$ partial dislocation cut into the γ'-phase will lead to the formation of APB; a $\frac{1}{6} < 112 >$ partial dislocation cut into the γ'-precipitates will result in a complex stacking fault (CSF); a $\frac{1}{3} < 112 >$ partial dislocation cut into the γ'-precipitates will lead to a superlattice intrinsic stacking fault (SISF). Generally, the barrier for partial dislocation cutting into the γ'-phase follows the order of CSF > APB > SISF [12]. In this work, the isolated SISFs were clearly observed in the deformed specimen at 650 °C, indicating the cutting of a $\frac{1}{3} < 112 >$ partial dislocation into the γ'-phase. One typical dislocation reaction model has been proposed as [20]:

$$\frac{1}{2}\left[\bar{1}01\right]+\frac{1}{2}\left[0\bar{1}1\right]\rightarrow\frac{1}{3}\left[\bar{1}\bar{1}2\right]+\frac{1}{6}\left[\bar{1}\bar{1}2\right] \tag{2}$$

The reaction of two $\frac{1}{2} < 110 >$ full dislocations in the γ-matrix results in a dislocation pair consisting of a $\frac{1}{3} < 112 >$ leading dislocation and a $\frac{1}{6} < 112 >$ trailing dislocation. At 650 °C, the dislocation glides first in the soft γ-matrix channels. With the accumulated dislocation density at the γ'/γ interface, the local stress concentration will activate a slip of partial dislocations from different slip systems, thus leading to the intersection of SSFs within the γ'-precipitates. Consequently, the CM247LC alloy exhibits a high work hardening ability at 650 °C. This is according to the Considère criterion [21], as expressed by:

$$\frac{d\sigma_T}{d\varepsilon_T} < \sigma_T \tag{3}$$

where σ_T denotes true stress and ε_T true strain. The necking instability will occur when the strain-hardening rate drops to the value of the true stress. In other words, a higher strain-hardening ability renders a higher tensile ductility. Therefore, as shown in Figure 5, the highest strain-hardening capability at 650 °C leads to a high uniform strain until fracture.

At 800 °C, the CM247LC alloy exhibits the highest yield and tensile strength, which can be attributed to the following reason. On the one hand, a K-W lock is formed in the γ'-precipitates at 800 °C, which is attributed to the cross-slip of dislocation with the help of thermal activations. The anomalous yield strengthening effect makes the cutting of partial dislocations into the γ'-precipitates much harder. On the other hand, the lattice misfit between γ' and the γ-phase, δ, is defined as:

$$\delta = 2 \times \frac{a_{\gamma'} - a_\gamma}{a_{\gamma'} + a_\gamma} \tag{4}$$

where $a_{\gamma'}$ and a_γ are the lattice parameters of the γ' and γ-phases, respectively. It has been proven that the expansion coefficient of γ is considerably higher than that of the γ'-phase [12,22]. Although the exact value of δ for the CM247LC alloy was not obtained by an experimental method in this work, the tendency δ versus temperature is similar for most Ni-based superalloys. For example, Harada et al. [23] demonstrated that the value of δ becomes more negative with the increasing temperature for single-crystal Ni-based superalloys, including TMS63, TMS12, and CMSX-4. The J-MatPro calculation result illustrates that $a_{\gamma'}$ = 0.3615 nm and a_γ = 0.3611 nm at 650 °C, which yields a positive δ of ~0.116% for the CM247LC alloy, while, $a_{\gamma'}$= 0.3638 nm and a_γ= 0.3643 nm at 950 °C, which yields a more negative δ of −0.125%. δ becomes more negative with the increasing temperature, thus leading to a higher coherency strain as the obstacle for dislocations motion. Therefore, the cutting of partial dislocations from the γ-matrix channel into the γ'-precipitate becomes more difficult. The accumulated dislocations near the γ'/γ interface, SSFs, and K-W lock lead to the strain-hardening effects. However, at the same time, the local stress concentration near the γ'/γ interface can be relieved by the cross-slip and climb of dislocations with the help of thermal activation, which is termed as the softening effect.

The feature of stress–strain curves depends on the competition between strain-hardening and softening effects. Initially, the strain-hardening effect plays the dominant role, thus leading to the quickly increased flow stress up to the ultimate tensile strength. Then, the flow stress decreases with the increasing strain due to the softening effects caused by thermal activation.

At 950 °C, the gliding dislocations were mainly constricted to the soft γ-matrix channel during tensile deformation. The tensile deformation at 950 °C is dominated by the climb and cross-slip of dislocations under the significant thermal activations in the γ-matrix to bypass over the γ'-precipiates. Therefore, the stress–strain curve illustrates an obvious softening phenomenon at 950 °C.

4. Conclusions

The CM247LC alloy was prepared with the directional solidification technique. The solidification characteristics, solution, heat-treated microstructure, and tensile properties of the CM247LC alloy are investigated. The following conclusions are listed as follows:

(1) The directionally-solidified specimen exhibited a representative dendritic microstructure. The γ-phase first solidified from the melt as the primary phase, followed with the solidification of MC carbide at 1347 °C. MC carbides enriched with Ta, Hf, and Ti mainly distributed in the interdendritic region. Due to the solute segregation of Ta, Ti, Al, etc., a γ'/γ eutectic with lamellar structure was found in the interdenritic region.
(2) After 1232 °C/2 h +1257 °C/2 h, A.C solutioning and 1080 °C/4 h, A.C., +870 °C/20 h, A.C., aging treatments, a homogenous distribution of γ'-precipitates embedded in the γ-matrix was obtained, along with the γ'-size of 0.31 μm and γ'-volume fraction of ~50.8%.
(3) At 650 °C, the tensile deformation was dominated by the shearing of partial dislocation into γ'-precipitates to form SSFs. At 800 °C, the K-W lock resulted in anomalous yield effects. The tensile specimen showed the highest σ_Y of 1021 MPa and σ_{UTS} of 1126 MPa at 800 °C. The tensile deformation was controlled by the dislocations bypassing the γ'-precipiates at 950 °C.

Author Contributions: Conceptualization, Z.G. and G.L.; investigation, S.L. (Shikun Li), Z.S. and D.S.; writing—original draft preparation, Z.G. and G.L.; writing—review and editing, G.Y. and J.Z.; supervision, S.L. (Shuhua Liang); All authors have read and agreed to the published version of the manuscript.

Funding: This research was funded by the fund of State Key Laboratory of Long-life High Temperature Materials (DEC8300CG202111716EE280355).

Data Availability Statement: Data is contained within the article.

Conflicts of Interest: The authors declare no conflict of interest.

References

1. Harris, K.; Erickson, G.L.; Schwer, R.E. Mar M 247 Derivations-CM 247 LC DS alloy and CMSX single crystal alloys: Properties and performance. In *Superalloys 1984, Proceedings of the 5th International Symposium on Superalloys, Champion, PA, USA, 7–11 October 1984*; TMS: Warrendale, PA, USA, 1984; pp. 221–230.
2. Huang, H.E.; Koo, C.H. Characteristics and mechanical properties of polycrystalline CM 247 LC superalloy casting. *Mater. Trans.* **2004**, *45*, 562–568. [CrossRef]
3. Rai, R.K.; Sahu, J.K. Strength-ductility paradox in a directionally solidified nickel base superalloy. *Mater. Lett.* **2018**, *220*, 90–93. [CrossRef]
4. Jeong, H.W.; Seo, S.M.; Choi, B.G.; Yoo, Y.S.; Ahn, Y.K.; Lee, J.H. Effect of long-term thermal exposures on microstructures and mechanical properties of directionally solidified CM247LC alloy. *Met. Mater. Int.* **2013**, *19*, 917–925. [CrossRef]
5. Zhou, H.; Harada, H.; Ro, Y.; Okada, I. Investigations on the thermo-mechanical fatigue of two Ni-based single-crystal superalloys. *Mater. Sci. Eng. A* **2005**, *394*, 161–167. [CrossRef]
6. Ye, W.M.; Hu, X.T.; Song, Y.D. The relationship between creep and tensile properties of a nickel-based superalloy. *Mater. Sci. Eng. A* **2020**, *774*, 138847. [CrossRef]

7. Alizadeh-Sh, M.; Marashi, S.P.H.; Ranjbarnodeh, E.; Shoja-Razavi, R.; Oliveira, J.P. Prediction of solidification cracking by an empirical-statistical analysis for laser cladding of Inconel 718 powder on a non-weldable substrate. *Opt. Laser Technol.* **2020**, *128*, 106244. [CrossRef]
8. Li, S.; Li, J.Y.; Jiang, Z.W.; Cheng, Y.; Li, Y.Z.; Tang, S.; Leng, J.Z.; Chen, H.X.; Zou, Y.; Zhao, Y.H.; et al. Controlling the columnar-to-equiaxed transition during directed energy deposition of Inconel 625. *Addit. Manuf.* **2022**, *57*, 102958. [CrossRef]
9. Rodrigues, T.A.; Farias, F.W.C.; Zhang, K.P.; Shamsolhodaei, A.; Shen, J.J.; Zhou, N.; Schell, N.; Capek, J.; Polatidis, E.; Santos, T.G.; et al. Wire and arc additive manufacturing of 316L stainless steel/Inconel 625 functionally graded material: Development and characterization. *J. Mater. Res. Technol.* **2022**, *21*, 237–251. [CrossRef]
10. Liu, D.Y.; Ding, Q.Q.; Zhou, Q.; Zhou, D.X.; Wei, X.; Zhao, X.B.; Zhang, Z.; Bei, H.B. Microstructure, mechanical properties and thermal stability of Ni-based single crystal superalloys with low specific weight. *Crystals* **2023**, *13*, 610. [CrossRef]
11. Harrison, J.; Withey, P.A. Precipitation of topologically closed packed phases during the heat-treatment of Rhenium containing single crystal Ni-based superalloys. *Crystals* **2023**, *13*, 519. [CrossRef]
12. Reed, R.C. *The Superalloys: Fundamentals and Applications*; Cambridge University Press: Cambridge, UK, 2006.
13. Kim, I.S.; Choi, B.G.; Seo, S.M.; Kim, D.H.; Jo, C.Y. Influence of heat treatment on microstructure and tensile properties of conventionally cast and directionally solidified superalloy CM247LC. *Mater. Lett.* **2008**, *62*, 1110–1113. [CrossRef]
14. Kim, I.S.; Choi, B.G.; Jung, J.E.; Do, J.; Seok, W.Y.; Lee, Y.H.; Jeong, I.Y. Effect of heat treatment on microstructural evolution and creep behaviors of a conventionally cast nickel-based superalloy. *Mater. Character.* **2020**, *165*, 110378. [CrossRef]
15. Sheng, L.Y.; Yang, F.; Guo, J.T.; Xi, T.F. Anomalous yield and intermediate temperature brittleness behaviors of directionally solidified nickel-based superalloy. *Trans. Nonferr. Met. Soc. China* **2014**, *24*, 673–681. [CrossRef]
16. Rai, R.K.; Sahu, J.K.; Jena, P.S.M.; Das, S.K.; Paulose, N.; Fernando, C.D. High temperature tensile deformation of a directionally solidified nickel base superalloy: Role of micro constituents. *Mater. Sci. Eng. A* **2017**, *705*, 189–195. [CrossRef]
17. Zhang, P.; Yuan, Y.; Gao, Z.H.; Gu, Y.F.; Li, J.; Yan, J.B.; Gong, X.F.; Lu, J.T.; Shi, X.B.; Fu, B.Q. Strain-rate insensitive yield strength and deformation mechanisms of Ni-base superalloy CM247LC at 600 °C. *J. Alloys Compd.* **2021**, *862*, 158478. [CrossRef]
18. Liu, G.; Liu, L.; Ai, C.; Ge, B.M.; Zhang, J.; Fu, H.Z. Influence of withdrawal rate on the microstructure of Ni-base single-crystal superalloys containing Re and Ru. *J. Alloys Compd.* **2011**, *509*, 5866–5872. [CrossRef]
19. Rai, R.K.; Sahu, J.K.; Jena, P.S.M.; Das, S.K.; Paulose, N.; Fernando, D.C. Micromechanism of High-Temperature Tensile Deformation Behavior of a Directionally Solidified Nickel Base Superalloy. *J. Mater. Eng. Perform.* **2018**, *27*, 659–665. [CrossRef]
20. Long, H.; Liu, Y.; Kong, D.; Wei, H.; Chen, Y.; Mao, S. Shearing mechanisms of stacking fault and anti-phase-boundary forming dislocation pairs in the γ' phase in Ni-based single crystal superalloy. *J. Alloys Compd.* **2017**, *724*, 287–295. [CrossRef]
21. Dieter, G.E.; Bacon, D. *Mechanical Metallurgy*; McGraw-Hill: New York, NY, USA, 1986.
22. Wang, G.L.; Liu, J.L.; Liu, J.D.; Wang, X.G.; Zhou, Y.Z.; Sun, X.D.; Zhang, H.F.; Jin, T. Temperature dependence of tensile behavior and deformation microstructure of a Re-containing Ni-base single crystal superalloy. *Mater. Des.* **2017**, *130*, 131–139. [CrossRef]
23. Harada, H.; Murakami, H. Design of Ni-base superalloys. In *Computational Materials Design*; Springer: Berlin/Heidelberg, Germany, 1999; pp. 39–70.

crystals

Article

Thickness Effects on Oxidation Behavior and Consequent γ' Degradation of a High-Al Ni-Based Single Crystal Superalloy

Haigen Zhao [1], Wenqi Guo [1], Wenyue Zhao [2,*], Yi Ru [2,3], Junwu Wang [1,4], Yanling Pei [2], Shengkai Gong [2,3] and Shusuo Li [1,3,*]

1 Research Institute of Aero-Engine, Beihang University, Beijing 100191, China
2 Frontier Research Institute of Innovative Science and Technology, Beihang University, Beijing 100191, China
3 AECC Guizhou Liyang Aviation Power Co., Ltd., Guizhou 550000, China
4 AECC Gui'yang Power Precision Casting Co., Ltd., Guizhou 550014, China
* Correspondence: wendyzhao56@buaa.edu.cn (W.Z.); lishs@buaa.edu.cn (S.L.)

Abstract: High temperature oxidation is considered to play an essential role in the thickness debit effect on the creep rupture life of Ni-based single crystal (SC) superalloys. In order to clarify thickness effects, thin-walled specimens of different thickness (t = 0.1, 0.3, 1.0 mm) were prepared. Cyclic and isothermal oxidation tests of a high-Al Ni-based SC superalloy IC21 were carried out at 900 °C and 1100 °C in order to study the thickness effects on the oxidation behavior and consequent microstructural degradation. Thin-walled specimens of S01-N exhibited a good oxidation resistance when the protective scale-forming elements were enough in the matrix. Specimen thickness tuned the oxidation kinetics by changing the spallation behavior but had few influences on the thermodynamics. The easier stress relief via creep deformation in thin specimens is the main reason behind this phenomenon. Moreover, the obvious temperature effects on the multilayer oxide scales caused the different thickness-related spallation behaviors. Weaker microstructural degradation appeared and was further mitigated by reduced specimen thickness. Sufficient Al content is considered to be indispensable for the formation of protective α-Al_2O_3 scale with less degradation of matrix during the high temperature oxidation of thin-walled Ni-based SC superalloy castings.

Keywords: superalloys; thickness; oxidation; high temperature; Al element

1. Introduction

Ni-based single crystal (SC) superalloys have been extensively applied in the turbine blades of advanced aero-engines owing to their outstanding creep resistance at high temperature [1]. In order to improve the service performances of these hot sections further, decreasing the casting wall thickness of blades has become an efficient way to meet the requirements of metal cooling schemes and lower overall weight [2,3]. However, reduced wall thickness has been verified to increase the strain rate and decrease the creep rupture life of Ni-based superalloys, which is known as the thickness debit effect and brings a new challenge for the materials design of superalloys [4–11]. Based on many previous studies focusing on this issue, high temperature oxidation has been considered to be one of the critical factors responsible for this effect [12–15]. The obviously shortened creep life of a thin specimen might be attributed to the notable microstructure degradation as well as the formation of brittle oxide scales in a service environment [4,11–15]. Nevertheless, the synergistic effects of other factors with high temperature oxidation make the mechanisms behind the phenomenon unclear. Therefore, it is essential to study the specimen thickness effects on the oxidation behavior of a high-aluminum Ni-based single crystal superalloy and consequent degradation of the γ'-Ni_3Al phase.

In the literature [16–19], many studies report the oxidation behavior of superalloys at lower (800~900 °C) and higher temperatures (1050~1150 °C). At higher temperatures, the oxide scale formed on alloy is composed of α-alumina, spinel and rutile, but that is not the case at lower temperature. At lower temperatures, the formation of a protective alumina scale may be not achieved. On the other hand, the outside of the blade was serviced under cyclic oxidation conditions at 1100 °C. However, the inside of the blades was subjected to lower temperatures [20]. In order to quantify the thickness effect on the oxidation kinetics at lower and higher temperatures, the typical temperatures of 900 °C and 1100 °C were used in this study. The oxidation resistances of Ni-based SC superalloys at high temperature are generally provided by the formation of protective alumina (Al_2O_3) and/or chromic oxide (Cr_2O_3) scales. Due to the lower diffusion in alumina and the certain amount of Al required to form the γ'-Ni_3Al strengthening precipitates, Al content is more crucial to maintain the oxidation resistances of superalloys, while Cr is usually micro-alloyed for further improvement. Previous studies have shown that the specimen thickness has negligible influence on the initial oxidation of Ni-based alloys before the oxide scale has reached a critical thickness [12]. However, the specimen thickness effects on the oxidation kinetics and spallation behavior become significant with increasing exposure time [12]. By applying a probabilistic spallation model, the thickness effect on the corrosion behavior of CMSX-4 was attributed to the differences in spallation mechanisms [21]. The distinct thermal stresses generated in the oxide scale of the specimens with different thicknesses, which resulted from the mismatch in thermal expansion and elastic modulus between oxide and matrix alloy, were considered to be the main reasons [12,21]. On the other hand, the near-surface microstructures of alumina-forming Ni-based SC superalloys were considered to be strongly altered by high-temperature oxidation, which has been verified both by modelling and experiments [13,14]. Moreover, this microstructure degradation was found to be enhanced with increasing temperature and decreasing specimen thickness. However, the thickness effects associated with high-temperature oxidation might be different due to varied compositions of superalloys, especially the Al content closely related to the formation of protective alumina scale. To our best knowledge, few studies focus on this composition-related thickness effect on the oxidation behavior and microstructural evolution, which are actually important for the materials design of modern Ni-based SC superalloys for thin-walled blades. The novelty of this research was combining thickness with different Al content together to suggest an alloy design for a thin-walled blade.

In the present work, the thickness effects on the oxidation behavior and consequent microstructure degradation of a newly designed Ni-based SC superalloy with high Al content (IC21) were studied via high-temperature oxidation tests. The oxidation behaviors at different temperatures were evaluated by focusing on the oxidation kinetics and spallation mechanisms. We also paid close attention to the composition effects of Al content on the γ' degradation caused by oxidation in thin specimens, based on extensive investigations on the specimens with different original microstructures. The rest of the present paper is organized as follows. The specimen preparation and experimental methods are described firstly in Section 2. Then, the oxidation behaviors of the specimens with different thicknesses at 900 °C and 1100 °C are evaluated by oxidation kinetics, and the composition and microstructure of the oxide scale are examined in Section 3.1. The oxidation mechanisms are also discussed from the aspects of thermodynamics and kinetics related to spallation behavior. In Section 3.2, the variation trends in the thickness of the γ' degradation zone caused by oxidation are analyzed and further compared among the alloy specimens with different thicknesses. The microstructural degradation during oxidation that varied with the original Al content in the thin specimen is also discussed in order to study the composition related thickness effects. Finally, all the main findings are summarized in Section 4.

2. Experimental Methods

2.1. Specimen Preparation

A newly designed Ni-based SC superalloy with the nominal composition of Ni-(6.5~8.2), Al-(8.0–12.6), Mo-(1.0–4.5), Ta-(0.8–1.8), Re-(1.3–3.2), Cr-(0.1–0.4) Hf -minor Ce and Y (in wt.%) is studied in the present work. The main feature of the studied alloy is its high content of Al, which results in a higher volume fraction of γ' precipitates up to 82%. A casting plate of this superalloy was prepared by high rate solidification. The specimens with the crystal orientation bias within 5° from [001] direction were chosen for the oxidation tests at high temperature. In order to eliminate the composition segregation, subsequent heat treatments were conducted following the regime below: 1315 °C/4 h + 1320 °C/6 h + 1325 °C/6 h (air cooling) + 1100 °C/2 h (air cooling) + 870 °C/32 h (air cooling). Different thicknesses (t = 0.1, 0.3, 1.0 mm) of specimens were cut from the core section of the heat-treated superalloy plate paralleling the solidification direction. Here, it is worth mentioning that we intended to obtain different microstructures from surface to core in the heat-treated plate by applying the highest solid solution temperature of 1325 °C in air. Additional thin specimens with a thickness of 0.1 mm were cut further from the plate with different distances away from the surface in order to obtain a variational Al content and microstructure during solid solution in an air environment. All the detailed information of the specimens for oxidation tests are shown in Table 1. Before the oxidation tests, all the specimen surfaces were ground with 2000-grit SiC paper and cleaned ultrasonically in acetone for 5 min.

Table 1. Detailed information of studied superalloy specimens for oxidation tests at high temperature.

Specimen Number	Thickness (mm)	Distance from Surface (μm) *	Morphology of γ'	Volume Fraction of γ' (%)	Average Size of γ' (nm)	Average Al Content (wt. %)
S01-N	0.1	>400	Cubic	82	450	7.6
S03-N	0.3	>400	Cubic	82	450	7.6
S10-N	1.0	>400	Cubic	82	450	7.6
S01-1	0.1	110	Spherical + Rounded cubic	54	270	4.4
S01-2	0.1	150	Cubic	75	331	6.2
S01-3	0.1	250	Cubic	80	365	7.0

*: measured from the symmetry mirror plane of the specimen to the surface of the alloy plate.

2.2. Oxidation Tests at High Temperature

Cyclic oxidation tests were conducted in a tube furnace at 900 °C and 1100 °C for 100 h. The length and width of the thin-walled specimen were 10 mm and 8 mm with a different thickness. The specimen was put in a pre-annealed Al_2O_3 crucible to protect it from pollution. During the cyclic oxidation, the specimen was exposed for 50 min in the furnace and cooled for 10 min to room temperature by an air fan. The heating rates and cooling rates were about 10 °C/s and 20 °C/s, respectively. The mass of every specimen was measured three times before and after different duration times of oxidation by an electronic balance with a precision of 10^{-5} g. The average values were used to calculate the mass gain per unit area and plot the kinetic curves. In addition, the mass change was also weighted in order to evaluate the spallation behavior. For the thin specimens with different original compositions and microstructures, isothermal oxidation tests were carried out at 900 °C and 1100 °C for 100 h as well.

The microstructural morphologies of oxide scales were observed by using a Supra 55 scanning electron microscopy (SEM), and all the images were collected in backscattered electron (BSE) mode. Composition analyses were also carried out by a D/Max type X-ray diffractometer (XRD), an energy-dispersive spectroscopy (EDS) and a JXA-8230 electron microprobe analysis (EPMA). In order to evaluate the spallation mechanism during oxidation, the residual stress in oxide scale was measured via the shifts of the corresponding XRD spectral peaks. The shift of the XRD spectral peak toward the low angle direction indicates the generation of tensile stress. The value of biaxial stress is calculated by using the so-called $\sin^2\psi$ method as follows,

$$\sigma_\phi = -\frac{E}{2(1+\nu)}\cot\theta_0\frac{\pi}{180}\frac{\partial(2\theta_{\phi\psi})}{\partial(\sin^2\psi)} \quad (1)$$

in which σ_ϕ is stress in direction ϕ, E is Young's modulus, ν is the Poisson ratio, θ_0 and θ are the standard and real diffraction angles, respectively, and ψ is the tilt angle.

For the oxides far away from the surface, which usually have weaker XRD spectral peaks, a laser Raman microprobe (LabRAM HR Evolution) was used to determine the residual stress in oxide scale instead. The measurements were conducted at ten different locations on the specimen surface after oxidation by using a He-Ne laser beam. The biaxial stress σ (in GPa) was calculated by the following equation,

$$\sigma = \Delta\nu / 5.07 \tag{2}$$

in which $\Delta\nu$ (in cm^{-1}) represents the frequency shift of the characteristic luminescence line of a specific oxide.

3. Results and Discussion

3.1. Thickness Effects on Oxidation Behavior at Different Temperatures

3.1.1. Oxidation Kinetics

The cyclic oxidation kinetics of the superalloy specimens with different thicknesses was evaluated by the mass gains per unit area as a function of exposure time at 900 °C and 1100 °C. In order to eliminate the effects of the original microstructure (i.e., composition effects), the specimens cut from the core section (S01-N, S03-N, S10-N) were tested. Figure 1 shows the microstructure of the core section (the matrix alloy) from which specimens S01-N, S03-N and S10-N were cut.

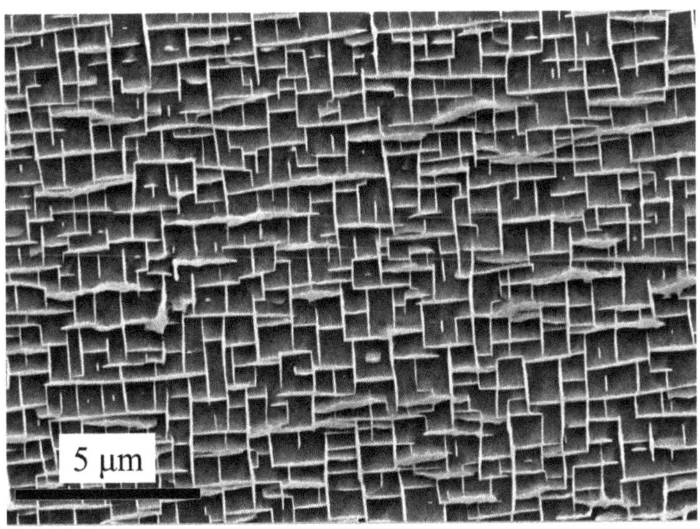

Figure 1. Microstructure of the core section from which the specimens S01-N, S03-N and S10-N were cut.

As shown in Figure 2a, the mass gain curves basically follow the parabolic law at 900 °C. However, the oxidations at 1100 °C reached a steady stage after 20 h, although their initial stage also followed the parabolic law but with obviously higher rates than those at 900 °C. In order to facilitate the comparison between different oxidation temperatures, the parabolic rate constant k_p was calculated based on the equation for parabolic law,

$$(\Delta w / A)^2 = k_p \cdot t + b \tag{3}$$

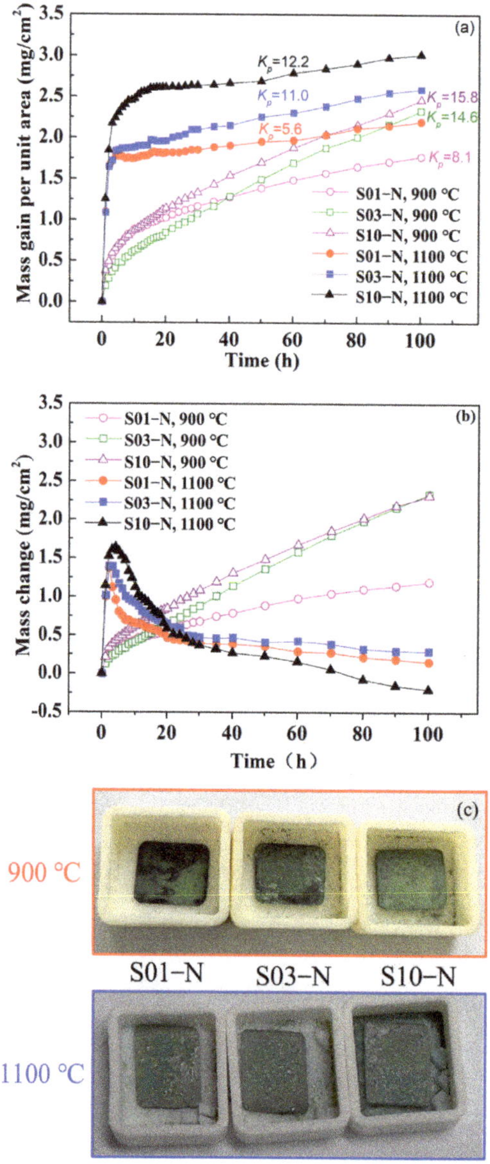

Figure 2. Cyclic oxidation kinetic curves of the specimens of IC21 alloy with different thicknesses at 900 °C and 1100 °C: (**a**) mass gain; (**b**) mass change. Parabolic rate constant k_p is also calculated according to Equation (2) and shown in (**a**) with a unit of 10^{-12} $g^2 \cdot cm^{-4} \cdot s^{-1}$; (**c**) macrostructure after 100 h cycle oxidation at 900 °C and 1100 °C.

The results shown in Figure 2 indicate that the parabolic rate constant was smaller for the specimens with smaller thicknesses both at 900 °C and 1100 °C. The mass gain of S01-N, S03-N and S10-N specimens were 1.77, 2.32 and 2.45 mg/cm^2 at 900 °C and 2.19, 2.59 and 3.01 mg/cm^2 at 1100 °C. Moreover, the differences in the oxidation rate caused by varied specimen thickness were more obvious for 900 °C because of the faster achievement of a steady stage at 1100 °C. On the other hand, the absolute values of mass gain per unit area at specific exposure time were also remarkably lower for the thinner specimens. This is especially true for the cyclic oxidation at 1100 °C with a larger change of 0.81 mg/cm^{-2} between S01-N and S10-N after 100 h compared with that of 0.69 mg/cm^{-2} at 900 °C. As a result, the mass gain of the thin specimen (S01-N) after 100 h of cyclic oxidation at 1100 °C was even smaller than those of the thicker specimens (S03-N and S10-N) at 900 °C. The spallation behaviors were further analyzed by measuring the mass of spalling oxides varied with exposure time (Figure 2b). The mass change values close to mass gain suggest that there was almost no spallation at 900 °C. However, powdery spallation of oxides was still observed in the crucibles containing S03-N and S10-N samples as Figure 2c showed. In contrast, oxide spallation is proved to evidently happen at 1100 °C, which was enhanced by longer exposure time and larger specimen thickness. The oxide spallation of S10-N was more obvious than S01-N and S03-N.

3.1.2. Composition and Microstructure of Oxide Scale

The oxidation products formed after 100 h of cyclic oxidation at 900 °C and 1100 °C were identified by XRD. As shown in Figure 3, NiO and Al_2O_3 were detected both at 900 °C and 1100 °C, but the spectral peak intensity of Al_2O_3 was higher for 1100 °C. However, Cr_2O_3, $NiMoO_4$ and MoO_3 only presented for the oxidation at 900 °C, while spectral peaks of $NiTa_2O_6$ were detected for that at 1100 °C. Moreover, the spinel oxide of $NiCr_2O_4$ formed at 900 °C mostly changed to $NiAl_2O_4$ for the oxidation at 1100 °C. It is worth noting that the type of oxides was quite similar for the specimens with different thicknesses oxidized at the same temperature except for the slight variations in content. This phenomenon suggests that the thermodynamics process of cyclic oxidation at a specific temperature was hardly changed by the specimen thickness.

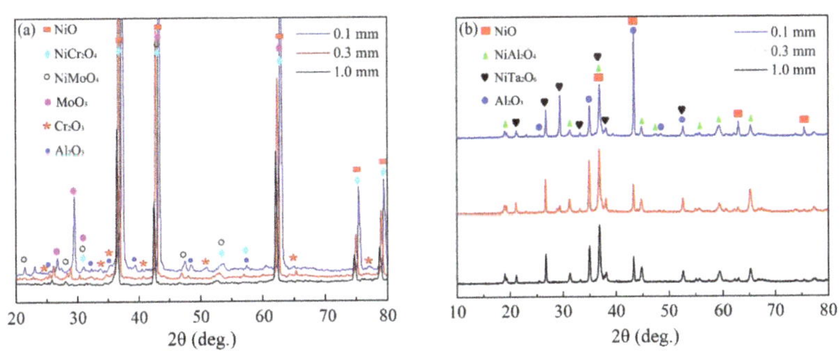

Figure 3. XRD patterns of oxides formed on the specimens of IC21 alloy with different thicknesses after 100 h of cyclic oxidation: (**a**) 900 °C; (**b**) 1100 °C.

The cross-section morphologies and compositions of the oxide scales formed after 100 h of cyclic oxidation were investigated and compared further among the specimens with different thicknesses as well as between 900 °C and 1100 °C. Multilayer oxide scales presented in all the specimens with an outmost layer of single oxide NiO (Figures 4 and 5). The columnar layer of NiO was discontinuous at 1100 °C due to the oxide spallation (Figure 5), while cracking was observed mainly at the interface between NiO and the oxide layer beneath in the thicker specimens for the cyclic oxidation at 900 °C (Figure 4b,c). Complex oxide layer of $NiAl_2O_4$ following a layer of Al_2O_3 formed beneath at 1100 °C, which became more continuous and denser for the thinner specimen. A small amount of oxide particles with relatively higher concentrations of Ta were detected at 1100 °C, which are consistent with the XRD spectral peaks of $NiTa_2O_6$. Instead, a complex oxide layer of $NiCr_2O_4$ and $NiMoO_4$ formed during the cyclic oxidation at 900 °C (Figure 4). A thin discontinuous layer of Cr_2O_3 and MoO_3 was also detected along with an internal oxidation zone of Al_2O_3 with dendritic morphology beneath. These two layers penetrated to each other at some locations of the thicker specimen (Figure 5b) and resulted in a blurred interface in between. Moreover, the internal oxidation of Al is considered to be enhanced in the thick specimen (Figure 5c) compared with that in the thin one (Figure 5a). Here, we should emphasize that there were only a few scattered internal Al_2O_3 formed after 100 h of cyclic oxidation at 1100 °C. Nevertheless, the preferable oxidation of Al in γ' still resulted in the formation of an Al-depletion zone between the oxide scale and the matrix alloy at 1100 °C, similar to the residual part among the dendritic internal oxides at 900 °C. This Al-depletion zone is commonly known as the γ'-free layer, and the near surface area of matrix alloy might have a reduced fraction of γ' precipitates as well (so-called γ'-reduced layer). The detailed behaviors of these microstructural degradations varied with specimen thickness and oxidation temperature and will be discussed separately in Section 3.2.

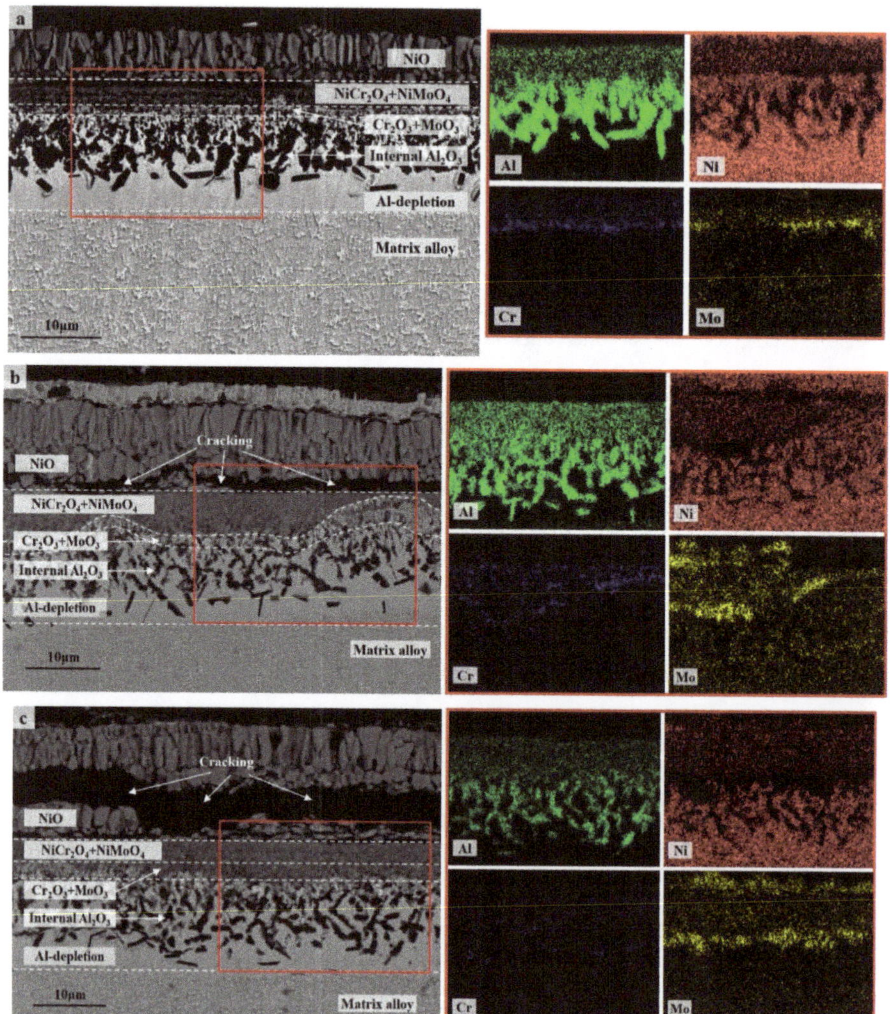

Figure 4. Cross-section morphologies (BSE) and composition distributions (EDS map scanning) of the oxide scales on the specimens of IC21 alloy with different thicknesses after 100 h of cyclic oxidation at 900 °C: (**a**) S01-N, 0.1 mm; (**b**) S03-N, 0.3 mm; (**c**) S10-N, 1.0 mm. The red square is the area of EDS map scanning.

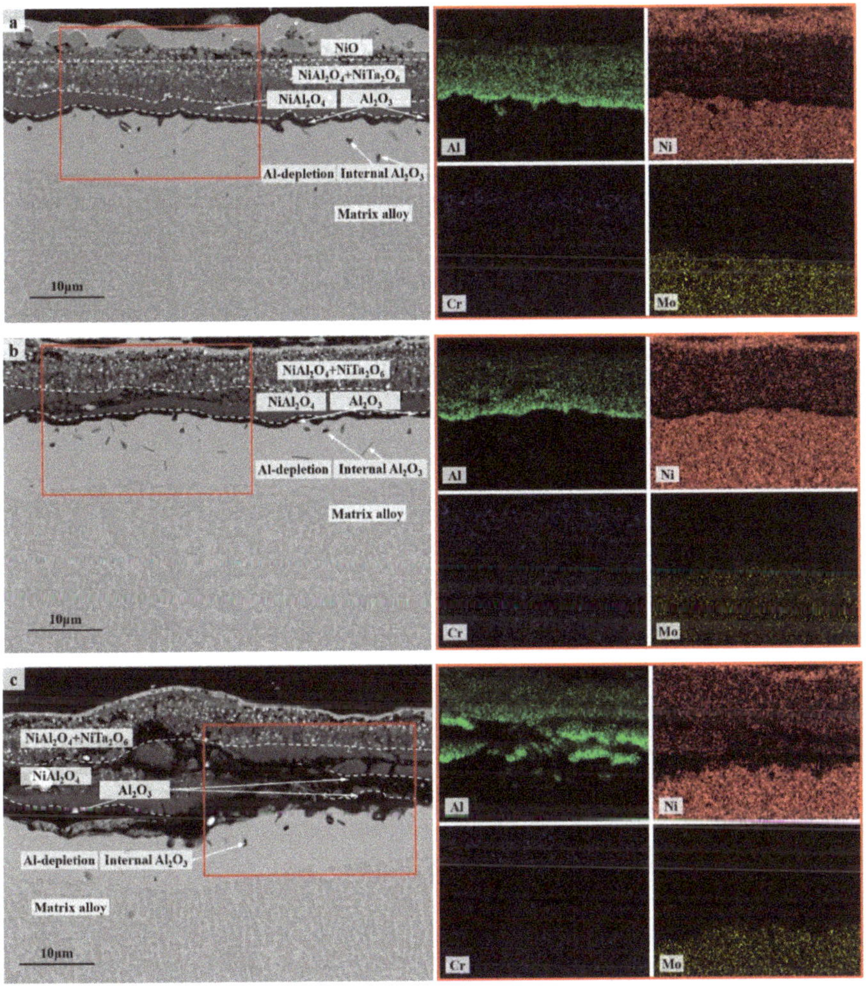

Figure 5. Cross-section morphologies (BSE) and composition distributions (EDS map scanning) of the oxide scales on the specimens of IC21 alloy with different thicknesses after 100 h of cyclic oxidation at 1100 °C: (**a**) S01-N, 0.1 mm; (**b**) S03-N, 0.3 mm; (**c**) S10-N, 1.0 mm. The red square is the area of EDS map scanning.

3.1.3. Oxidation Mechanisms

Thermodynamics

Based on the results of the oxidation products and oxide scales above, the oxidation mechanisms of IC21 alloy are considered to be different for 900 °C and 1100 °C. The relationship between the parabolic rate constant and the temperature is able to roughly predict the type of oxide formed for Ni-based superalloys [22,23]. The curves for the formations of NiO, Cr_2O_3, θ- and α-Al_2O_3 approximated in linear law are plotted in Figure 6 according to previous data [24]. As shown in Figure 6, the parabolic rate constants of IC21 alloy for the oxidation at 900 °C are all close to the line for Cr_2O_3. For the oxidation at 1100 °C, the rate constants in the initial stage locate between the lines for NiO and Cr_2O_3, while those in steady stage evidently move toward the Al_2O_3 zone (θ- and α-Al_2O_3). Based on the fast transition from θ-Al_2O_3 to α-Al_2O_3 during the cyclic oxidation of the IC21 alloy at high temperature [25], these results are in good agreement with the formation of Cr_2O_3 at a lower temperature but the occurrence of a protective α-Al_2O_3 layer at a higher temperature. In general, formation of Al_2O_3 is preferable over that of Cr_2O_3 especially at temperatures above 1000 °C due to the slower diffusion of reactive elements in Al_2O_3 and the volatility of Cr_2O_3 [26]. As a result, lower rates of the oxidation steady state appeared for 1100 °C, with even smaller mass gain than that at 900 °C for long-time exposure (Figure 2a). Moreover, $NiMoO_4$ and meta-stable MoO_3 were only detected with the effective protection of Cr_2O_3 at 900 °C, owing to the accelerated volatilization of these oxides at a higher temperature. Unfortunately, the weaker protection of discontinuous Cr_2O_3 still caused the formation of internal Al_2O_3 owing to the faster inward diffusion of oxygen ions. Nevertheless, the specimen thickness hardly changed the formation propensities of oxides at 900 °C and 1100 °C. This has been verified by almost the same oxide products with similar cross-section microstructures forming on the specimens with different thicknesses at a specific temperature.

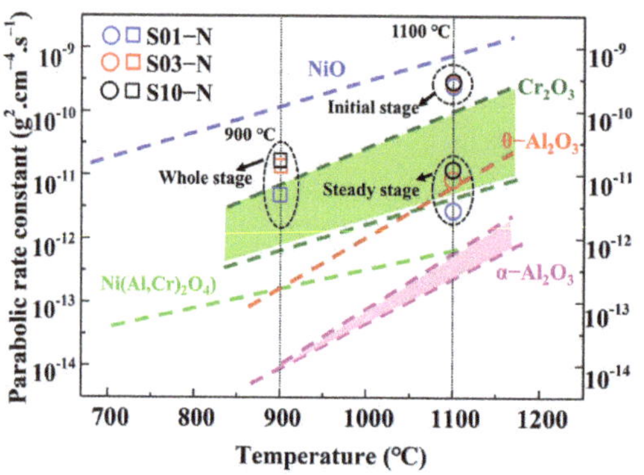

Figure 6. Comparison of the parabolic rate constants k_p for the specimens of IC21 alloy with different thicknesses at 900 °C and 1100 °C with the k_p for pure oxides varied with the temperature [24].

Kinetics Tuned by Spallation Behavior

The oxidation kinetics of the studied alloy is considered to be tuned by changing the oxide spallation behaviors with specimen thickness, especially at 1100 °C. For the oxidation at 900 °C, the residual stress in the outmost layer of NiO was evaluated by the shifts of its XRD spectrum compared with the standard one. As shown in Table 2, the results indicate that tensile stress presented in NiO decreased with increasing specimen thickness. The larger stress relaxation due to more cracking happening in the thicker specimen (Figure 4b,c) is considered to be responsible for this phenomenon. Consequently, more oxygen ions diffused inward via the cracks and enhanced the internal oxidation of Al in the thicker specimen due to the weak protection of discontinuous Cr_2O_3. On the other hand, the residual stress in the Al_2O_3 layer at 1100 °C was measured by a Raman microprobe instead due to the extensive spallation of NiO and the farther location of Al_2O_3 from the surface. Compressive stresses were detected with much higher absolute values than those in NiO formed at 900 °C. Moreover, lower compressive stress presented in the severe spallation area of the thicker specimen, which was similar to the case of NiO formed at 900 °C. However, a contrary trend appeared in the area with scarce spallation and weak residual stress relaxation. In other words, decreasing specimen thickness reduced the stress concentration in the oxide scale, which in turn decreased the amount of spallation and improved the oxidation resistance of the IC21 alloy at high temperature. This is also verified by less mass gain and a more continuous Al_2O_3 layer in the thin specimen.

Table 2. Residual stresses (GPa) in the oxide scales of the studied alloy specimens with different thicknesses.

Specimen Number	Residual Stress (GPa) *		
	900 °C, 100 h (NiO **)	1100 °C, 100 h (Al_2O_3 ***)	
	No Spallation	Less Spallation	Severe Spallation
S01-1	0.26	**−3.16**	−2.52
S01-2	0.24	**−3.35**	−2.38
S01-3	0.19	**−3.82**	−2.20

* Positive and negative values represent tensile and compressive stresses respectively; ** normal stress perpendicular to specimen surface was measured via X-ray diffraction spectra analysis; *** in-plane stress parallel to specimen surface was measured via Raman spectra analysis.

Oxide spallation is generally caused by misfits in thermal expansion and elastic deformation between oxide scale and matrix alloy [27–29]. However, the much larger thermal expansion coefficient of NiO compared to those of other oxides (e.g., Cr_2O_3 and Al_2O_3) [30–32] made the exfoliation of NiO take place firstly along the weaker interface between oxide layers via a buckling route [27,29]. As a result, tensile stress normal to the alloy surface was generated in NiO, while compressive stress resided in the oxide layer beneath during cooling. The specimen thickness effects on oxide spallation behavior can be ascribed to the easier stress relief in the thin specimen via creep deformation [21]. The internal or continuous Al_2O_3 oxides adhered to the Al-depletion zone rendered the cooperative deformation of the bottomed oxide layers and matrix alloy. Moreover, the less spallation but more cracking found at 900 °C compared with 1100 °C is considered to be caused by the different types of oxides formed under the NiO layer as well as the smaller temperature drop during cyclic oxidation.

3.2. Composition Related Thickness Effects on Microstructural Degradation

3.2.1. Thickness Effects under Fixed Composition

Besides the specimen thickness effects on oxidation behavior, the microstructural degradation caused by high-temperature oxidation is also crucial to the creep resistances of superalloys, especially for thin-walled components. Based on the cross-section microstructures after cyclic oxidation at 900 °C and 1100 °C illustrated in Figures 4 and 5, the cubic morphology of the matrix alloy in all the specimens hardly changed, except for the γ'-free layer with depletion of Al. However, a careful investigation of the statistics of the volume fraction of γ' precipitates along the depth of the specimen confirms the existence of a γ'-reduced layer after 100 h of cyclic oxidation at 1100 °C (Figure 7), which is in agreement with the cases in other traditional Ni-based superalloys [13–15,21]. The γ'-reduced layer consisted of an 8 μm wide region with a sharply decreased volume fraction of γ' right beneath the γ'-free layer and another much wider region with gentle variation. Although the sharply γ'-reduced region was almost identical for the specimens with different thicknesses, a narrower γ'-free layer and a gently γ'-reduced region with a smaller linear slope (S_l) presented obviously in the thin specimen (S01-N). Here, we should mention that the bottom of the γ'-reduced layer in the thin specimen was already close to its core (mirror plane) because of its limited original thickness (0.1 mm). Moreover, the volume fraction of γ' in the core of the thin specimen (~70% in S01-N) was still lower than those in the thicker specimens (~80% in S03-N and S10-N), which were almost the same as the original one before oxidation (82%). The higher consumption of Al to promote the fast formation of α-Al_2O_3 in the thin specimen is considered to be the reason behind this finding. It is important to emphasize that the γ'-reduced layer in the studied IC21 alloy was much narrower than those found in CMSX-4 an3d René N5 [14,21,22], regardless of specimen thickness. In addition, there was even no γ'-reduced layer formed during the oxidation of the IC21 alloy at 900 °C. These discrepancies in the γ' degradation zones after high temperature oxidation among the IC21 alloy and other Ni-based superalloys are ascribed to the high-Al content in the studied alloy, which will be discussed in detail below.

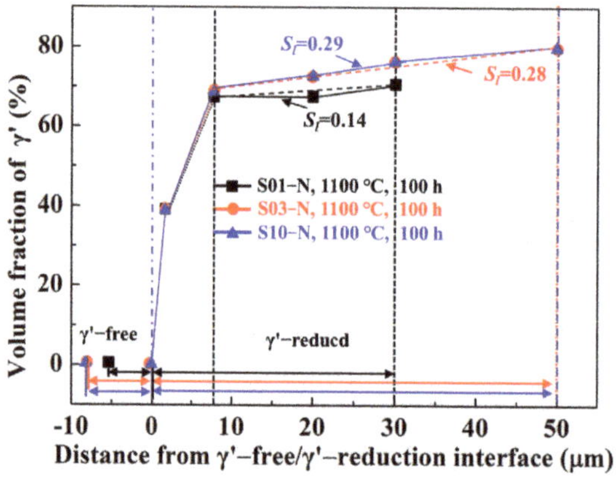

Figure 7. Volume fractions of γ' precipitates along the depth of the specimens of the IC21 alloy with different thicknesses after 100 h of cyclic oxidation at 1100 °C. The γ'-free layer was defined as the region with zero volume fraction of γ', while the γ'-reduced layer was defined as the region with a lower volume fraction of γ' than the original one (or that in the core). The fitted linear slopes of the gentle variation region in the γ'-reduced layer S_l are shown as well.

3.2.2. Composition Effects in Thin-Walled Specimen

The composition effects on the microstructural degradation were studied by the oxidation tests of a series of specimens with different original Al contents and γ/γ' morphologies. The variations in composition and microstructure were achieved by cutting the specimens from the heat-treated plate with different distances away from the surface. We paid close attention to the microstructural evolution in the thin-walled situation by only isothermal oxidizing the specimens with a thickness of 0.1 mm at 1100 °C for 100 h. As the detailed information of these thin specimens (S01-1, 2, 3, N) shows in Table 1, the increasing original Al content resulted in increasing the volume fraction and average size of γ' precipitates, the morphologies of which changed from sphere to cube. However, inhomogeneous Al contents and γ/γ' microstructures might exist in each single specimen due to the relatively larger scale of the specimen thickness (0.1 mm) compared to those of the γ' degradation regions near the surface after heat treatments. After 100 h of cyclic oxidation at 1100 °C, similar oxide products formed in all the specimens, but a much denser α-Al_2O_3 layer was observed in the specimen with higher original Al content. In other words, there was a critical value of Al content to support the formation of a protective and continuous α-Al_2O_3 scale to maintain the oxidation resistance of the superalloy.

On the other hand, the microstructural degradation caused by the isothermal oxidation was affected by the original Al content of the specimen even more. As shown in Figure 8, most of the matrix alloy in S01-1 became the γ'-free layer, while residual γ/γ' microstructures were still left in the core of the specimens with higher original Al content.

The matrix of the S01-N specimen still had a coarsened γ' content of 70 vol% and a thickness of 74 μm matrix residual after 100 h cycle oxidation. However, the spherical combined with rounded cubic morphologies of γ' precipitates in S01-2 changed to spherical morphologies with a larger size of 1 μm. Moreover, γ' precipitated with a strip shape formed after oxidation in S01-3 instead of the original cubic morphology. It is worth noting that only a slight coarsening of γ' precipitates happened in S01-N, which also had the thickest residual γ/γ' zone but the thinnest γ'-free layer. Further analysis results on the thicknesses of the residual matrix alloy, especially the residual γ/γ' zone, reveal their upward trends with increasing original Al content (Figure 9). In addition, the slope of the thickness of the residual γ/γ' zone was higher than that of the whole residual matrix alloy. As a result, the thickness of the γ'-free layer reduced in turn. Accordingly, the Al content at the γ'-free/γ'-reduced interface after isothermal oxidation also followed a similar increasing trend but with a much smaller slope than that in the core as a function of the original Al content (Figure 10). Consequently, the difference in the Al content between the γ'-reduced layer and the core section was larger for the thin specimen with higher original Al content. In other words, the formation of protective α-Al_2O_3 can only be supplied by the sufficient Al contents in the near surface area without deteriorating the γ/γ' microstructure in the core which was the same as that reported in the literature [33–35]. The obtained results discussed above verified that the high-Al content was the main reason for the weaker microstructural degradation during the high temperature oxidation of the IC21 alloy. Furthermore, this composition effect of Al was even more important for the oxidation behavior and microstructural evolution of the thin specimen. Nevertheless, only the variation trend of the γ' degradation zones has been disclosed in this study, while further works need to be carried out to determine the critical value of Al content quantitatively. The present study lays a foundation for the design of high-Al Ni-based SC superalloys, which are beneficial to improve oxidation resistance and mitigate the thickness debit effects in a service environment. In order to decease the degree of thin-wall blade oxidation, a method was proposed by adopting a NiPtAl coating and a thermal barrier deposited by EB PVD (electron beam physical vapor deposition). However, the inside of the blades which were subjected to lower temperatures may use CVD (chemical vapor deposition coating) to protect the matrix.

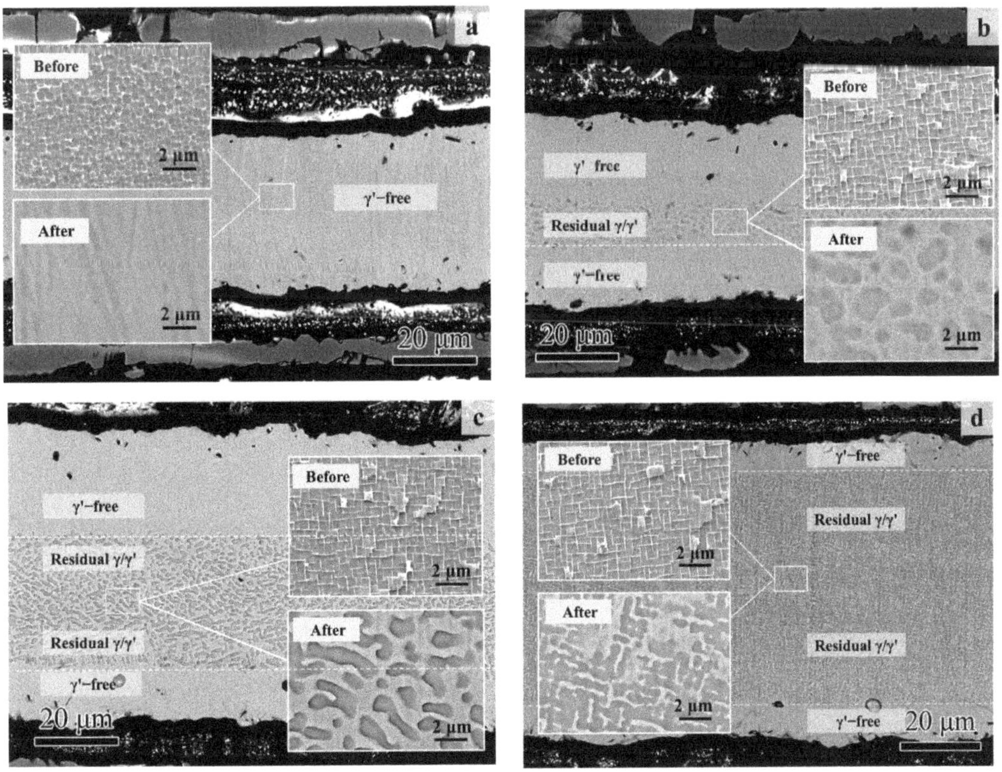

Figure 8. Cross-section morphologies of the thin specimens (thickness of 0.1 mm) with different original Al contents after 100 h of isothermal oxidation at 1100 °C: (**a**) S01-1; (**b**) S01-2; (**c**) S01-3; (**d**) S01-N. The magnified morphologies in the core are shown as inner figures in order to reveal the microstructure degradation more clearly. The original microstructures before oxidation are also shown for comparison.

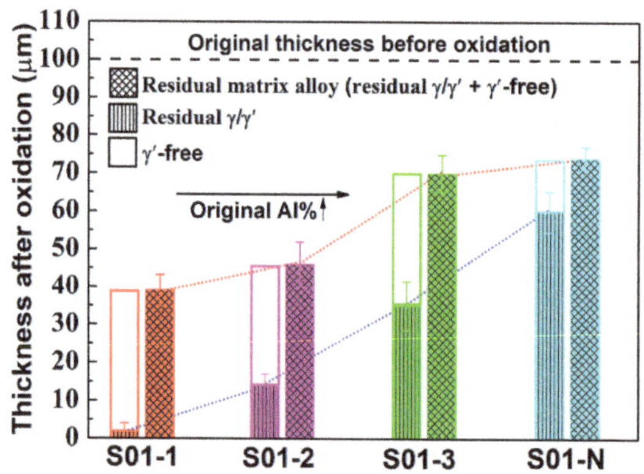

Figure 9. Thicknesses of the residual matrix alloy region in the thin specimens (thickness of 0.1 mm) with different original Al contents after 100 h of isothermal oxidation at 1100 °C. The thicknesses of the residual γ/γ′ zone and the γ′-free zone, which make up the residual matrix alloy region, are also plotted.

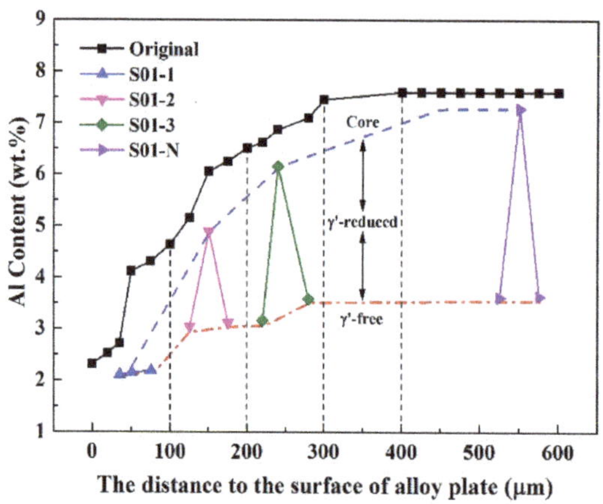

Figure 10. Variation of Al content in the thin specimens (thickness of 0.1 mm) with different original Al contents after 100 h of isothermal oxidation at 1100 °C. The values measured in the core and at the γ′-free/γ′-reduced interface are plotted in accordance with the distances to the surface of alloy plate, from which the specimens were cut. The vertical dashed lines are plotted to distinguish the sampling areas with different original Al contents. The original Al contents in the alloy plate as a function of distance are also plotted for comparison.

4. Conclusions

The thickness effects on the oxidation behavior and microstructural degradation of a high-Al Ni-based SC superalloy IC21 were studied via cyclic and isothermal oxidation tests at 900 °C and 1100 °C. The mass gain of S01-N, S03-N and S10-N specimens were 1.77, 2.32 and 2.45 mg/cm^2 at 900 °C and 2.19, 2.59 and 3.01 mg/cm^2 at 1100 °C. Temperature was found to have obvious influences on the oxidation thermodynamics and kinetics of the IC21 alloy. Compared with the discontinuous Cr_2O_3 and internal dendritic Al_2O_3 observed after the cyclic oxidation at 900 °C, the continuous Al_2O_3 layer without oxides of Mo formed instead at 1100 °C. As a result, the IC21 alloy achieved a steady stage of oxidation faster at 1100 °C, within 20 h. Specimen thickness also showed evident effects with higher oxidation resistance presented in the thinner specimen both at 900 °C and 1100 °C. However, the specimen thickness hardly changed the oxidation thermodynamics but did tune the kinetics by altering the oxide spallation behavior of the IC21 alloy. The easier stress relief in the thin specimen via creep deformation is considered to be the main mechanism, while the severe spallation at 1100 °C was ascribed to the different oxidation products as well as the larger temperature variation. Moreover, the microstructural degradation during oxidation, which was characterized by the γ'-free and γ'-reduced layers in the residual matrix alloy, was weaker in the studied IC21 alloy than those in CMSX-4 and René N5 due to its high Al content. This γ' degradation was further mitigated by smaller specimen thickness due to the higher consumption of Al. The matrix of the S01-N specimen still had a coarsened γ' content of 70 vol% and a thickness of 74 μm matrix residual after a 100 h cycle oxidation. The composition effects on the microstructural degradation studied via the isothermal oxidation tests of thin specimens with different original microstructures verified the indispensable role of sufficient Al in the achievement of higher oxidation resistance and microstructural stability, especially for a thin-walled situation. The results obtained in the present study shed light on the mechanisms of the composition-related thickness debit effects and lay a foundation for the materials design of modern Ni-based SC superalloys.

Author Contributions: Conceptualization, H.Z., W.Z., J.W. and S.G.; Methodology, H.Z., Y.R., S.G. and S.L.; Validation, Y.R.; Formal analysis, W.G., W.Z. and Y.P.; Investigation, Y.R.; Resources, J.W.; Writing—original draft, H.Z.; Writing—review & editing, W.G. and W.Z.; Project administration, S.L.; Funding acquisition, W.G., Y.P., S.G. and S.L. All authors have read and agreed to the published version of the manuscript.

Funding: This paper is supported by National Natural Science Foundation (No. 52103358), National Science and Technology Major Project (2017-VI-0012-0084) and Science Center for Gas Turbine Project (No. P2021-A-IV-001-003).

Data Availability Statement: The data presented in this study are available on request from the corresponding and first author. The data are not publicly due to [Alloy material sensitivity problem].

Conflicts of Interest: The authors declare no conflict of interest.

References

1. Reed, R.C. *The Superalloys: Fundamentals and Applications*; Cambridge University Press: Cambridge, MA, USA, 2006.
2. Koff, B.L. Gas turbine technology evolution: A designers perspective. *J. Propuls. Power* **2004**, *20*, 577–595. [CrossRef]
3. Xu, L.; Bo, S.; Hongde, Y.; Lei, W. Evolution of Rolls-Royce air-cooled turbine blades and feature analysis. *Procedia Eng.* **2015**, *99*, 1482–1491. [CrossRef]
4. Hu, Y.; Zhang, L.; Cheng, C.; Zhao, P.; Cao, T.; Guo, G.; Zhao, J. Influence of specimen thickness on the creep behavior of a directional solidification nickel-based superalloy. *Vacuum* **2018**, *150*, 105–115. [CrossRef]
5. Srivastava, A.; Needleman, A. Phenomenological modeling of the effect of specimen thickness on the creep response of Ni-based superalloy single crystals. *Acta Mater.* **2013**, *61*, 6506–6516. [CrossRef]
6. Srivastava, A.; Gopagoni, S.; Needleman, A.; Seetharaman, V.; Staroselsky, A.; Banerjee, R. Effect of specimen thickness on the creep response of a Ni-based single-crystal superalloy. *Acta Mater.* **2012**, *60*, 5697–5711. [CrossRef]
7. Wen, Z.; Pei, H.; Li, D.; Yue, Z.; Gao, J. Thickness influence on the creep response of DD6 Ni-based single-crystal superalloy. *High Temp. Mater. Process.* **2016**, *35*, 871–880. [CrossRef]
8. Brunner, M.; Bensch, M.; Völkl, R.; Affeldt, E.; Glatzel, U. Thickness influence on creep properties for Ni-based superalloy M247LC SX. *Mater. Sci. Eng. A* **2012**, *550*, 254–262. [CrossRef]
9. Hüttner, R.; Gabel, J.; Glatzel, U.; Völkl, R. First creep results on thin-walled single-crystal superalloys. *Mater. Sci. Eng. A* **2009**, *510*, 307–311. [CrossRef]
10. Cassenti, B.; Staroselsky, A. The effect of thickness on the creep response of thin-wall single crystal components. *Mater. Sci. Eng. A* **2009**, *508*, 183–189. [CrossRef]
11. Seetharaman, V.; Cetel, A.D. Thickness debit in creep properties of PWA 1484 [A]. In Proceedings of the 10th International Symposium on Superalloys (Superalloys 2004), Champion, PA, USA, 19–23 September 2004; pp. 207–214.
12. Duan, R.; Jalowicka, A.; Unocic, K.; Pint, B.A.; Huczkowski, P.; Chyrkin, A.; Grüner, D.; Pillai, R.; Quadakkers, W.J. Predicting oxidation-limited lifetime of thin-walled components of NiCrW alloy 230. *Oxid. Met.* **2017**, *87*, 11–38. [CrossRef]
13. Bensch, M.; Konrad, C.H.; Fleischmann, E.; Rae, C.M.; Glatzel, U. Influence of oxidation on near-surface γ' fraction and resulting creep behaviour of single crystal Ni-base superalloy M247LC SX. *Mater. Sci. Eng. A* **2013**, *577*, 179–188. [CrossRef]
14. Bensch, M.; Preußner, J.; Hüttner, R.; Obigodi, G.; Virtanen, S.; Gabel, J.; Glatzel, U. Modelling and analysis of the oxidation influence on creep behaviour of thin-walled structures of the single-crystal nickel-base superalloy René N5 at 980 °C. *Acta Mater.* **2010**, *58*, 1607–1617. [CrossRef]

15. Dryepondt, S.; Monceau, D.; Crabos, F.; Andrieu, E. Static and dynamic aspects of coupling between creep behavior and oxidation on MC2 single crystal superalloy at 1150 °C. *Acta Mater.* **2005**, *53*, 4199–4209. [CrossRef]
16. Pour-Ali, S.; Tavangar, R.; Akhtari, F.; Hejazi, S. High-temperature oxidation behavior of GTD-111 Ni-based superalloy with an ultrafine-grained surface at 900 °C. *Corros. Sci.* **2022**, *212*, 110935. [CrossRef]
17. Hu, Y.; Cheng, C.; Cao, T.; Zhang, L.; Zhao, J. A study on the multiple stages of oxidation kinetics in a single crystal nickel-based superalloy. *Corros. Sci.* **2021**, *188*, 109512. [CrossRef]
18. Li, P.; Jin, X.; Zhao, J.; Lu, P.; Hu, N.; Liu, D.; Dong, J.; Fan, X. Oxidation behaviors and compressive strength evolution of DD6 Ni-based single-crystal superalloy at 1100 °C. *Corros. Sci.* **2022**, *208*, 110684. [CrossRef]
19. Pistor, J.; Hagen, S.P.; Virtanen, S.; Körner, C. Influence of the microstructural homogeneity on the high-temperature oxidation behavior of a single crystalline Ni-base superalloy. *Scr. Mater.* **2022**, *207*, 114301. [CrossRef]
20. Perez, T.; Monceau, D.; Desgranges, C. Kinetic oxidation model including the transient regime for a single crystal nickel-based superalloy over the temperature range 750–1300 °C. *Corros. Sci.* **2022**, *206*, 110485.
21. Orosz, R.; Krupp, U.; Christ, H.J.; Monceau, D. The influence of specimen thickness on the high temperature corrosion behavior of CMSX-4 during thermal-cycling exposure. *Oxid. Met.* **2007**, *68*, 165–176. [CrossRef]
22. Bensch, M.; Sato, A.; Warnken, N.; Affeldt, E.; Reed, R.; Glatzel, U. Modelling of high temperature oxidation of alumina-forming single-crystal nickel-base superalloys. *Acta Mater.* **2012**, *60*, 5468–5480. [CrossRef]
23. Sato, A.; Chiu, Y.-L.; Reed, R.C. Oxidation of nickel-based single-crystal superalloys for industrial gas turbine applications. *Acta Mater.* **2011**, *59*, 225–240. [CrossRef]
24. Qin, L.; Pei, Y.; Li, S.; Zhao, X.; Gong, S.; Xu, H. Role of volatilization of molybdenum oxides during the cyclic oxidation of high-Mo containing Ni-based single crystal superalloys. *Corros. Sci.* **2017**, *129*, 192–204. [CrossRef]
25. Yang, T.T.; Zhou, X.; Li, S.S.; Pei, Y.L.; Gong, S.K. Cyclic oxidation behavior of Ni_3Al-based single crystal alloy IC21. *Rare Met.* **2017**, 1–7. [CrossRef]
26. Akhtar, A.; Hegde, S.; Reed, R.C. The oxidation of single-crystal nickel-based superalloys. *JOM* **2006**, *58*, 37–42. [CrossRef]
27. Evans, H.E. Modelling oxide spallation. *Mater. High Temp.* **1994**, *12*, 219–227. [CrossRef]
28. Jedliński, J.; Bennett, M.J.; Evans, H.E. Experimental data on the spallation of protective oxide scales: A brief literature survey. *Mater. High Temp.* **1994**, *12*, 169–175. [CrossRef]
29. Evans, H.E.; Lobb, R.C. Conditions for the initiation of oxide-scale cracking and spallation. *Corros. Sci.* **1984**, *24*, 209–222. [CrossRef]
30. Wang, Y.; Fang, H.; Zacherl, C.L.; Mei, Z.; Shang, S.; Chen, L.-Q.; Jablonski, P.D.; Liu, Z.-K. First-principles lattice dynamics, thermodynamics, and elasticity of Cr_2O_3. *Surf. Sci.* **2012**, *606*, 1422–1425. [CrossRef]
31. Nielsen, T.H.; Leipold, M.H. Thermal expansion of nickel oxide. *J. Am. Ceram. Soc.* **1965**, *48*, 164. [CrossRef]
32. Touloukian, Y.S. *Thermophysical Properties of High Temperature Solid Materials. Volume 4. Oxides and Their Solutions and Mixtures. Part 1. Simple Oxygen Compounds and Their Mixtures*; Thermostatical and Electronic Properties Information Analysis Center: Lafayette, Indiana, 1966.
33. Shen, Y.; Ju, Q.; Xu, G.; Du, X.; Zhang, Y.W.; Zhu, Y.; Huang, J.; Wang, T.Y.; Liu, Z. Improved oxidation resistance and excellent strength of nickel-based superalloy at 1100 °C by determining critical Cr-Al value. *Mater. Lett.* **2022**, *328*, 133226. [CrossRef]
34. Yun, D.; Seo, S.; Jeong, H.; Yoo, Y.S. Effect of refractory elements and Al on the high temperature oxidation of Ni-base superalloys and modelling of their oxidation resistance. *J. Alloys Compd.* **2017**, *710*, 8–19. [CrossRef]
35. Yu, H.; Ukai, S.; Hayashi, S.; Oono, N. Effect of Al content on the high-temperature oxidation of Co-20Cr-(5, 10) Al oxide dispersion strengthened superalloys. *Corros. Sci.* **2017**, *118*, 49–59. [CrossRef]

crystals

MDPI

Article

Thickness Debit Effect in Creep Performance of a Ni_3Al-Based Single-Crystal Superalloy with [001] Orientation

Shuangqi Zhang [1], Guoquan Ma [1], Haibo Wang [2], Wenqi Guo [3], Haigen Zhao [3], Yong Shang [2], Yanling Pei [2], Shusuo Li [3,4,*] and Shengkai Gong [2,4]

1 School of Materials Science and Engineering, Beihang University, Beijing 100191, China
2 Frontier Research Institute of Innovative Science and Technology, Beihang University, Beijing 100191, China
3 Research Institute of Aero-Engine, Beihang University, Beijing 100191, China
4 AECC Guizhou Liyang Aviation Power Company Limited, Guiyang 550014, China
* Correspondence: lishs@buaa.edu.cn

Abstract: With the complexity of the structure of aero-engine turbine blades, the blade wall thickness continues to decrease. It is found that when the blade wall thickness decreases to a certain extent, its mechanical properties will decline significantly. It is extremely important to study this phenomenon of a significant decline in mechanical properties caused by wall thickness. In this paper, the creep behavior of a second-generation Ni_3Al-based single crystal superalloy with different wall thicknesses and [001] orientation at 980 °C/220 MPa has been studied and compared with the creep life of Φ4 round bar. The experimental results show that the second orientation and the surface affected zone are not the main reasons for the reduction of the life of thin-walled samples under this experimental condition. By analyzing the fracture morphology and deformed microstructure of thin-walled samples with different thicknesses, it is found that the thickness debit effect of the single crystal alloy occurs since the effective stress area of the alloy changes due to internal defects and surface affected zone during the creep process. For thicker samples, the creep life of the alloy can be extended by making the samples undergo certain plastic deformation through better plastic deformation coordination ability, while for thinner samples, the plastic coordination ability is poor, and the ability to extend the creep life through plastic deformation is also weaker when the effective stress area of the alloy changes, which leads to the thinner samples being more prone to fracture.

Keywords: single crystal; thickness debit effect; creep; Ni_3Al-based superalloys

1. Introduction

As an intermetallic compound phase, Ni_3Al has a high specific strength and specific stiffness, especially good high-temperature mechanical properties. Ni_3Al phase contains high Al content, which has a low density compared with other alloy elements. Therefore, Ni_3Al-based single-crystal superalloys also have the advantage of low density. Ni_3Al-based single crystal superalloy mainly consists of γ and γ' phases. Under the condition of high temperature and stress, the two phases will undergo complex changes. This change in microstructure will affect the mechanical properties of the material. Therefore, it is very important to study Ni_3Al-based single crystal superalloy [1–4].

Because of the excellent properties of Ni_3Al-based single-crystal superalloy, it has attracted extensive attention as a candidate material for aero-engine turbine blades. In recent years, researchers have paid attention to the lightweight of turbine blades to meet the increasing design requirements of aero-engine turbine blades [5]. To make the blade lighter and thinner, researchers have continuously reduced the section size of specific parts of the blade and found that when the section size is reduced to a certain extent, the mechanical properties of these parts will decline significantly, which seriously affects the performance of the aero-engine. Therefore, people began to study the reason for performance degeneration caused by the change in section size [1,6–8]. The thickness debit effect is also called the section size effect, which means that when the size of the section direction of the part decreases to a certain extent, its mechanical properties will change significantly compared with the standard test bar [9,10].

The thickness debit effect of single crystal superalloys has been studied by researchers [11–16]. Some researchers believe that the thickness debit effect of single-crystal alloys is mainly caused by surface oxidation behavior [17,18]. Brunner et al. believed that the thin-walled sample has a high proportion of surface area, resulting in its performance being greatly affected by surface changes [19]. It is obvious that oxidation will be affected by the surface state of the alloy, such as secondary orientation. Zhao studied the relationship between the second orientation and the properties of thin wall samples of DD6 single crystal superalloy at 850 °C/560 MPa and 980 °C/250 MPa. It was found that when the primary orientation was [001], the greater the deviation of the second orientation from the [010] direction, the more the creep properties decreased [7,20]. At present, there are many kinds of research on the effects of primary orientation on the properties of tubes, but there is a lack of research on the effects of different secondary orientations on the properties of thin walls.

At present, studies on the thickness debit effect of single-crystal superalloys mainly focus on Ni-based single-crystal alloys, and no uniform explanation has been provided for the cause of the thickness debit effect. Furthermore, studies on the thickness debit effect of Ni_3Al-based single crystal alloys are even fewer [7,21]. Therefore, based on a second-generation Ni_3Al-based single crystal superalloy, the creep life of the alloy with three kinds of wall thickness samples of 0.3, 0.5, and 0.7 mm at 980 °C/220 MPa was studied in this paper. By comparing the creep life with that of Φ4 round bar, whether the three samples will produce the thickness debit effect is analyzed. The main influencing factors of the thickness debit effect of the alloy are revealed by analyzing the microstructure, which will provide some references for the subsequent research on the thickness debit effect.

2. Experimental

The alloy used in the test was a second-generation Ni_3Al-based single-crystal superalloy. After being refined at about 1600 °C in a directional solidification furnace, it was cast into the mold shell. Then the mold shell was pulled out of the insulation area at a speed of 4.5 mm/min, and the single crystal test bar was obtained by removing the mold shell after cooling. The single crystal test bar was etched with hydrochloric acid hydrogen peroxide solution to check the integrity of the single crystal. The main essential components are listed in Table 1. Test bars with good single crystal integrity for standard heat treatment (1300 °C, 2 h/1310 °C, 2 h/1320 °C, 2 h/1325 °C, 4 h/1330 °C, 6 h/argon gas cooling/1040 °C, 6 h/argon gas cooling/870 °C, 6h/furnace cooling) were selected.

Table 1. Composition of the used Ni_3Al-based single-crystal superalloy (mass %).

Element	Ni	Al	Cr	Mo	Re	Ta	Y
Content	Excess	7.6–8.3	1.5–2.5	9–13	0.5–1.5	2.4–4.0	0.01

The X-ray backscattering Laue method was used to conduct the crystal orientation test along the axis of the test bar. The test bar with the primary orientation deviating less than 5 ° from the [001] direction was selected. With the consideration of the secondary orientation, the secondary orientation perpendicular to the side of the sample was controlled to deviate less than 5 ° from the [110] and [010] directions, respectively. The specific sampling method and sample size are shown in Figures 1 and 2.

In order to ensure the surface quality of the thin wall sample, the 1 mm thick sample was processed by wire cutting, and then the surface and side of the sample were ground with 400, 600, 800, 1000, 1200, and 1500 silicon carbide sandpaper in turn. The error in the thickness direction of the sample was ±0.02 mm. Finally, the surface of the sample was polished with a diamond polish of 0.5 nm particles. The surface of the treated sample was required to be free of obvious scratches and other defects.

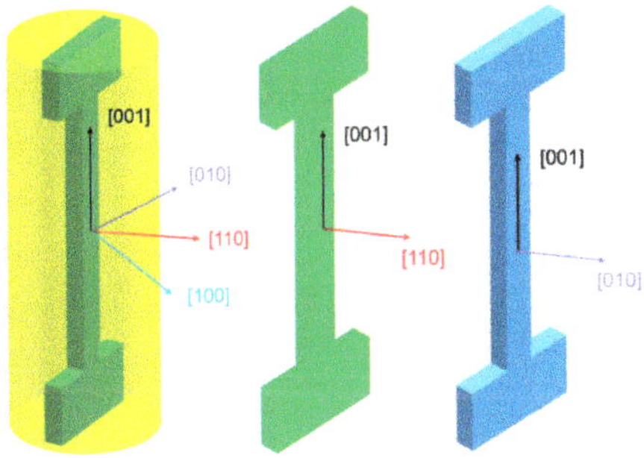

Figure 1. The schematic of samples with [001] primary orientation and different secondary orientation with [110] and [010].

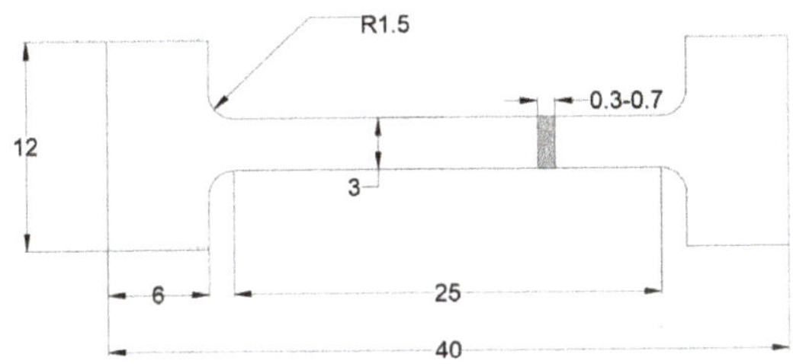

(**a**)

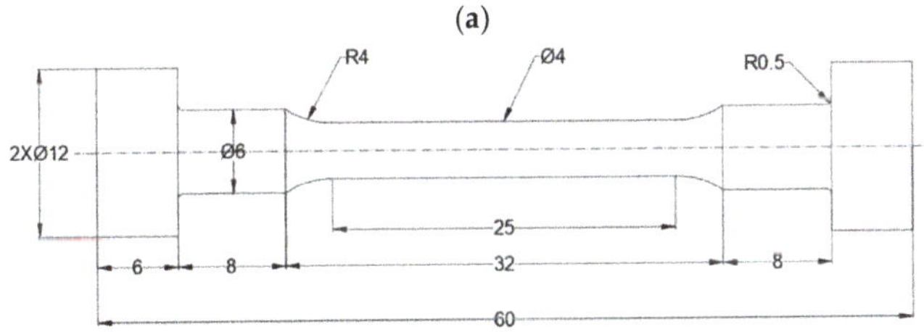

(**b**)

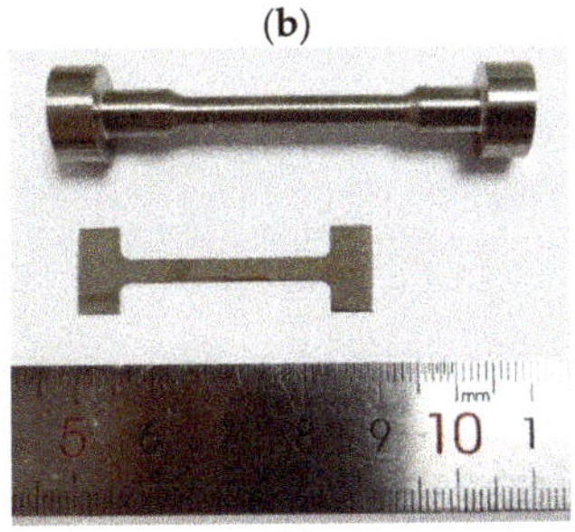

(**c**)

Figure 2. Test pieces' sizes: (**a**) Thin wall sample size, (**b**) Φ4 round bar size, (**c**) picture of the sample.

All creep tests were conducted according to the uniaxial tensile creep test method for metallic materials (GB/T 2039-2012), and the test conditions were 980 °C/220 MPa. After the test, samples were taken from the fracture area and test section of the sample, respectively, for polishing. The reagent prepared by CuSO4+100mL HCl+100mL C2H5OH was used for corrosion. All the microstructure characterizations were conducted by scanning electron microscope (SEM, Apreo S LoVac, FEI, Czech) equipped with an electron backscatter diffraction (EBSD) system (orientation analysis) operated at 25 kV and an energy dispersive spectroscopy (EDS) system operated at 20 kV. The fracture surface of the sample was treated by ultrasonic cleaning, the fracture morphology and microstructure were observed by SEM, and the surface oxide composition was analyzed by EDS. To further analyze the crystal change, EBSD was used to characterize the crystal rotation near the fracture surface of the sample.

3. Results and Discussion

In order to study the influence of wall thickness and secondary orientation on the creep property of the sample, thin wall samples with the second orientation of [110] and [010] are selected for testing. The creep life of thin wall samples with different thicknesses and Φ4 samples is shown in Figure 3.

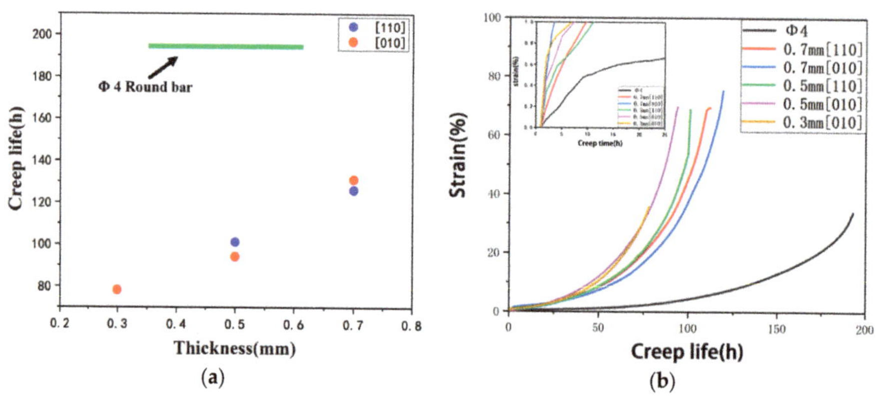

Figure 3. Creep life of thin-walled samples with different thicknesses and Φ4 round bar samples at 980 °C/220 MPa. (**a**) Relationship between wall thickness and creep life. (**b**) The creep curves at 980 °C/220 MPa.

It can be seen from Figure 3a that the creep life of the 0.3–0.7 mm thin-walled sample is far less than Φ4 round bar sample. The creep life of the thin wall sample with a wall thickness of 0.7 mm is 38% lower than that of the Φ4 round bar sample. The creep life of the 0.5 mm thin wall sample is 48% lower than that of the Φ4 round bar sample. The creep life of 0.3 mm thin wall sample is 60% lower than that of the Φ4 round bar sample. Since the creep life has decreased by 38% at 0.7 mm, which is much smaller than that of the Φ4 round bar sample, it can be determined that the Ni_3Al-based single crystal superalloy has produced the thickness debit effect when the wall thickness is smaller than 0.7 mm. At the same time, there is little difference between the creep life of the thin-walled sample with the second orientation of [110] and [010], that is, the secondary orientation has no obvious effect on the creep life of the thin-walled sample under this test condition. It can be seen from Figure 3b that the strain of the Φ4 round bar sample is about 34%, while the average strain of 0.5 and 0.7 mm thin-walled sample is about 69%, and the strain of 0.3 mm thin-walled sample is about 36%. It can be seen from the strain that when the thickness debit effect is produced, the strain will also decrease significantly when the wall thickness reaches a certain value. Thin-walled samples take much shorter periods of 1% strain than round-bar samples. It can also be seen from the figure that the thin-walled sample has no obvious second stage of creep, and its strain and strain rate increase with time until the sample breaks.

Figure 4 is the fractured image of the sample with primary orientation [001] and secondary orientation [010]. It can be seen from Figure 4a–c that the fracture surfaces of 0.3–0.7 mm thin wall samples are rectangular, and the thickness of the fracture surfaces are 0.23, 0.32, and 0.48 mm, respectively. The height difference between the left and right sides of the fracture surface is very small, and there are dimples inside. The fracture surface of the standard round bar sample is basically circular, and the diameter changed from Φ4 to

Φ3.4. The interior is full of tearing edges. It can be seen from the fracture surface of the thin-walled sample that the fracture surface thickness of the 0.3 mm sample decreases by 23%, and the average fracture surface thickness of the 0.5 and 0.7 mm samples decreases by 33.5%. Therefore, the deformation of the 0.3 mm sample in the length and thickness direction is smaller than that of the other two thickness samples, the differences regarding deformation are revealed in the following discussion part.

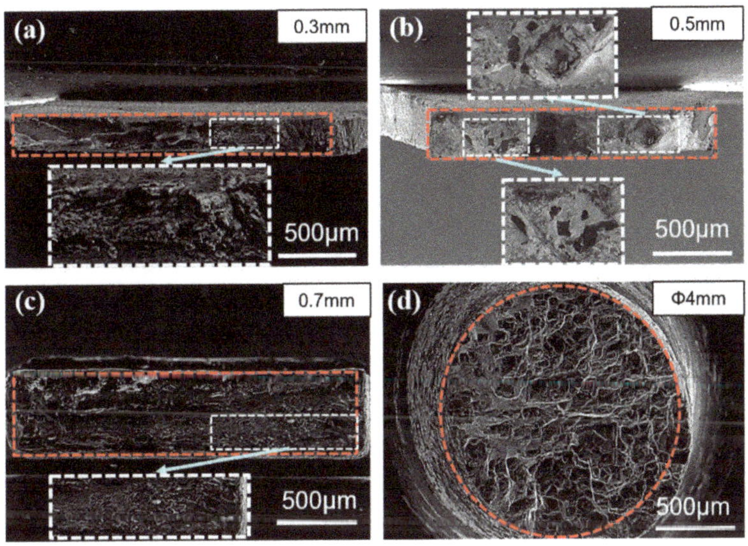

Figure 4. Thin-walled samples with different thicknesses and Φ4 round bar at 980 °C/220MP fracture of sample (**a**) fracture surface of 0.3 mm sample, (**b**) fracture surface of 0.5 mm sample, (**c**) fracture surface of 0.7 mm sample, (**d**) fracture surface of Φ4 round bar.

The white box in Figure 4a is an obvious dimple area by observing the fracture surface characteristics, while a large area of cleavage surface appears on the left side. Therefore, it is speculated that the crack will initiate and expand from the right side. When the crack expands to the left side, the sample will break instantaneously due to the smaller load-bearing area. In Figure 4b, a square cleavage surface is found in the white boxes on the left and right sides with tear edges around it, while the middle of the sample is a transient fracture zone with cleavage characteristics. A small dimple area is found in the white box in Figure 4c, and there is an obvious strip-like transient fracture area in the middle of the fracture. In Figure 4d tearing edges are distributed evenly at the fracture surface, and some cleavage surfaces are found on the left side of the fracture surface. Compared with Figure 4a, the proportion of cleavage surface in Figure 4d is far less than that in Figure 4a, indicating that the instantaneous fracture zone in the round bar sample is smaller than that in the thin wall sample. It can be seen from the analysis in Figure 4 that the three wall thickness samples all show the characteristics of mixed ductile-brittle fracture, of which the 0.3 mm thick sample has the largest transient fracture zone, indicating that the sample is more prone to fracture when the effective stress area changes in this thickness.

Figure 5 shows the composition and thickness comparison diagram of the affected zone of the sample test section, and the affected zone is the average value of the test section. It can be seen from Figure 5a that the affected zone of the alloy thin wall sample consists of the NiO zone, Al and Ni oxides zone, and γ'- free zone. Figure 5b shows the thickness of the affected zone in the test section of the thin-walled sample and the Φ4 round bar sample with the second orientation of [010]. It can be seen that the thickness of the affected zone of the Φ4 round bar sample is larger, about twice that of the thin-walled sample, but its overall proportion in the diameter direction is only 0.94%, far less than that of the thin-walled sample. The thickness of the affected zone of 0.3–0.7 mm thick, thin-walled samples has little difference, and the proportion in the thickness direction is 3.4–7.2%. Creep experiments found that the creep life of the 0.3 mm thick sample is about 70% of that of the 0.7 mm thick sample, but the thickness of the affected zone is not much different, so the thickness of the affected zone is not the main reason for the difference in the creep life of the two thin-walled samples.

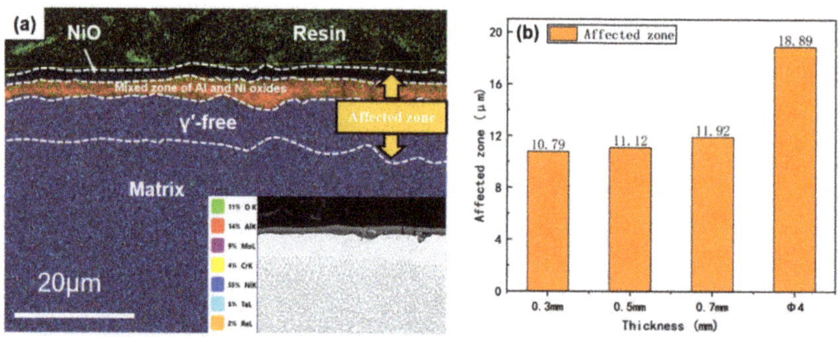

Figure 5. Thickness of affected zone in the test section of thin wall sample and Φ4 round bar sample with the secondary orientation of [010] (**a**) composition of the affected area, (**b**) thickness comparison of the affected zone.

Figure 6 shows the comparison of the affected zone in the test section of 0.7 mm thick samples with different secondary orientations. It can be seen from the figure that the thickness difference of the affected zone of the two thin-walled samples is not obvious, indicating that the second orientation of the sample in this experiment has no significant influence on the thickness of the affected zone.

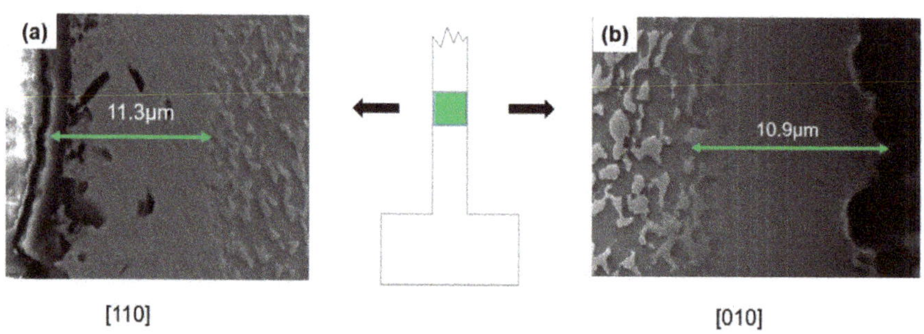

Figure 6. Thickness of affected zone of 0.7 mm thin walls (**a**) with the second orientation of [110], (**b**) with the second orientation of [010].

The microstructure comparison of the thin wall sample at 1 mm from the fracture surface is shown in Figure 7. It can be seen from the figure that the fracture microstructure of the 0.3–0.7 mm thin-walled samples presents a fine γ phase, and γ phase of 0.3 mm and 0.5 mm samples is smaller than that of 0.7 mm samples. This kind of fine γ phase is surrounded by γ' phase, forming many "islands", that is, "Topology inversion" [22]. In the evolution of γ/γ' phase morphology, the volume fraction of γ' raft changes [23]. The γ' phase is the main strengthening phase in single crystal superalloy, which is beneficial to the mechanical properties of the alloy at high temperatures, and the broken γ phase will form more γ/γ' two-phase interfaces [24]. The γ/γ' two-phase interface is conducive to forming an interfacial dislocation network, which effectively hinders the dislocation movement and improves the mechanical properties of the alloy [25].

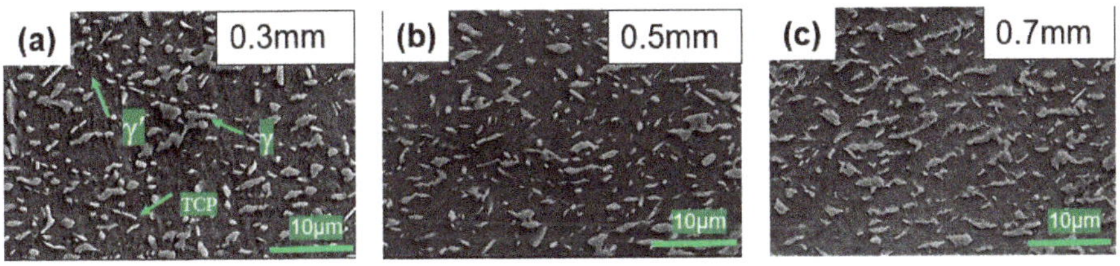

Figure 7. Microstructure of thin wall sample 1 mm from the fracture surface (**a**) 0.3 mm sample, (**b**) 0.5 mm sample, (**c**) 0.7 mm sample.

The same as in other tests, it was found in this experiment that the maximum strain variable of thin-walled samples would increase with the increase in wall thickness [8,16]. From the perspective of maximum strain, the 0.7 mm sample has a longer creep life than the 0.3 mm sample may be due to its stronger deformation coordination ability. When the plastic strain of the alloy increases due to defects such as micro holes during the creep process of the sample, the thicker sample can extend the life of the sample through stronger deformation coordination ability, while the thinner sample is difficult to extend the creep life of the sample through deformation due to poor deformation coordination ability, so it will fracture when the alloy plastic strain is large, which is also consistent with the test results of the 0.3 mm sample with deformation of less than 0.7 mm sample mentioned above. At the same time, this is consistent with the study of Huttner et al., that the creep fracture strain and creep life decrease with the decrease of the wall thickness of the sample 1–0.3 mm [26].

To verify this prediction, we analyzed the crystal rotation from the misorientation. EBSD was used to observe the misorientation at 1 mm of the fracture of 0.3 and 0.7 mm samples. The direction was parallel to the loading direction of the samples, and the length was about 650 μm. As can be seen from Figure 8a, the maximum misorientation of the 0.3 mm sample in the Z direction is 2.08°. From Figure 8b, the maximum misorientation of the 0.7 mm sample in the Z direction is 2.9°, that is, the thick sample has a greater degree of misorientation in the Z direction, and the thin sample has a smaller misorientation at fracture. This is consistent with the above results, the thinner the sample, the smaller the plastic deformation.

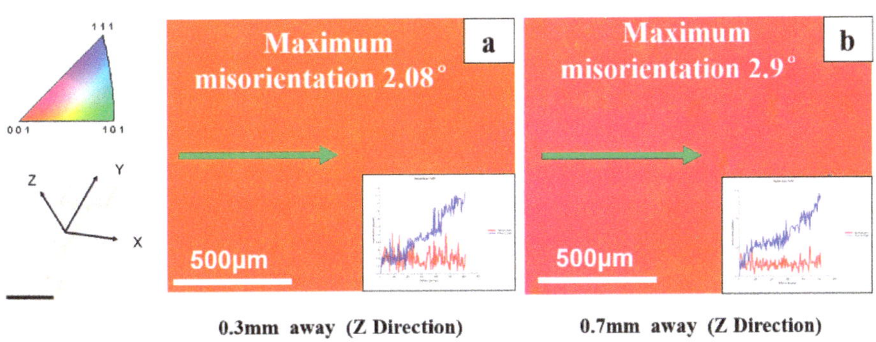

Figure 8. EBSD inverse pole figure of 0.3 and 0.7 mm sample 1 mm away from the fracture surface (**a**) Z direction of 0.3 mm sample, (**b**) Z direction of 0.7 mm sample.

From the above research, it can be seen that the second orientation has little effect on the creep life of the alloy sample with a wall thickness of 0.3–0.7 mm. The thickness of the affected zone of the samples with different wall thicknesses is similar, and there is no significant difference, which indicates that the affected zone is not the main reason for affecting the creep life of the alloy. Through the analysis of the morphology, deformation, and microstructure of the fracture surface of the thin-walled sample, it can be inferred that the causes of the thickness debit effect of the single crystal alloy thin-walled sample are as follows: during the creep process, due to internal defects and surface affected zone, the effective force area of the alloy changes. According to Wen [27], the necking degree of thin-walled specimens increases with the increase of wall thickness at high temperatures. Combined with the above research on the wall thickness change at the fracture, the increase of necking degree is equivalent to plastic deformation, for thicker samples, plastic deformation can be made to prolong the creep life of the alloy by better plastic deformation coordination ability, but the plastic coordination ability of thinner samples is poor. When the effective force area of the alloy changes, the way of prolonging the creep life by plastic deformation is weaker, and the plastic deformation sample of the after-creep fracture is smaller. The relationship between the thickness debit effect and deformation coordination ability has been studied by researchers. We know that the plastic deformation of the alloy is closely related to its activated slip system. Lv et al. [21] studied the thickness debit effect from the slip systems, they believed that the six slip systems of the {111}<110>type and one slip system of the {111}<112>type were activated during the creep of the thin wall sample. The eight slip systems of {111}<110>type and the two slip systems of {111}<112>type of the thick sample were activated. Due to the different activated numbers of slip systems, the deformation coordination ability of thin samples is poor, which is consistent with the conclusion of this paper. The study of Huttner et al. [26] also shows that there is a relationship between sample thickness and strain, and the strain of samples decreases with the decrease of wall thickness, which is consistent with the poorer plastic compatibility of thinner samples in this paper.

4. Conclusions

In this study, the thickness debit effect in creep performance of a Ni_3Al-based single crystal superalloy was studied. Through comparative analysis of sample orientation, affected zone, and microstructure, the following main conclusions are obtained:

1. The Ni_3Al-based single crystal superalloy studied in this experiment has an obvious thickness debit effect for 0.3–0.7 mm samples at 980 °C/220 MPa. It is found through the test that the second orientation [110] and [010] have no significant effect on the creep life of the thin wall samples.

2. By comparing the thickness of the affected zone of the sample with 0.3–0.7 mm thin wall, it is found that the thickness difference of the affected zone of the samples is not significant, indicating that the affected zone is not the main reason for the reduced life of the sample with a thin wall.

3. Based on the analysis of the microstructure of the thin-walled sample and the plastic deformation of the sample after fracture, a possible cause of the thickness debit effect was proposed. The thicker sample has better deformation coordination ability than the thinner one. When the stress condition of the sample changes due to defects in the creep process, the thicker sample can produce plastic deformation through its better deformation coordination ability and thus prolong the creep life, but the thinner sample can only prolong the creep life with smaller plastic deformation amount due to its poor deformation coordination ability. As a result, its creep life is shorter, and its fracture strain is smaller.

Author Contributions: Conceptualization, S.L. and S.G.; methodology, W.G.; formal analysis, Y.S.; investigation, H.Z. and Y.P.; data curation, H.W.; writing—original draft preparation, S.Z.; writing—review and editing, G.M. All authors have read and agreed to the published version of the manuscript.

Funding: This paper is supported by Science Center for Gas Turbine Project (NO. P2021-A-IV-001-003), National Natural Science Foundation (NO. 52103358), and National Science and Technology Major Project (2017-VI-0012-0084), Science Center for Gas Turbine Project (NO. P2022-B-IV-009-001).

Data Availability Statement: The data presented in this study are available on request from the corresponding author. The data are not publicly available due to [Alloy material sensitivity problem].

Conflicts of Interest: The authors declare no conflict of interest.

References

1. Xiong, W.; Ai, X.; Wang, J.; Wang, Q.; Zhao, Y.; Zhu, H.; Cheng, H.; Zhang, S. Study of the Creep Behavior of Nickel-Based Single Crystal Superalloy Micro Samples with Dimensional Effects. *Crystals* **2022**, *12*, 592. [CrossRef]
2. Chen, Y.; Zhang, W.; Zhao, Y.; Zhai, Y.; Zhang, B.; Lu, H.; Yang, G.; Yang, L.; Li, A. Oxidation-induced rhenium evaporation in Ni-based single crystal superalloy thin lamella. *Scr. Mater.* **2021**, *203*, 114106. [CrossRef]
3. He, X.; Zhang, J.; Peng, Y.; Li, J.; Ding, J.; Liu, C.; Xia, X.; Chen, X.; Liu, Y. Microstructure Evolution of Primary γ' Phase in Ni_3Al Based Superalloy. *Acta Metall. Sin.* **2020**, *33*, 1709–1726. [CrossRef]
4. Jiang, L.; Yang, Y.; Wu, M.; Cai, M. Anisotropy Study on Creep Behavior of a Ni_3Al Based Single Crystal Superalloy at 1100 °C/137 MPa. *Rare Met.* **2021**, *45*, 1025–1033.
5. Liu, W.; Zhu, O. Study on Thin Wall Effect of Single Crystal Blade for Aeroengine. *Cast. Technol.* **2017**, *38*, 2571–2575.
6. Hüttner, R.; Gabel, J.; Glatzel, U.; Völkl, R. First creep results on thin-walled single-crystal superalloys. *Mater. Sci. Eng. A* **2009**, *510–511*, 307–311. [CrossRef]
7. Hu, Y.; Zhang, L.; Cheng, C.; Zhao, P.; Cao, T.; Guo, G.; Zhao, J. Influence of sample thickness on the creep behavior of a directional solidification nickel-based superalloy. *Vacuum* **2018**, *150*, 105–115. [CrossRef]
8. Hu, Y.; Zhang, L.; Cao, T.; Cheng, C.; Zhao, P.; Guo, G.; Zhao, J. The effect of thickness on the creep properties of a single-crystal nickel-based superalloy. *Mater. Sci. Eng. A* **2018**, *728*, 124–132. [CrossRef]
9. Zheng, Y. Size effect of a thin section of single crystal turbine blade alloy. *Mater. Eng.* **2007**, *7*, 74–77.
10. Yu, Z.Y.; Wang, X.M.; Liang, H.; Li, Z.X.; Li, L.; Yue, Z.F. Thickness debit effect in Ni-based single crystal superalloys at different stress levels. *Int. J. Mech. Sci.* **2020**, *170*, 105357. [CrossRef]
11. Li, Y. *Creep Anisotropy of a Third Generation Nickel Base Superalloy*; University of Science and Technology of China: Hefei, China, 2019.
12. Li, Q. *Analysis of the Relationship between High Temperature Rupture Strength and Wall Thickness Effect of DD6 Alloy*; Dalian University of Technology: Dalian, China, 2016.
13. Yu, C.; Yu, J.; Yu, F.; Shi, F.; Sun, F. Thin wall effect on stress rupture properties of DD499 single crystal alloy. *Casting* **2014**, *63*, 479–483.
14. Fourie, J.; Baldan, A. *Size Effects in the Mechanical Properties of Superalloy Single Crystals*; TMS: Philadelphia, PA, USA, 1992.
15. Wen, Z.; Liang, J.; Liu, C.; Pei, H.; Wen, S.; Yue, Z. Prediction method for creep life of thin-wall sample with film cooling holes in Ni-based single-crystal superalloy. *Int. J. Mech. Sci.* **2018**, *141*, 276–289. [CrossRef]
16. Brice, C.; Alexander, S. The effect of thickness on the creep response of thin-wall single crystal components. *Mater. Sci. Eng. A* **2008**, *508*, 183–189.
17. Zhang, L.; Yu, H.; Guo, G.; Zhao, J.; Zhao, P. Stress rupture properties and fracture behavior of thin-walled samples of oriented DD6 single crystal alloy. *J. Aerodyn.* **2019**, *34*, 627–634.
18. Srivastava, A.; Gopagoni, S.; Needleman, A.; Seetharaman, V.; Staroselsky, A.; Banerjee, R. Effect of sample thickness on the creep response of a Ni-based single-crystal superalloy. *Acta Mater.* **2012**, *60*, 5697–5711. [CrossRef]
19. Brunner, M.; Bensch, M.; Völkl, R.; Affeldt, E.; Glatzel, U. Thickness influence on creep properties for Ni-based superalloy M247LC SX. Materials science & engineering. *Struct. Mater. Prop. Microstruct. Process.* **2012**, *550*, 254–262.
20. Zhao, J. Effect of secondary orientation on the rupture properties of single crystal superalloy DD6. In Proceedings of the China Materials Conference 2021, Xiamen, China, 9 July 2021. Available online: https://kns.cnki.net/kcms/detail/detail.aspx?FileName=ZGCZ202107001041&DbName=CPFD2021 (accessed on 3 January 2023).
21. Lv, J.; Zhao, Y.; Wang, S.; Zhao, X.; Zhao, J.; Zheng, L.; Guo, Y.; Schmitz, G.; Ge, B. Stress state mechanism of thickness debit effect in creep performances of a Ni-based single crystal superalloy. *Int. J. Plast.* **2022**, *159*, 103470. [CrossRef]
22. Ru, Y.; Hu, B.; Zhao, W.; Zhang, H.; Pei, Y.; Li, S.; Gong, S.; Xu, H. Topologically inverse microstructure in single-crystal superalloys: Microstructural stability and properties at ultrahigh temperature. *Mater. Res. Lett.* **2021**, *9*, 497–506. [CrossRef]
23. Murakumo, T.; Kobayashi, T.; Koizumi, Y.; Harada, H. Creep behaviour of Ni-base single-crystal superalloys with various gamma′ volume fraction. *Acta Mater.* **2004**, *52*, 3737–3744. [CrossRef]

24. Chen, J.; Cao, L.; Tang, X.; Xue, M. A kind of Ni_Microstructure and high plastic deformation behavior of 3Al based single crystal superalloy. *J. Mater. Heat Treat.* **2016**, *37*, 33–37.
25. Li, Y.; Wang, L.; He, Y.; Zheng, W.; Lou, L.; Zhang, J. Role of interfacial dislocation networks during secondary creep at elevated temperatures in a single crystal Ni-based superalloy. *Scr. Mater.* **2022**, *217*, 114769. [CrossRef]
26. Hüttner, R.; Völkl, R.; Gabel, J.; Glatzel, U. Creep behavior of thick and thin walled structures of a single crystal nickel-base superalloy at high temperatures—Experimental method and results. *Superalloys* **2008**, *2008*, 719–723.
27. Wen, Z.; Pei, H.; Li, D.; Yue, Z.; Gao, J. Thickness Influence on the Creep Response of DD6 Ni-Based Single-Crystal Superalloy. *High Temp. Mater. Process.* **2016**, *35*, 871–880. [CrossRef]

crystals

MDPI

Article

Topologically Closed Packed Phase and Its Interaction with Dislocation Movement in Ni–Based Superalloy during High–Temperature Creep

Wenqi Guo [1], Haigen Zhao [1], Yi Ru [2,3], Yanling Pei [2], Junwu Wang [1], Qiaomu Liu [2,4], Xuehang Li [5], Haibo Wang [2], Shuangqi Zhang [5], Shengkai Gong [2,3] and Shusuo Li [1,3,*]

1 Research Institute of Aero–Engine, Beihang University, Beijing 100191, China
2 Frontier Research Institute of Innovative Science and Technology, Beihang University, Beijing 100191, China
3 AECC Guizhou Liyang Aviation Power Company Limited, Guiyang 550000, China
4 AECC Sichuan Gas Turbine Establishment, Chengdu 610500, China
5 School of Materials Science and Engineering, Beihang University, Beijing 100191, China
* Correspondence: lishs@buaa.edu.cn

Abstract: In superalloys, topologically close–packed (TCP) phases, which contain refractory elements, usually significantly influence the mechanical properties. The current work investigates the structure and composition of the TCP phase in an Al–Mo–rich Ni–based single crystal superalloy. It is shown that after 40 h of thermal exposure, a large number of strip–like TCP phases are formed, which are enriched in Mo and Re. The structure of the TCP phase is identified as the tetragonal σ phase with the lattice parameter a being 0.93 nm and c being 0.50 nm. During the creep process, the single crystal tilts obviously and leads to orientation variation from <1 1 0> direction. Two groups of dislocations are observed in the deformed sample. One group contains straight dislocation lines and another group contains dislocation networks. The interaction between TCP phase and dislocation in the single crystal superalloy is studied to reveal the effect of the TCP phase on the deformation behavior. During creep, the σ phase hinders the dislocation movement, which may contribute to the propagation of the cracks and the final fracture.

Keywords: single crystal superalloys; topologically close–packed phase; crystal structure; dislocation movement; transmission electron microscope

1. Introduction

Ni–based single crystal (SC) superalloys usually include many elements, such as Ni, Al, Mo, Cr, Co, W, Ti, Ta, Re and Ru [1]. These constituent elements can be classified into two categories, i.e., γ' phase forming elements and γ phase forming elements [2–7]. The γ' phase, $Ni_3(Al, Ta)$, is a simple cubic L_{12} crystal structure with definite occupation of Al(Ta) and Ni atoms. Al(Ta) atoms are at the corners of the cube and Ni atoms are at the center of the plane. Thus the γ' stoichiometric composition is $Ni_3(Al,Ta)$. The γ phase forming elements refer to alloying elements distributed mainly in the γ matrix. The representative elements include Mo, Co Cr, W, Re and Ru [8]. These γ phase forming elements could significantly increase the solidus temperature and decrease the stacking fault energy, enhancing thermal stability and creep properties [9,10]. In addition, γ phase forming elements will have a great influence on the microstructure, diffusion and dislocation motion of SC superalloys, which could bring tailored mechanical properties. For example, Re is often added into the γ phase to slow down the dislocation motion and affect the mechanical properties [11–14]. According to Wu, the Re enrichment in dislocations provides direct evidence of solute drag and pipe diffusion, resulting in a reduced dislocation velocity and transport of matrix elements into the γ' precipitates [15].

However, the addition of refractory elements (e.g., Re, W and Mo) [15] often results in the precipitation of brittle topologically close–packed (TCP) phases (σ, μ, P, and R, etc.) [16,17] due to the congregation during high–temperature service, and these TCP phases are usually harmful to creep properties. Therefore, to guarantee the creep performance of SC superalloys, it is necessary to investigate the evolution of the TCP phase, as well as its influence on the deformation behavior. TCP phases are extensively studied in traditional Ni–based single crystal superalloys, such as the morphology of the TCP phase [18], the orientation relationships between TCP phases and matrix [19], and the effect of time and temperature on the TCP precipitation [20]. In recent years, single crystal superalloys with high Al and Mo contents draw more researchers' attention. These single crystal superalloys usually have higher γ' volume fraction and good creep performance at an ultrahigh temperature [21,22]. Meanwhile, there is a large tendency for the precipitation of the TCP phase in these alloys, since the low γ volume fraction easily leads to supersaturation of refractory elements and the precipitation of the TCP phase.

However, there is limited research on the structure and evolution of the TCP phase in single crystal superalloys with high Al and Mo contents. Ai Cheng et al. [23] studied the microstructure stability of TCP in Al–Mo–rich Ni–based single crystal superalloys under unstressed long–term (250 h) conditions, and the TCP phases in both long–term aged cellular and dendritic samples were identified as P phases. Whether the structure of the TCP phase will remain stable or change during thermal exposure is still unknown. Furthermore, the interaction of the TCP phase and dislocations during the creep process also remains unclear. In this work, we systematically investigate the structure of the TCP phase in the Al–Mo–rich Ni–based model SC superalloy and analyze the evolution of the TCP phase during the thermal exposure process at 1100 °C. The dislocation evolution and the interaction with the TCP phase of the Al–Mo–rich Ni–based SC superalloy are also investigated.

2. Experimental

The experimental alloy used in this work was an Al–Mo–rich Ni–based model SC superalloy with the nominal composition Table 1. Directional solidification experiments were carried out by a high rate solidification (HRS) apparatus. After directional solidification, the model SC superalloy underwent a solution treatment (1300 °C/2 h + 1305 °C/2 h + 1310 °C/2 h + 1315 °C/2 h + 1320 °C/4 h + 1325 °C/6 h, air cooling). Creep tests were carried out according to GB–2039–2012. The alloy composition is shown in Table 1. For the thermal exposure experiment, the sample after solution treatment was exposed to an air atmosphere at 1100 °C for 40 h. A normal creep (maximum strain is ~80%) experiment was conducted using the sample after solution treatment at 1100 °C and 140 MPa, and slices were cut from 1 mm and 10 mm away from the fracture surface for microstructure observation.

Table 1. Composition of the used Ni_3Al–based single–crystal superalloy (mass %).

Element	Ni	Al	Cr	Mo	Re	Ta
Content	Excess	7.6–8.3	1.5–2.5	9–13	0.5–1.5	2.4–4.0

The cut surface was mechanically ground with silicon carbide abrasive paper (P200 to P3000), and then polished with diamond paste to a mirror level. The etching solution used to reveal the γ' phase is 20 g $CuSO_4$ + 100 mL HCl + 100 mL C_2H_5OH. Microstructure characterizations were conducted by Apreo S LoVac scanning electron microscope (SEM) equipped with an energy dispersive spectroscopy (EDS) system operated at 20 kV and electron backscatter diffraction (EBSD) system (orientation analysis) operated at 25 kV. EDS experiments were conducted to analyze the composition of the TCP phase, and EBSD experiments were conducted to analyze the orientation variation after deformation. In order to further analyze the structure of the TCP phase, focused ion beam technology was used to make a transmission electron microscope sample using Helios G4 CX equipment. Then, the morphologies of TCP phase and dislocations of SC superalloy were identified by a JEM 2100 TEM operated at 200 kV.

3. Results and Discussion

Figure 1 shows the microstructure of the solution–treated Al–Mo–rich Ni-based SC superalloy. The microstructure consists of cubic γ'–precipitates embedded in the γ–matrix. The fractions of two phases are obtained by statistically counting white (γ'–phase) in the images. The volume fraction of γ'–precipitate of the solution–treated SC superalloy is calculated as 72 $\pm$ 3%, the γ'–cube sizes as 405 $\pm$ 20 nm, and the γ–channel width as 60 $\pm$ 6 nm. No TCP phase is observed after solution treatment. Figure 1c shows the creep time–strain curve under 1100 °C/140 MPa and the average rupture time is ~42 h and the average strain is ~86%. Figure 2a,b exhibit the microstructure of Al–Mo–rich Ni-based SC superalloy after 40 h thermal exposure. When observing from the (1 1 0) plane, a large amount of stripe–like TCP phases is regularly arranged, which can be classified into two types with different widths of 400 $\pm$ 25 nm and 125 $\pm$ 15 nm. Figure 2c shows the EDS results of spot 1 to spot 4 in Figure 2b, and both the two types of TCP phases are enriched in Re and Mo elements.

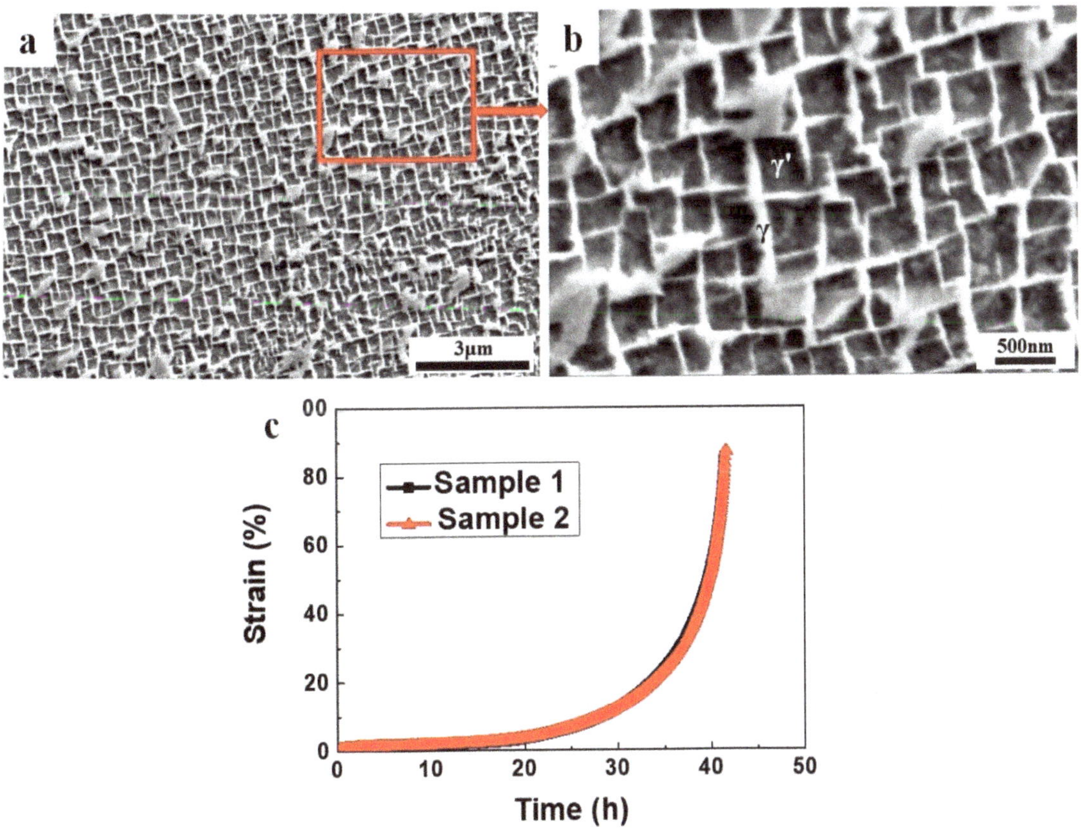

Figure 1. (**a**) Microstructure of the Al–Mo–rich Ni-based SC superalloy; (**b**) enlarged image of (**a**) showing γ phase and γ' phase; (**c**) creep time–strain curve under 1100 °C/140 MPa.

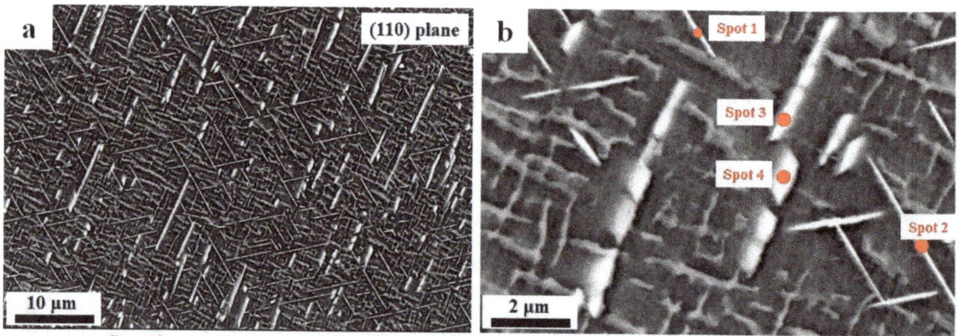

Spot 1

Element	Weight %	Atomic %
AlK	5.86	12.99
TaM	2.19	0.72
ReM	4.45	1.43
MoL	11.43	7.12
CrK	2.21	2.54
NiK	73.87	75.20

Spot 2

Element	Weight %	Atomic %
AlK	5.07	11.87
TaM	2.38	0.83
ReM	7.99	2.71
MoL	16.10	10.60
CrK	2.45	2.98
NiK	66.00	71.00

Spot 3

Element	Weight %	Atomic %
AlK	4.06	9.93
TaM	2.14	0.78
ReM	11.07	3.92
MoL	18.41	12.66
CrK	3.07	3.89
NiK	61.25	68.82

Spot 4

Element	Weight %	Atomic %
AlK	4.61	11.14
TaM	2.59	0.93
ReM	10.18	3.57
MoL	18.23	12.40
CrK	2.58	3.24
NiK	61.80	68.71

Figure 2. (**a**) Microstructure of Al–Mo–rich Ni–based SC superalloy after hot exposure; (**b**) enlarged image of (**a**); (**c**) EDS results of spot 1–spot 4 in (**b**).

TEM is employed to study the structure of the TCP phase. Figure 3a shows the SEM image of Al–Mo–rich Ni–based SC superalloy after hot exposure. FIB is used to cut a TEM sample from the red rectangle region in Figure 3a, and the TEM lamellar sample is shown in Figure 3b with a TCP phase in the center. Figure 3c exhibits the SC superalloy's bright field TEM image, which contains an interface of matrix and TCP phase. Figure 3d shows the diffraction patterns of the matrix and interface with the beam from [1 1 1] direction, and the TCP is confirmed as the tetragonal σ phase. According to the diffraction patterns, it has been determined that the crystallography relationship of $(1\ 1\ 1)_{\gamma}//(0\ 0\ 1)_{\sigma}$ is maintained between the γ and σ phases.

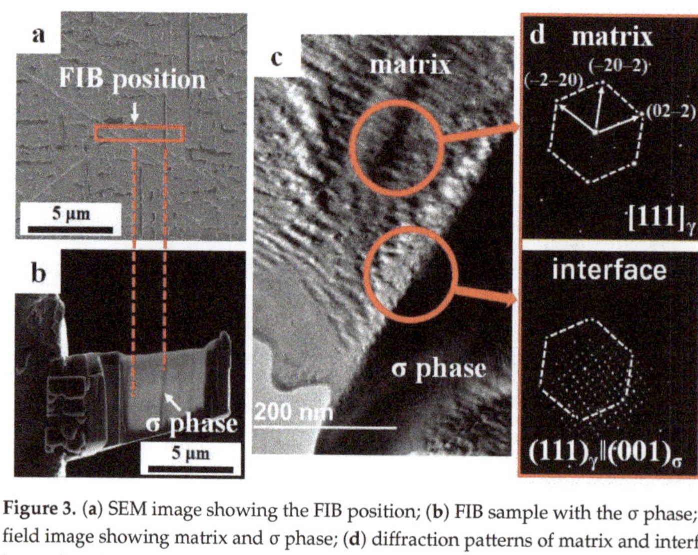

Figure 3. (**a**) SEM image showing the FIB position; (**b**) FIB sample with the σ phase; (**c**) TEM bright field image showing matrix and σ phase; (**d**) diffraction patterns of matrix and interface with [1 1 1] beam direction.

In order to further characterize the crystal parameter of the σ phase, high–resolution TEM is employed. Figure 4a shows the high–resolution TEM image of the σ phase, and Figure 4b is the fast Fourier transform patterns of the red rectangle in Figure 4a, and the red circles in Figure 4b are the masks. Figure 4c exhibits the inverse fast Fourier transform image containing the crystal lattice. The crystal plane space in (0 0 1) plane of σ phase of Al–Mo–rich Ni–based SC superalloy after 40 h thermal exposure is calculated to be 0.93 nm, indicating that lattice parameter a of the σ phase is 0.93 nm.

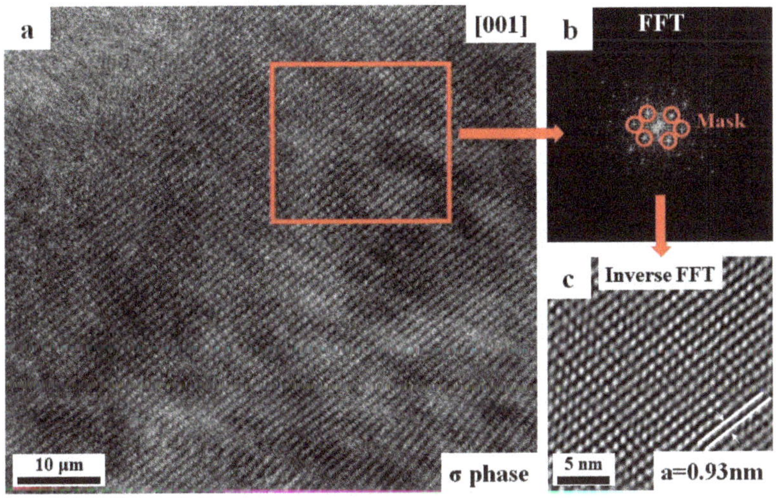

Figure 4. (**a**) The high–resolution TEM image of σ phase in (0 0 1) plane while the γ phase is in (1 1 1) plane; (**b**) fast Fourier transform patterns of the red rectangle in (**a**); (**c**) inverse fast Fourier transform image showing that lattice parameter a is 0.93 nm.

In comparison, the TCP phase in Mo–rich Ni–based SC superalloy after 250 h thermal exposure treatment is identified as P phase [23]. Thus it is speculated that the temporality of the TCP phase evolution is from σ phase to P phase. Similarly, according to RC Reed's work [24], in traditional Ni–based SC superalloy, the flaky σ phase is first precipitated and then transformed into the P phase. Increasing the molybdenum stabilizes P phase at the expense of μ phase and σ phase. In our Al–Mo–rich Ni–based SC superalloy, the initially precipitated σ phase is rich in refractory elements Mo and Re. As the precipitated phase grows up, the surrounding γ′ phase restricts the diffusion of refractory elements to the precipitated phase, which impedes the growth of the TCP phase. Meanwhile, the phase transformation (σ phase to P phase) is promoted by self–diffusion of the refractory element in the σ phase.

After creep tests, EBSD is used to study the orientation variation from <1 1 0> direction of the SC superalloy sample. Figure 5a–c shows the inverse pole figure of (1 −1 0) plane from X direction, Y direction and Z direction of the region which is 10 mm away from the fracture surface, respectively. The inserts are the misorientation angle of the line in each figure, and the maximum misorientation across the line (~400 μm) is ~8°. While Figure 5d–f shows the inverse pole figure of (1 −1 0) plane from X direction, Y direction and Z direction of the region which is 1 mm away from the fracture surface, respectively, and the maximum misorientation across the line (~400 μm) is ~13°. This misorientation indicates the single crystal is obviously twisted during creep, and the deformation mechanism and dislocation behavior are revealed in the following discussion part.

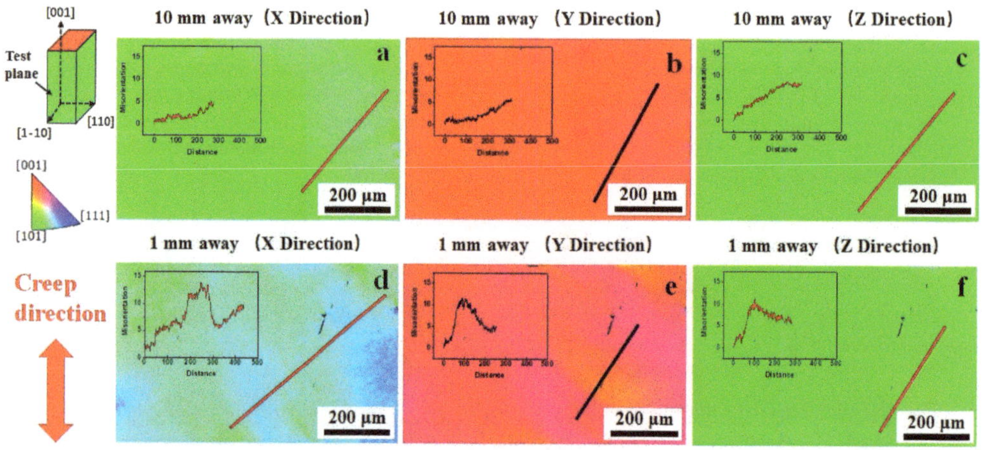

Figure 5. EBSD inverse pole figure of the region which is 10 mm away from the fracture surface (**a**) X direction; (**b**) Y direction; (**c**) Z direction; EBSD inverse pole figure of the region which is 1 mm away from the fracture surface (**d**) X direction; (**e**) Y direction; (**f**) Z direction.

Figure 6 exhibits the bright field TEM image of the region which is 10 mm away from the fracture surface, and the insert is a diffraction pattern with the beam from the [1 1 0] direction. Two groups of dislocations are observed in the deformed sample. One group contains straight dislocation lines parallel to each other, which are shown in Area_1. Another group contains dislocation networks in Area_2, which is near the σ phase. We observed a series of images and did not find any twins, which indicates that the creep mechanism of the SC superalloy is dislocation motion. According to our previous work and other researchers' work, the creep mechanism of Al–Mo–rich Ni–based SC superalloy is mainly dislocation slip. Figure 7 shows the enlarged TEM image of Area_2 in Figure 6. Figure 7a–c shows the bright field TEM images of the dislocation networks of the region which is 10 mm away from the fracture surface with two beam conditions. According to the extinction law in Figure 7d, the dislocations networks which are near the strip–like σ phase exhibit a b = a/2<1 −1 0> or b = a/2<0 1 −1> Burgers vector. Figure 8 shows the enlarged TEM image of area 1 in Figure 6. Figure 8a–c shows the bright field TEM images of the straight dislocation lines. According to the extinction law in Figure 7d, the straight dislocation lines exhibit a b = a/2<1 −1 0> or b = a/2< 1 0 1> Burgers vector. This suggests that during creep, the dislocations piled up near the strip–like σ phase may lead to the stress concentration, which will promote the initiation and propagation of microcracks and accelerate the fracture of the SC superalloy [25,26].

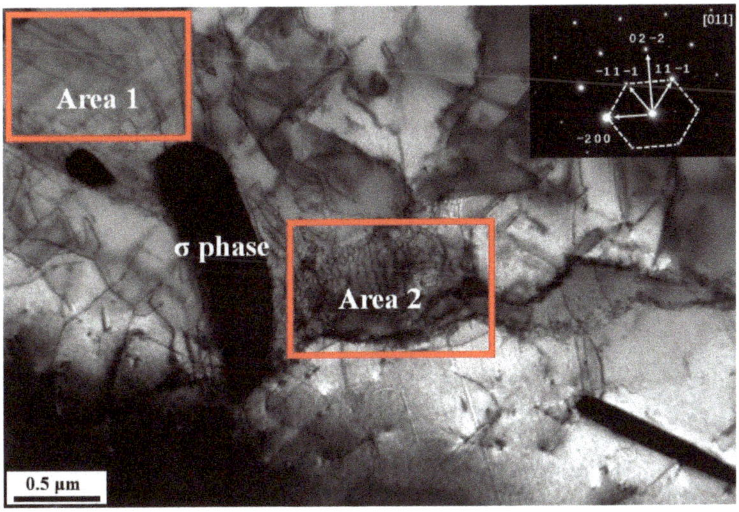

Figure 6. Bright field TEM image and diffraction pattern of the region with the beam from the [0 1 1] direction, which is 10 mm away from the fracture surface.

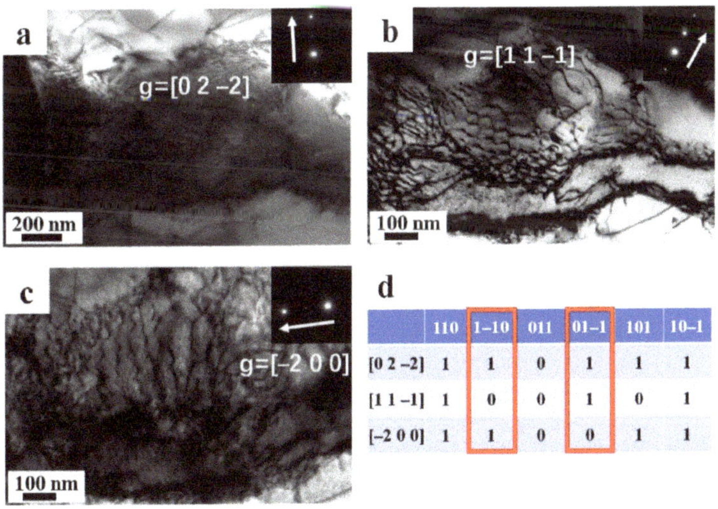

Figure 7. (**a**) Enlarged TEM image of Area_2 in Figure 6, which is 10 mm away from the fracture surface (**a**) diffraction pattern; bright field TEM image with (**b**) g = [0 2 −2]; (**c**) g = [1 1 −1]; (**d**) [−2 0 0].

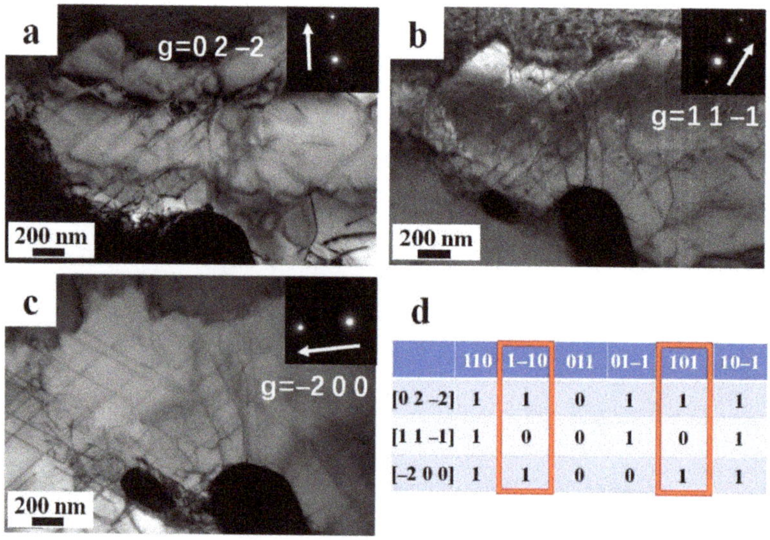

	110	1-10	011	01-1	101	10-1
[0 2 -2]	1	1	0	1	1	1
[1 1 -1]	1	0	0	1	0	1
[-2 0 0]	1	1	0	0	1	1

Figure 8. (**a**) Enlarged TEM image of Area_1 in Figure 6, which is 10 mm away from the fracture surface (**a**) diffraction pattern; bright field TEM image with (**b**) g = [0 2 −2]; (**c**) g = [1 1 −1]; (**d**) [−2 0 0].

Figure 9 shows the interaction of the σ phase and dislocations in the deformed Al–Mo–rich Ni–based SC superalloy. Figure 9a exhibits the bright field image of the deformed sample 10 mm away from the fracture surface, and several bending dislocations are observed near the σ phase, indicating the stress is easily concentrated in this region, which will promote the initiation and propagation of the cracks to accelerate the fracture. The crystal structure of σ phase is confirmed by the diffraction patterns in Figure 9b,c. Figure 9e shows the diffraction pattern of the interface between σ phase and γ matrix in Figure 9d, which indicates the orientation relationship of $[1\ 1\ 0]_\gamma//[1\ 1\ 0]_\sigma$. The lattice parameter c is calculated to be 0.50 nm. According to RC Reed's work [24], there is a consistent orientation relationship between σ and the γ matrix, which is also confirmed by our results, and dislocations in the interface which extend from the edges of the precipitates are indications of a high degree of coherency in the interface between σ and the γ matrix. In order to observe the dislocation movement, we tilt α in the range of $-35°$ to $35°$ and record the σ phase every $2°$. Figure 9f,g are bright field images of the σ phase with ~6° α tilt variation, and throughout emerging Figure 9f,g, a stereoscopic morphology is obtained in Figure 9h. Dislocations can be observed in the region which is near the σ phase. The σ phase which is enriched in Re and Mo experiences random nucleation and diffusion–controlled growth [20]. The growth of σ phase greatly consumes the surrounding elements to form a depleted zone that surrounds the σ phase. As the growth primarily consumes γ–rich elements, e.g., Mo and Re, the depleted zone is the intrinsic γ' phase. Since the large depleted zone is prone to stress concentration, dislocations that emit from the interface between TCP and the depleted zone facilitate dislocation interaction and microcrack initiation in the large depleted zone, promoting the propagation of the cracks and accelerating the fracture. In the future, more quantitative research, e.g., dislocation–based phase field [27–29], should be made to further understand the interaction between dislocation and phase microstructures of Ni–based superalloys.

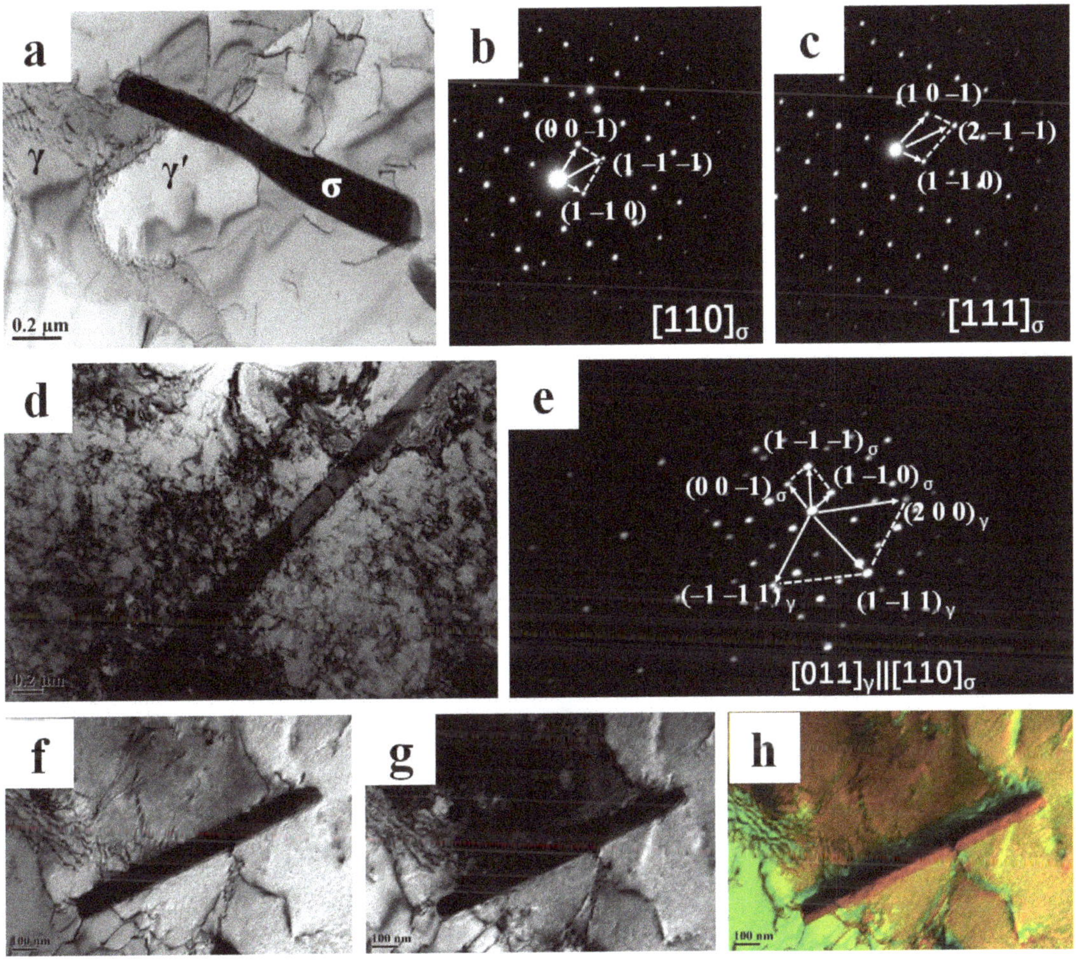

Figure 9. TEM results of the region which is 10 mm away from the fracture surface; (**a**) bright field image showing the interaction of σ phase and dislocations; (**b**) diffraction pattern of σ phase with the beam from [1 1 0] direction; (**c**) diffraction pattern of σ phase with the beam from [1 1 1] direction; (**d**,**e**) bright field image and diffraction pattern showing the interface between σ phase and γ matrix; (**f**) bright field image with beam close to [1 1 0] direction; (**g**) bright field image with ~6° α tilt; (**h**) merged image of (**f**,**g**).

4. Conclusions

In the current work, the structure of the TCP phase in the Al–Mo–rich Ni–based model single crystal superalloy is systematically investigated, as well as analyzing the possible evolution of the TCP phase. Meanwhile, the dislocation behavior of the Al–Mo–rich Ni–based SC superalloy is studied to reveal the role the TCP phase played during the creep.

In Al–Mo–rich Ni–based model SC superalloy, no TCP phase is observed after solution treatment. After thermal exposure for 40 h, a large number of strip–like TCP phases enriched in Mo and Re elements are formed. The structure of the TCP phase is identified as the tetragonal σ phase with the lattice parameter a being 0.93 nm and c being 0.50 nm.

During the creep process, the single crystal is tilted to result in obviously orientation variation from <1 −1 0> direction. Two groups of dislocations are observed in the deformed sample. One group contains straight dislocation lines with Burgers vector of b = a/2< 1 −1 0> or b = a/2<0 1 −1>. Another group contains dislocation networks with Burgers vector of b = a/2<1 −1 0> or b = a/2< 1 0 1>. During creep, dislocations piled up near the strip-like σ phase lead to the stress concentration, which may promote the initiation and propagation of microcracks and accelerate the fracture of the SC superalloy.

Author Contributions: Methodology, H.W. and S.Z.; Project administration, Y.P. and Q.L.; Resources, Y.R. and J.W.; Supervision, S.G.; Writing—original draft, W.G.; Writing—review & editing, H.Z., X.L. and S.L. All authors have read and agreed to the published version of the manuscript.

Funding: This research was funded by National Natural Science Foundation (No. 52103358), Science Center for Gas Turbine Project (No. P2021–A–IV–001–003), and National Science and Technology Major Project (2017–VI–0012–0084).

Conflicts of Interest: The authors declare no conflict of interest.

References

1. Xia, W.; Zhao, X.; Yue, L.; Zhang, Z. A review of composition evolution in Ni–based single crystal superalloys. *J. Mater. Sci. Technol.* **2020**, *44*, 76–95. [CrossRef]
2. Kawagishi, K.; Sato, A.; Kobayashi, T.; Harada, H. Effect of alloying elements on the oxidation resistance of 4th generation Ni–base single–crystal superalloys. *J. Jpn. Inst. Met.* **2005**, *69*, 249–252. [CrossRef]
3. Sato, A.; Harada, H.; Yokokawa, T.; Murakumo, T.; Koizumi, Y.; Kobayashi, T.; Imai, H. The effects of ruthenium on the phase stability of fourth generation Ni–base single crystal superalloys. *Scr. Mater.* **2006**, *54*, 1679–1684. [CrossRef]
4. Reed, R.C.; Tao, T.; Warnken, N. Alloys–by–design: Application to nickel–based single crystal superalloys. *Acta Mater.* **2009**, *57*, 5898–5913. [CrossRef]
5. Wu, Q.; Li, S. Alloying element additions to Ni3Al: Site preferences and effects on elastic properties from first–principles calculations. *Comput. Mater. Sci.* **2012**, *53*, 436–443. [CrossRef]
6. Yan, J.; Gu, Y.; Dang, Y.; Zhao, X.; Lu, J.; Yuan, Y.; Yin, H. Effect of carbon on the microstructure evolution and mechanical properties of low Si–containing centrifugal casting 20Cr32Ni1Nb alloy. *Mater. Chem. Phys.* **2016**, *175*, 107–117. [CrossRef]
7. Jiang, W.; Shao, W.; Sha, J.; Zhou, C. Experimental studies and modeling for the transition from internal to external oxidation of three–phase Nb–Si–Cr alloys. *Prog. Nat. Sci. Mater. Int.* **2018**, *28*, 740–748. [CrossRef]
8. Long, H.; Mao, S.; Liu, Y.; Zhang, Z.; Han, X. Microstructural and compositional design of Ni–based single crystalline superalloys—A review. *J. Alloys Compd.* **2018**, *743*, 203–220. [CrossRef]
9. Christofidou, K.A.; Jones, N.G.; Pickering, E.J.; Flacau, R.; Hardy, M.C.; Stone, H.J. The microstructure and hardness of Ni–Co–Al–Ti–Cr quinary alloys. *J. Alloys Compd.* **2016**, *688*, 542–552. [CrossRef]
10. Liu, C.P.; Zhang, X.N.; Ge, L.; Liu, S.H.; Wang, C.Y.; Yu, T.; Zhang, Z. Effect of rhenium and ruthenium on the deformation and fracture mechanism in nickel–based model single crystal superalloys during the in–situ tensile at room temperature. *Mater. Sci. Eng. A* **2017**, *682*, 90–97. [CrossRef]
11. Wollgramm, P.; Buck, H.; Neuking, K.; Parsa, A.B.; Schuwalow, S.; Rogal, J.; Eggeler, G. On the role of Re in the stress and temperature dependence of creep of Ni–base single crystal superalloys. *Mater. Sci. Eng. A* **2015**, *628*, 382–395. [CrossRef]
12. Karunaratne, M.; Reed, R. Interdiffusion of the platinum–group metals in nickel at elevated temperatures. *Acta Mater.* **2003**, *51*, 2905–2919. [CrossRef]
13. Wu, R.; Qian, Y.; Wang, J. Effect of Re on mechanical properties of single crystal Ni–based superalloys: Insights from first–principle and molecular dynamics. *J. Alloys Compd.* **2021**, *862*, 158643. [CrossRef]
14. Wu, X.; Makineni, S.K.; Liebscher, C.H.; Dehm, G.; Rezaei Mianroodi, J.; Shanthraj, P.; Gault, B. Unveiling the Re effect in Ni–based single crystal superalloys. *Nat. Commun.* **2020**, *11*, 1–13. [CrossRef]
15. Zhao, P.; Xie, G.; Chen, C.; Wang, X.; Zeng, P.; Wang, F.; Du, K. Interplay of chemistry and deformation–induced defects on facilitating topologically–close–packed phase precipitation in nickel–base superalloys. *Acta Mater.* **2022**, *236*, 118109. [CrossRef]
16. Park, K.; Withey, P. General View of Rhenium–Rich Particles along Defect Grain Boundaries Formed in Nickel–Based Single–Crystal Superalloy Turbine Blades: Formation, Dissolution and Comparison with Other Phases. *Crystals* **2021**, *11*, 1201. [CrossRef]
17. Rae CM, F.; Karunaratne MS, A.; Small, C.J.; Broomfield, R.W.; Jones, C.N.; Reed, R.C. Topologically close packed phases in an experimental rhenium–containing single crystal superalloy. *Superalloys* **2000**, *2000*, 767–776.
18. Zhang, Z.; Wen, Z.; Yue, Z. Effects of tensile/compressive creeps on microstructure evolution of nickel–based single crystal superalloys. *J. Alloys Compd.* **2021**, *851*, 156767. [CrossRef]
19. Jin, H.; Zhang, J.; Zhang, Y.; Zhang, W.; Ma, S.; Mao, S.; Wang, Q. Effects of the orientation relationships between TCP phases and matrix on the morphologies of TCP phases in Ni–based single crystal superalloys. *Mater. Charact.* **2022**, *183*, 111609. [CrossRef]

20. Xia, W.; Zhao, X.; Yue, Q.; Xuan, W.; Pan, Q.; Wang, J.; Zhang, Z. Competitive deformation induced by TCP precipitation and creep inconsistency on dendritic structures in a nickel–based single crystal superalloy crept at high temperatures. *Mater. Charact.* **2022**, *187*, 111855. [CrossRef]
21. Ru, Y.; Zhao, H.; Zhang, H.; Pan, X.; Zhao, W.; Pei, Y.; Gong, S. Design for anomalous yield in γ'–strengthening superalloys. *Mater. Des.* **2019**, *183*, 108082. [CrossRef]
22. Ru, Y.; Hu, B.; Zhao, W.; Zhang, H.; Pei, Y.; Li, S.; Xu, H. Topologically inverse microstructure in single–crystal superalloys: Microstructural stability and properties at ultrahigh temperature. *Mater. Res. Lett.* **2021**, *12*, 497–506. [CrossRef]
23. Ai, C.; Li, S.; Zhao, X.; Zhou, J.; Guo, Y.; Sun, Z.; Gong, S. Influence of solidification history on precipitation behavior of TCP phase in a completely heat–treated Ni3Al based single crystal superalloy during thermal exposure. *J. Alloys Compd.* **2017**, *722*, 740–745. [CrossRef]
24. Rae, C.M.; Reed, R.C. The precipitation of topologically close–packed phases in rhenium–containing superalloys. *Acta Mater.* **2001**, *49*, 4113–4125. [CrossRef]
25. Zhang, Z.; Yue, Z. TCP phases growth and crack initiation and propagation in nickel–based single crystal superalloys containing Re. *J. Alloys Compd.* **2018**, *746*, 84–92. [CrossRef]
26. Sugui, T.; Minggang, W.; Tang, L.; Benjiang, Q.; Jun, X. Influence of TCP phase and its morphology on creep properties of single crystal nickel–based superalloys. *Mater. Sci. Eng. A* **2010**, *527*, 5444–5451. [CrossRef]
27. Wu, R.; Zaiser, M. Cyclic–loading microstructure–property relations from a mesoscale perspective: An example of single crystal Nickel–based superalloys. *J. Alloys Compd.* **2019**, *770*, 964–971. [CrossRef]
28. Wu, R.; Zhang, Y. Phase–field, dislocation based plasticity and damage coupled model: Modelling and application to single crystal superalloys. *Int. J. Plast.* **2022**, *157*, 103376. [CrossRef]
29. Cottura, M.; Appolaire, B.; Finel, A. Coupling the Phase Field Method for diffusive transformations with dislocation density–based crystal plasticity: Application to Ni–based superalloys. *J. Mech. Phys. Solids* **2016**, *94*, 473–489. [CrossRef]

crystals

MDPI

Article

Temperature Effects on the Deformation Mechanisms in a Ni-Co-Based Superalloys

Rui Hu [1,*], Jiaheng Zhao [1], Cheng Yang [1,2], Jinhui Du [2], Xian Luo [1], Zhongnan Bi [2] and Bin Gan [2,*]

1 State Key Laboratory of Solidification Processing, Northwestern Polytechnical University, Xi'an 710072, China
2 Beijing Key Laboratory of Advanced High Temperature Materials, Central Iron and Steel Research Institute, Beijing 100081, China
* Correspondence: rhu@nwpu.edu.cn (R.H.); ganbin@cisri-gaona.com.cn (B.G.)

Abstract: The tensile properties of a Ni-Co-based superalloy were investigated from room temperature to 900 °C. From 25 to 650 °C, the yield strength and tensile strength of the alloy decreased slightly, while the elongation decreased sharply. From 760 °C to 900 °C, the yield strength and tensile strength were greatly reduced, while the elongation also had a low value. With the increase in temperature, the deformation mechanism transformed from anti-phase boundary shearing to stacking fault shearing, and then from deformation twinning to Orowan bypassing, respectively. Deformation twins were generated in the deformed alloy with high-density stacking faults and they can contribute to the high strength. The alloy in this study has good mechanical properties and hot working characteristics below 760 °C and can be used as a turbine disk, turbine blade, combustion chamber, and other aircraft structural parts.

Keywords: nickel-based superalloy; deformation mechanism; microstructure; intermediate-temperature brittleness

1. Introduction

Nickel-based superalloys are widely used in aircraft engines because of their excellent strength and creep resistance at high temperatures [1,2]. The outstanding strength of these alloys mainly stems from solid solution strengthening elements and high volume fractions of γ' precipitates [3,4]. The superalloy turbine discs are used at temperatures of 650~700 °C and sometimes reach 815 °C, according to the actual service conditions [5]. The temperature-bearing capacity and mechanical properties of turbine disks determine the thermal efficiency and service life of the engine system. Conventional strengthening mechanisms, such as solid-solution strengthening, work hardening, grain boundaries strengthening, and precipitation hardening, have previously been used to improve the properties of superalloys [6]. However, the above-mentioned defects are not thermally stable at high temperatures. Lu et al. reported that nanoscale coherent twin boundaries (TB) can effectively enhance nano and ultra-fine grained materials without adversely affecting the ductility [7,8]. The addition of Co will reduce the stacking fault energy (SFE) of superalloys [9]. The decrease of SFE can change the deformation mechanism of the alloys, which may lead to twin boundary strengthening [6]. Therefore, it is necessary to study the deformation mechanism and mechanical properties of Ni-Co-based superalloys from room temperature to high temperatures.

The intermediate and high-temperature deformation mechanisms have been extensively investigated in the past decades [10–17]. The research results of Yuan et al. [18] show that the addition of the Co element reduces the stacking fault (SF) energy of the Ni-based superalloy and influences its deformation mechanism. The dominant deformation mechanism of superalloys is that a pair of dislocations shear γ' precipitates at low temperatures, while SF is formed by the movement of partial dislocations at intermediate temperatures. Xu et al. [19] studied the variation trend of SF energy and SF density with temperatures, showing that the SF density increased with the increase in temperatures. Yuan et al. [20] reported that the mechanisms of antiphase boundary (APB) cutting and SF cutting both appeared in the alloy. With the increase in temperature, deformation twins are easier to form than APB.

In this study, the temperature dependence of the tensile behavior of a Ni-Co-based superalloy was investigated. On the basis of the microstructure analysis, the transformation of the deformation mechanism (with temperature) and the intermediate temperature brittleness were discussed.

2. Experimental Procedures

The studied Ni-Co-based superalloy has the following chemical compositions: 25.0 Co, 14.0 Cr, 2.8 Mo, 1.2 W, 8.0 (Al, Ti, Nb), 0.02 C, 0.02 B, 0.03 Zr, and balanced Ni (wt%). The alloy was prepared by vacuum induction melting and forging. The samples were cut by electric spark cutting and homogenized at 1100 °C to eliminate the segregation. Aging treatments were carried out as follows: 650 °C/24 h/air cooling + 760 °C/16 h/air cooling. The equipment used for the heat treatment was a KSL-1400X-A1 high-temperature box furnace. Specimens with a gauge length of 25 mm and a diameter of 12 mm were machined out for tensile tests. The tensile testing equipment was an electronic universal material testing machine produced by INSTRON Company. The tensile tests were conducted with a strain rate of 3×10^{-4} s^{-1} at various temperatures, i.e., 25 °C, 650 °C, 760 °C, 850 °C, and 900 °C, respectively. A temperature fluctuation not exceeding ±2 °C was maintained over the gauge length. At least three identical specimens were tested at each temperature. After the tensile tests, the fracture surfaces of the specimens were investigated using a Zeiss Gemini 500 field emission scanning electron microscope (FESEM) operated at 15 kV. Slices were cut perpendicular to the tensile direction from the deformed samples and mechanically thinned down to 50 μm, and then thinned by ion-beam milling. The microstructures of the deformed samples were investigated using a Talos F200X transmission electron microscope (TEM) operated at 200 kV. It was also equipped with an X-ray energy dispersion analyzer for chemical composition analysis.

3. Results and Discussion

3.1. Mechanical Properties Analysis

The tensile properties of the superalloys at different temperatures are shown in Figure 1. The yield strength (YS) and ultimate tensile strength (UTS) of the superalloy had similar variation trends with the temperature. The YS and UTS decreased slightly when the temperature rose to 650 °C and then decreased rapidly above this temperature. The elongation decreased rapidly with temperature, from room temperature to 650 °C, and then maintained a low value above 650 °C, demonstrating an intermediate temperature brittleness (ITB) behavior.

The γ' precipitation has a unique feature in that its strength increases with the increase in temperature [21–23]. The superalloy studied in this work contained a high-volume fraction of γ' precipitates. The decrease in strength of the γ matrix was compensated by the increased strength of γ' precipitates with the increase in temperature [24], due to the thermally-activated cross-slip of dislocations from {111} planes to {110} planes [21,25].

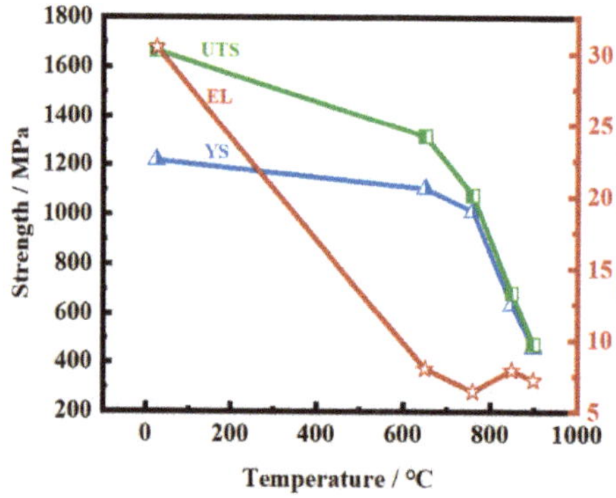

Figure 1. Tensile properties of the superalloy at different temperatures.

The YS of the alloy depended greatly on the testing temperature. According to References [25,26], the yielding behavior at a high temperature is a thermally activated process. Therefore, the Arrhenius type of relationship may be suitable for characterizing the plastic flow behavior of this alloy, i.e.,

$$\sigma_y/E = A\{\exp[Q/(RT)]\} \quad (1)$$

where σ_y is the yield strength, E is the elastic modulus, Q is the activation energy of the deformation process, R is the gas constant (8.314 J mol^{-1} K^{-1}), T is the temperature, and A is the material constant. Equation (1) was applied to several theoretical and experimental studies of superalloys [27,28]. A plot of the ratio of normalized values of YS by the elastic modulus vs. the reciprocal of temperature is shown in Figure 2. It is obvious that there are three different stages as functions of temperatures. At high temperatures (above 760 °C), the curve had a positive slope, at intermediate temperatures, the curve exhibited a negative slope, and at low temperatures (below 650 °C), the curve dropped slowly. This indicates that the rate-controlling processes for the deformation mechanisms had great changes. The main strengthening mechanism of the alloy was the γ' precipitation, which could effectively block dislocation movement. So, at low and intermediate temperatures, the high applied stress could force dislocations to cut into γ' precipitates. With the increase in temperature, the applied stress value is less than the critical stress required for dislocation cutting γ' precipitates, and then the enhanced thermal activation causes the dislocation climbing mechanism [29].

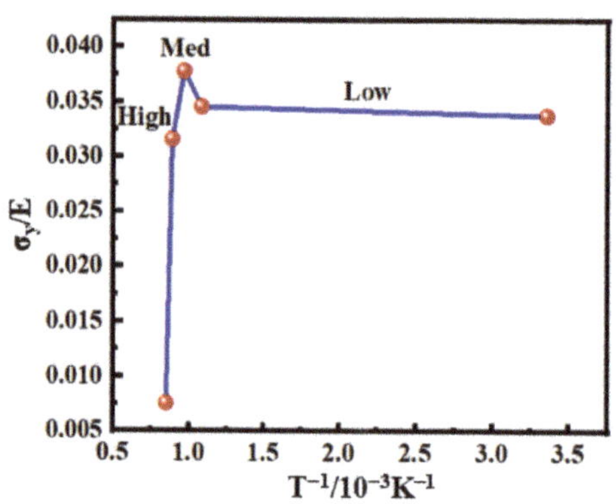

Figure 2. A plot of the ratio of the normalized value of YS by σ_y/E vs. the reciprocal of temperature.

3.2. Mechanical Property Analysis

3.2.1. Initial Microstructure

A typical microstructure of the alloy after the heat treatment is shown in Figure 3. One can see that the γ' precipitates are uniformly distributed in the alloy. According to the forming sequence, the γ' precipitates in the alloy can be divided into primary, secondary, and tertiary γ' precipitates. As shown in Figure 3a,c,e, the primary γ' precipitates tend to appear at grain boundaries with larger sizes, while the secondary γ' precipitates are located within moderately sized grains. In addition, a large number of nanoscale tertiary γ' precipitations can be seen inside the grains. The γ' precipitates are $L1_2$ structures confirmed by the SAED patterns (Figure 3b,d,f) and are coherent with the γ matrix.

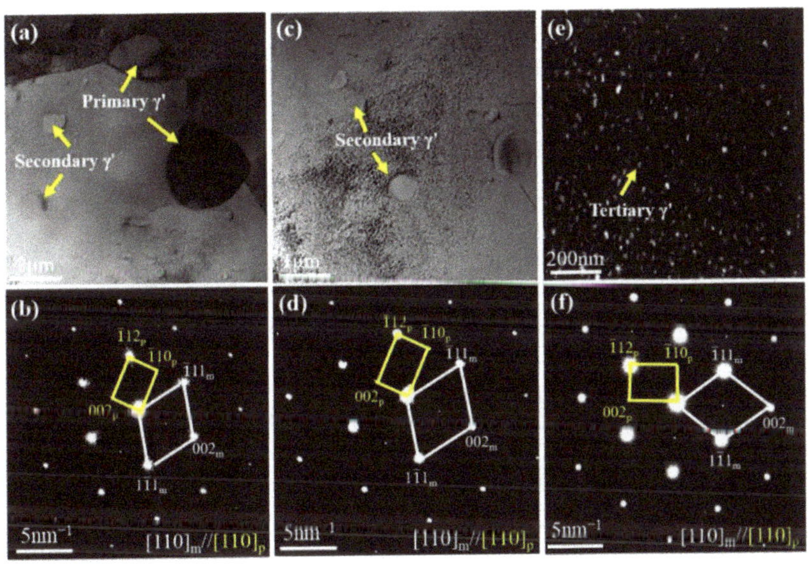

Figure 3. TEM micrographs of the heat-treated superalloy: (**a**,**c**,**e**) are the primary, secondary, and tertiary γ' precipitates, respectively; (**b**,**d**,**f**) are their corresponding SAED patterns, respectively.

By calibrating the super diffraction spots and the matrix diffraction spots, the orientation relationships between the precipitates and the matrix can be obtained as follows (m represents matrix, p represents γ' precipitates):

$$[110]m//[110]p \quad (002)m//(002)p \quad (111)_m//(112)_p$$

The element content in the alloy was analyzed by TEM equipped with an X-ray energy dispersive analyzer; the results are shown in Table 1. The contents of C, B, and other light elements are difficult to be measured by the energy spectrometer, so only some elements are listed in Table 1. It can be seen that Co, Cr, Mo, and W are enriched in the γ matrix and play the role of solid solution strengthening, while Ti, Al, and Ni are enriched in the γ' precipitates. These three elements mainly form $(Ni,Co)_3(Al,Ti)$ during the heat treatment process, and the γ' precipitates can play a role in precipitation strengthening.

Table 1. Alloy element distribution (wt %).

	Ni	Co	Cr	Ti	Al	Mo	W
Primary γ'	66.1	17.2	3.0	8.7	3.6	0.7	0.7
Secondary γ'	63.0	18.7	7.0	6.4	2.4	1.5	1.0
γ matrix	50.8	24.8	13.6	4.8	1.9	2.8	1.3
$C_{primary\ \gamma'}/C_{\gamma}$	1.301	0.694	0.221	1.813	1.895	0.250	0.538
$C_{secondary\ \gamma'}/C_{\gamma}$	1.240	0.754	0.515	1.333	1.263	0.536	0.769

3.2.2. Microstructure Analysis of the Deformed Samples

Figure 4 shows the deformed microstructure of the room temperature-tested sample observed by TEM. Apparently, there are some dislocations in both the γ matrix and the γ' precipitation at room temperature. Most of the dislocations move alone, some in pairs. Due to the smaller size of the tertiary γ' precipitate, its density is higher [14]. When a partial dislocation is cut into the γ' precipitation, high-energy APBs are generated due to the a/2<110> displacement of the superlattice. So dislocations occur through the γ' precipitation in closely spaced pairs to minimize the APB [14].

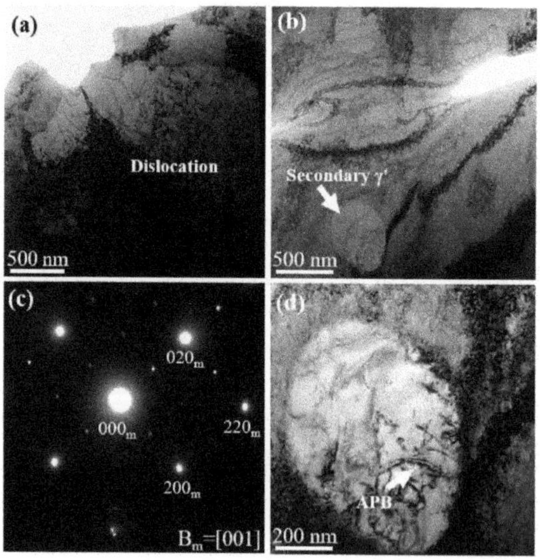

Figure 4. Deformed microstructure of the room temperature-tested sample: (**a**,**b**) high-density dislocations in γ matrix and γ' precipitates, (**c**) SAED pattern, (**d**) APB in the secondary γ' precipitates.

The TEM observations of this alloy tested at different temperatures are shown in Figures 5–7. Figure 5 presents the deformed microstructures after a tensile test at 650 °C. When the testing temperature is 650 °C, the dislocation density becomes high and a number of SFs are produced both inside the γ' precipitates and the γ matrix. Moreover, the formation of dislocation entanglement in the γ matrix indicates that the deformation occurs mainly in the γ matrix. The SFs were observed in two different directions, which formed structures similar to Lomer–Cottrell locks. As indicated by the arrows in Figure 5b, these SFs on different planes intersect and interact with each other. The observed SFs have been investigated in some alloys [29]. Chu et al. [30] believed that the SFE of DZ951 alloy decreased with temperature from 20 °C to 760 °C. The transition temperature from APB shearing to the SF shearing mechanism decreases due to the combination of higher APB energy and lower SFE [20]. Therefore, SFs will appear as the temperature increases.

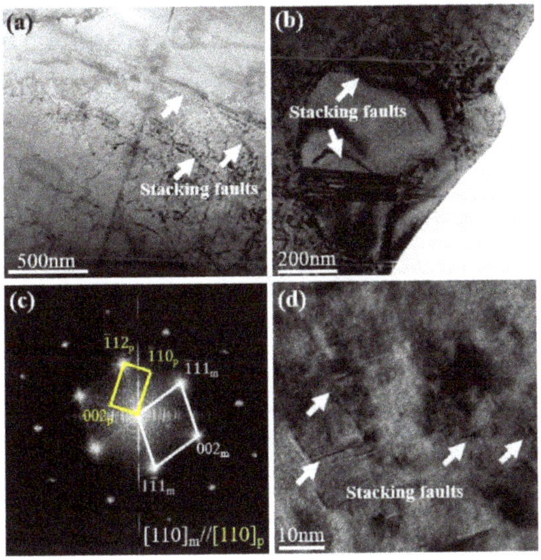

Figure 5. Deformation microstructures after the tensile test at 650 °C: (**a**) the SFs in the γ matrix; (**b**) the SF in the γ' precipitates; (**c**) a SAED pattern corresponding to (**a**); (**d**) HRTEM image showing SFs.

When the test temperature is 760 °C, it can be seen that the dislocation density in the γ matrix further increases, and they become entangled with each other. In addition, when the test temperature is increased, a large number of deformation twins are generated in the alloy. A study of FCC crystals showed that SFs and deformation twins were sequentially generated in the alloy with increasing plastic strains and deformation temperatures [31]. Figure 6d shows a high-resolution transmission electron microscope (HRTEM) image of the superalloy. The twin boundaries are indicated by green lines. The thickness of the twinned lamella is 16 layers of atoms.

When the test temperature was 850 °C, it can be seen that more dislocations were formed in the γ matrix and tangled with each other (Figure 7a,b), but it is difficult to find any deformation twins, and the stacking faults parallel to each other are clearly visible after the tensile test at 850 °C. When the tensile temperature was increased from 760 °C to 850 °C, there were many dislocation loops, as seen in Figure 7b. Figure 7c,d show that the deformation mechanism mainly involves the dislocation bypassing the γ' precipitation through the Orowan process, and the dislocations pile up around the γ' precipitation at high temperatures. A large number of dislocations surrounded the γ' precipitates, while only a few dislocations were located in the γ' precipitates. In contrast to the deformation at room temperature, the deformation was dominated by Orowan bypassing at 900 °C. When the test temperature increased, the applied stress was less than the critical stress required for dislocation cutting the γ' precipitate, then the enhanced thermal activation caused the dislocation climbing mechanism. It can be seen that as the temperature increases, the deformation activation energy decreases [29].

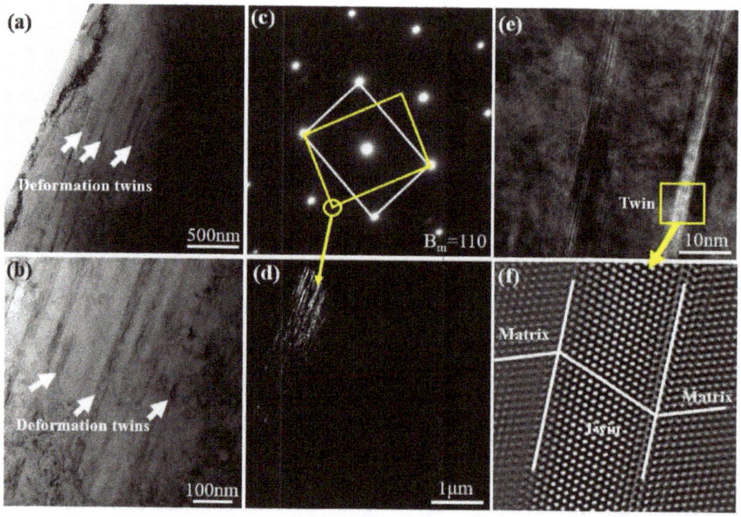

Figure 6. Deformed microstructures after tensile testing at 760 °C: (**a**) bright field image with a lower magnification; (**b**) bright field image with a higher magnification; (**c**) a SAED pattern; (**d**) dark field image corresponding to (**c**); (**e**) HRTEM image showing a twin lamella; (**f**) inverse Fourier transform image corresponding to (**e**).

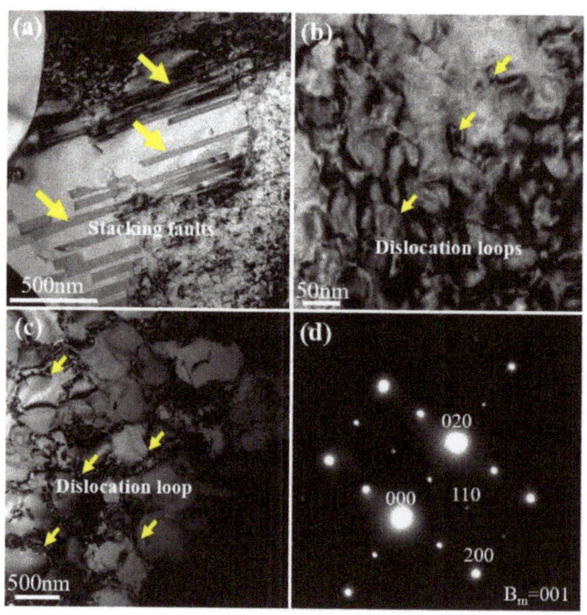

Figure 7. Deformed microstructures after tensile testing at 850 °C and 900 °C: (**a**,**b**), 850 °C; (**c**,**d**), 900 °C.

3.2.3. Fracture Surface Analysis

The morphologies of the fracture surfaces of the tensile specimens tested at different temperatures are shown in Figure 8. Clearly, the deformation is homogeneous, and the fracture has a large number of dimples. It can be seen that the tear-off dimples are elongated, so the plasticity is good, as shown in Figure 8a,b. This is consistent with the results obtained for higher elongation after room temperature tensile testing. When the testing temperature increased to 650 °C, the fracture morphology changed, as shown in Figure 8c,d. Clearly, the main features of the specimen tested at 650 °C were the decohesion combined with some dimples, as shown in Figure 8c. Although there were some dimples, the tear-off dimples were not elongated, so the deformation was limited. Further observations showed that there were many secondary cracks and debonding phenomena along the γ' precipitate/γ matrix interfaces on the fracture surface. Secondary cracks readily propagated along rigid precipitates and the matrix, which is detrimental to ductility [32–35]. Therefore, it is easy to understand why the elongation of the alloy is lower at 650 °C. The fracture of the alloy tested at 760 °C is shown in Figure 8e,f. It can be seen that the sample exhibited a heavier brittle feature, with cleavage fracture being the main feature, as shown in Figure 8e. The secondary cracks propagated along the grain boundary. Moreover, small dimples and precipitates were distributed on the cleavage facets. The deformation was not homogeneous, so the elongation was low. The morphologies of the fracture surfaces of the tensile specimens tested at 850 °C and 900 °C are shown in Figure 8g,h, respectively. The fracture pattern was mainly in the intergranular mode. Decohesion along the γ' precipitates/γ matrix interfaces existed on the fracture surface.

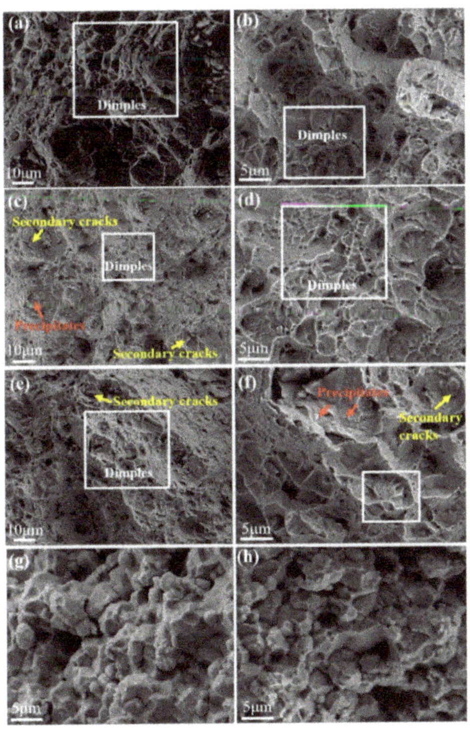

Figure 8. SEM images showing the fracture surface morphologies after tensile tests at different temperatures: (**a**,**b**) RT; (**c**,**d**) 650 °C; (**e**,**f**) 760 °C; (**g**) 850 °C; (**h**) 900 °C. The yellow and red arrows, respectively, indicate the secondary cracks and the precipitates. The white square indicates dimples.

4. Discussion about the Mechanism of Intermediate-Temperature Brittleness

Although the elongation is high at room temperature, the elongation is greatly decreased when the test temperature is higher than 650 °C. The intermediate temperature brittleness was observed in several superalloys with high volume fractions of γ' precipitates. There are a number of reasons for this behavior, and the most important factors for superalloys are [36]: (1) carbide particles are rich in trace elements or oxygen, resulting in the embrittlement of grain boundaries; (2) changes in the deformation mechanisms lead to strain localization; (3) the instability of γ' precipitates that are exposed to high temperatures. Clearly, no carbide particles are found in the present superalloy, so intermediate-temperature brittleness is not caused by carbide particles. Chu et al. [30] showed that deformation was mainly dominated by pairs of a/2<110> dislocation shearing γ' precipitation at low temperatures, and it was mainly dominated by Orowan bypassing at high temperatures. They found the intermediate temperature brittleness at 760 °C was due to strain localization mainly caused by SFs. Kim et al. [13] suggested that the generation of deformation twins has an important effect on the intermediate temperature brittleness. At the same time, they showed that deformation twins are easy to form in superalloys with low SFE.

In general, when a new deformation mechanism appears, the ductility decreases simultaneously [37]. The study of the deformed microstructure provides information for analyzing possible fracture mechanisms. The dominant deformation mechanisms is that the γ' precipitates is cut by dislocations at low temperatures (below 650 °C). Orowan bypass is the main deformation mechanism at high temperatures (above 900 °C). At 760 °C, a high density of dislocations was formed in the γ matrix and many of them were tangled. The operation of a multi-slip system will generate the delivery and reaction of dislocations, thereby creating more barriers for cross-slips. Most importantly, there are a large number of SFs and deformation twins, which can also create barriers for cross-slips. The deformation is very inhomogeneous, and the local strain reaches the maximum simultaneously, resulting in intermediate temperature brittleness at 760 °C. Similarly, there are a number of SFs both at 650 °C and 850 °C. So the intermediate temperature brittleness is mainly caused by the strain localization caused by SFs or deformation twinning.

5. Conclusions

Through the above comprehensive analysis of the microstructural changes of the Ni-Co-based superalloy (after tensile testing at different temperatures), the following conclusions can be drawn:

(1) From room temperature to 650 °C, the YS and TS of the alloy decrease slightly, while the elongation decreases sharply. From 760 °C to 900 °C, YS and TS are greatly reduced; the elongation also has a low value. There is an intermediate temperature brittleness.

(2) After heat treatment, the alloy has three different γ' precipitate sizes, which play important roles in precipitation strengthening. With the increase in temperature, the deformation mechanism changes from anti-phase boundary shearing to stacking fault shearing, and then deformation twins are generated in the deformed alloy with high-density stacking faults. The alloy has good mechanical properties and hot working characteristics below 760 °C and can be used as a turbine disk, turbine blade, combustion chamber, and other aircraft structural parts.

(3) From the analysis of the results, the mechanical properties of the alloy decrease sharply from 850 °C to 900 °C, and the deformation mechanism also changes to Orowan bypass.

Author Contributions: Conceptualization, R.H., J.Z., Z.B. and B.G.; methodology, R.H. and J.Z.; validation, R.H., J.Z. and C.Y.; formal analysis, R.H., J.Z. and J.D.; investigation, R.H., J.Z., J.D., Z.B. and B.G.; data curation, J.Z., C.Y. and B.G.; writing—original draft preparation, J.Z. and C.Y.; writing—review and editing, R.H. and B.G.; supervision, R.H., X.L. and B.G.; project administration, R.H., X.L. and B.G.; funding acquisition, B.G. All authors have read and agreed to the published version of the manuscript.

Funding: This research was funded by the National Key Research and Development Program of China, no. 2017YFA0700703 and the National Natural Science Foundation of China, no. 92060102.

Institutional Review Board Statement: Not applicable.

Informed Consent Statement: Not applicable.

Data Availability Statement: Not applicable.

Conflicts of Interest: The authors declare no conflict of interest.

References

1. Reed, R.C.; Rae, C.M.F. *Physical Metallurgy of the Nickel-Based Superalloys*; Elsevier: Amsterdam, The Netherlands, 2014.
2. Pollock, T.M. Alloy design for aircraft engines. *Nat. Mater.* **2016**, *15*, 809. [CrossRef]
3. Jackson, M.; Reed, R. Heat treatment of UDIMET 720Li: The effect of microstructure on properties. *Mater. Sci. Eng. A* **1999**, *259*, 85–97. [CrossRef]
4. Reed, R.C. *The Superalloys Fundamentals and Applications*; Cambridge University Press: Cambridge, UK, 2006.
5. Williams, J.C.; Starke, J.E.A. Progress in structural materials for aerospace systems. *Acta Mater.* **2003**, *51*, 5775–5799. [CrossRef]
6. Yuan, Y.; Gu, Y.; Osada, T.; Zhong, Z.; Yokokawa, T.; Harada, H. A new method to strengthen turbine disc superalloys at service temperatures. *Scr. Mater.* **2012**, *66*, 884–889. [CrossRef]
7. Lu, K.; Lu, L.; Suresh, S. Strengthening Materials by Engineering Coherent Internal Boundaries at the Nanoscale. *Science* **2009**, *324*, 349–352. [CrossRef]
8. Lu, L.; Chen, X.; Huang, X.; Lu, K. Revealing the maximum strength in Nanotwinned copper. *Science* **2009**, *323*, 607–610. [CrossRef]
9. Yuan, Y.; Gu, Y.; Cui, C.; Osada, T.; Zhong, Z.; Tetsui, T.; Yokokawa, T.; Harada, H. Influence of Co content on stacking fault energy in Ni–Co base disk superalloys. *J. Mater. Res.* **2011**, *26*, 2833–2837. [CrossRef]
10. Francis, E.M.; Grant, B.M.; Da Fonseca, J.Q.; Phillips, P.J.; Mills, M.J.; Daymond, M.R.; Preuss, M. High-temperature deformation mechanisms in a polycrystalline nickel-base superalloy studied by neutron diffraction and electron microscopy. *Acta Mater.* **2014**, *74*, 18–29. [CrossRef]
11. Viswanathan, C.; Sarosi, P.M.; Whitis, D.H.; Mills, M.J. Deformation mechanisms at intermediate creep temperatures in the Ni-base superalloy René 88 DT. *Mater. Sci. Eng. A* **2005**, *400*, 489–495. [CrossRef]
12. Yuan, Y.; Gu, Y.; Zhong, Z.; Osada, T.; Cui, C.; Tetsui, T.; Yokokawa, T.; Harada, H. Creep mechanisms of a new Ni-Co-base disc superalloy at an intermediate temperature. *J. Microsc.* **2012**, *248*, 34. [CrossRef]
13. Yuan, Y.; Gu, Y.; Osada, T.; Zhong, Z.; Yokokawa, T.; Harada, H. Deformation mechanisms in a new disc superalloy at low and intermediate temperatures. *Scr. Mater.* **2012**, *67*, 137–140. [CrossRef]
14. Fu, B.; Du, K.; Han, G.; Cui, C.; Zhang, J. Deformation mechanisms in a Co-rich nickel based superalloy with different size of γ' precipitates. *Mater. Lett.* **2015**, *152*, 272–275. [CrossRef]
15. Daymond, M.; Preuss, M.; Clausen, B. Evidence of variation in slip mode in a polycrystalline nickel-base superalloy with change in temperature from neutron diffraction strain measurements. *Acta Mater.* **2007**, *55*, 3089–3102. [CrossRef]
16. Unocic, R.; Kovarik, L.; Shen, C.; Sarosi, P.; Wang, Y.; Li, J.; Ghosh, S.; Mills, M. Deformation mechanisms in Ni-base disk superalloys at higher temperatures. *Superalloys* **2008**, *8*, 377–385.
17. Kovarik, L.; Unocic, R.; Li, J.; Sarosi, P.; Shen, C.; Wang, Y.; Mills, M. Microtwinning and other shearing mechanisms at intermediate temperatures in Ni-based superalloys. *Prog. Mater. Sci.* **2009**, *54*, 839–873. [CrossRef]
18. Yuan, Y.; Gu, Y.; Zhong, Z.; Yokokawa, T.; Harada, H. Enhanced strength at intermediate temperatures in a Ni-base disk superalloy with high Co addition. *Mater. Sci. Eng. A* **2012**, *556*, 595–600. [CrossRef]
19. Xu, Y.; Qi, D.; Du, K.; Cui, C.; Ye, H. Stacking fault effects on dynamic strain aging in a Ni–Co-based superalloy. *Scr. Mater.* **2014**, *87*, 37–40. [CrossRef]
20. Yuan, Y.; Gu, Y.F.; Zhong, Z.H.; Osada, T.; Yokokawa, T.; Harada, H. Controlling the deformation mechanism in disk superalloys at low and intermediate temperatures. *Superalloys* **2012**, *2012*, 35–42.
21. Stoloff, N.S.; Liu, C.T. The physical and mechanical metallurgy of Ni_3Al and its alloys. *Phys. Metall. Process. Intermet. Compd.* **1996**, *1*, 212–296.
22. Sheng, L.; Zhang, W.; Guo, J.; Wang, Z.; Ovcharenko, V.; Zhou, L.; Ye, H. Microstructure and mechanical properties of Ni_3Al fabricated by thermal explosion and hot extrusion. *Intermetallics* **2009**, *17*, 572–577. [CrossRef]
23. Cui, C.; Gu, Y.; Ping, D.; Harada, H. Microstructural evolution and mechanical properties of a Ni-based superalloy, TMW-4. *Metall. Mater. Trans. A* **2009**, *40*, 282–291. [CrossRef]
24. Kear, B.H. Dislocation configurations and work hardening in Cu_3Au crystals. *Acta Metall.* **1964**, *12*, 555–569. [CrossRef]
25. Kolbe, M.; Neuking, K.; Eggeler, G. Dislocation reactions and microstructural instability during 1025 °C shear creep testing of superalloy single crystals. *Mater. Sci. Eng. A* **1997**, *234*, 877–879. [CrossRef]
26. Sengupta, A.; Putatunda, S.K.; Bartosiewicz, L.; Hangas, J.; Nailos, P.J.; Peputapeck, M.; Alberts, F.E. Tensile behavior of a new single-crystal nickel-based superalloy (CMSX-4) at room and elevated temperatures. *J. Mater. Eng. Perform.* **1994**, *3*, 73–81. [CrossRef]
27. He, L.Z.; Zheng, Q.; Sun, X.F. Low ductility at intermediate temperature of Ni–base superalloy M963. *Mater. Sci. Eng. A* **2004**, *380*, 340–348. [CrossRef]
28. Pu, Z.J.; Wu, K.H.; Shi, J.; Zou, D. Development of constitutive relationships for the hot deformation of boron microalloying TiAl–Cr–V alloys. *Mater. Sci. Eng. A* **1995**, *192*, 780–787. [CrossRef]

29. Sheng, L.Y.; Fang, Y.A.; Guo, J.T.; Xi, T.F. Anomalous yield and intermediate temperature brittleness behaviors of directionally solidified nickel-based superalloy. *Trans. Nonferrous Met. Soc. China* **2014**, *24*, 673–681. [CrossRef]
30. Chu, Z.; Yu, J.; Sun, X.; Guan, H.; Hu, Z. Tensile property and deformation behavior of a directionally solidified Ni-base superalloy. *Mater. Sci. Eng. A* **2010**, *527*, 3010–3014. [CrossRef]
31. Niewczas, M. Dislocations and twinning in face centered cubic crystals. *Dislocat. Solids* **2007**, *13*, 263–364.
32. Sheng, L.Y.; Yang, F.; Guo, J.T.; Xi, T.F.; Ye, H.Q. Investigation on NiAl-TiC-Al_2O_3 composite prepared by self-propagation high temperature synthesis with hot extrusion. *Compos. Part B Eng.* **2013**, *45*, 785–791. [CrossRef]
33. Sheng, L.; Yang, F.; Xi, T.; Guo, J. Investigation on microstructure and wear behavior of the NiAl–TiC–Al_2O_3 composite fabricated by self-propagation high-temperature synthesis with extrusion. *J. Alloys Compd.* **2013**, *554*, 182–188. [CrossRef]
34. Sheng, L.Y.; Guo, J.T.; Ren, W.L.; Zhang, Z.X.; Ren, Z.M.; Ye, H.Q. Preliminary investigation on strong magnetic field treated NiAl-Cr(Mo)-Hf near eutectic alloy. *Intermetallics* **2011**, *19*, 143–148. [CrossRef]
35. Sheng, L.Y.; Zhang, W.; Guo, J.T.; Wang, Z.S.; Ye, H.Q. Microstructure evolution and elevated temperature compressive properties of a rapidly solidified NiAl–Cr(Nb)/Dy alloy. *Mater. Des.* **2009**, *30*, 2752–2755. [CrossRef]
36. Copley, S.M.; Kear, B.H.; Rowe, G.M. The temperature and orientation dependence of yielding in Mar-M200 single crystals. *Mater. Sci. Eng.* **1972**, *10*, 87–92. [CrossRef]
37. Bettge, D.; Österle, W.; Ziebs, J. Temperature dependence of yield strength and elongation of the nickel-base superalloy IN 738 LC and the corresponding microstructural evolution. *Int. J. Mater. Res.* **1995**, *86*, 190. [CrossRef]

crystals

MDPI

Article

The Effect of Cooling Rate from Solution Treatment on γ' Reprecipitates and Creep Behaviors of a Ni-Based Superalloy Single-Crystal Casting

Jiapeng Huang [1], Cheng Ai [2], Yi Ru [1], Yong Shang [1], Yanling Pei [1], Shusuo Li [1], Shengkai Gong [1] and Heng Zhang [1,*]

1 School of Material Science and Engineering, Beihang University, Beijing 100191, China
2 School of Materials Science and Engineering, Chang'an University, Xi'an 710064, China
* Correspondence: hengzz@buaa.edu.cn

Abstract: Slowing down the coarsening of the γ' phase and suppressing the precipitation of the topologically close-packed (TCP) phase is crucial for optimizing the creep properties of Ni-based single crystal superalloys, which are affected by the solution treatment history. In the present study, the effect of cooling rate on the morphology, size and lattice misfit of γ' reprecipitates after solution treatment, as well as the microstructural evolution (e.g., the coarsening of γ' reprecipitate and precipitation of the TCP phase) and creep properties of samples under different cooling rates at 1100 °C were investigated. The findings suggested that as the cooling rate increasing, the size of γ' reprecipitates decreased, while the morphology transformed from polygonal to cubic. Additionally, faster cooling rate, on the one hand, the lower the degree of lattice misfit of γ/γ' phases, which is beneficial to slow down the coarsening of the γ' phase; on the other hand, the supersaturation of the γ-phase was reduced, i.e., the Mo and Re contents in the γ matrix were lower compared to the slow-cooling sample, which led to a lower TCP phase area fraction during thermal exposure at 1100 °C. It is crucial that the creep life of the alloy significantly improved by increasing the cooling rate after solution treatment; this is facilitated by the formation of rafts from finer cubic γ' phase and reduction in the TCP phase as a source of microcracks. In conclusion, the findings of this study provide new insights into suppressing the precipitation of the TCP phase and optimizing alloy heat treatment processes to improve creep properties.

Keywords: Ni-based superalloy; single-crystal casting; γ' reprecipitates; solution treatment; cooling rate; TCP; creep

1. Introduction

Ni-based single crystal (SX) superalloys are extensively used for modern areo-engines due to their excellent microstructural stability, mechanical properties and environmental tolerance at elevated temperatures [1,2]. Generally, the excellent mechanical properties of Ni-based SX superalloys at elevated temperature derives from their unique two-phase equilibrium microstructure, consisting of ordered Ni_3Al (γ' phase)-strengthening precipitates with an $L1_2$ structure, which are coherently embedded in the face-centered cubic (FCC) matrix γ-phase [3,4]. In addition, high temperature creep strength is a key parameter with which to evaluate the high mechanical properties of Ni-based SX superalloys, which depends on the interaction of dislocations with the γ' precipitates and interface of γ/γ' phases [5–8]. However, the γ–γ' microstructure undergoes degradation during the prolonged high-temperature exposure, including coarsening of γ' precipitates and precipitation of the topologically close-packed (TCP) phase [9–11], which makes the superalloy enter the rapid deformation stage and fracture. Although a proper initial γ–γ' microstructure is obtained, it is necessary to consider slowing down the coarsening of γ'

precipitates and inhibiting the precipitation of TCP phase, which are very important for improving the high-temperature creep properties of the alloy.

The coarsening of γ' precipitates is driven by the reduction in the interfacial energy and coherent strain energy of the γ/γ' phases [12], where the former is related to its size and the latter is related to the distribution of alloying elements in the γ/γ' phases. In addition, whether the TCP phase can be precipitated depends on the enrichment degree of Re, Mo, Cr and other elements in the γ matrix of the superalloy [13,14]. Therefore, reducing the degree of segregation of alloying elements in dendrites structure or γ/γ' phases is beneficial for slowing down the coarsening of γ' precipitates and inhibiting the precipitation of the TCP phase.

Generally, a proper heat treatment is required before service for Ni-based SX superalloys to eliminate the γ–γ' eutectic, reduce the microsegregation of elements such as Re, Mo, Cr [15] and optimize the size and morphology of the γ' reprecipitations (secondary γ' phase) [16], thereby obtaining excellent properties for the alloy [17–19]. Among them, an appropriate solution treatment (ST) process (including austenitizing temperature, holding time and cooling rate, etc.) is the basis for subsequent microstructural evolution and regulation. Elimination of residual microsegregation is usually performed by increasing the austenitizing temperature or prolonging the holding time, but this will lead to the formation of more and larger homogenized pores [20,21], so that the purpose of improving the high-temperature creep performance cannot be achieved; furthermore, Hegde [22] and Karunaratne et al. [23] suggested that the microsegregation does not change monotonically with the increase in the solution temperature and the prolongation of the solution time, and the microsegregation of Re, Cr and Mo elements increased due to the uphill diffusion of the γ–γ' eutectic in the inter-dendrites. However, it has been reported that by increasing the cooling rate after solution treatment from supersolvus temperature, on the one hand, the size of the γ' reprecipitates becomes smaller [24] (the interface energy of γ–γ' phases is larger), but its morphology changes from cubic to irregular shape. Similar results were reported by Bhowal [7] and Yu [25]; on the one hand, they report how the secondary γ' precipitates with non-equilibrium compositions formed at high cooling rate due to the limited time available for diffusion and reduction in mobility of elements [26,27]. Indeed, this is beneficial to reduce the degree of elemental segregation between γ- and γ' phases, as confirmed by the work of Conner [28] and Mitchell [29]. Nonetheless, the high-temperature coarsening behavior of γ' reprecipitates with non-equilibrium components is still unclear at present. Secondly, the effects of γ–γ' microstructure evolution and the precipitation behavior of the TCP phase at higher cooling rates after solution treatment on high-temperature creep properties are currently lacking systematic studies.

The purpose of this paper is to investigate the effect of cooling rates (water quenching and air cooling) after solution treatment from supersolvus temperature on the coarsening of γ' reprecipitates, the precipitation behavior of the TCP phase and high-temperature creep properties (1100 °C/137 MPa). The variation in size and morphology of the γ–γ' phase microstructure and microsegregation behavior under different cooling rates were analyzed in detail, and the relationship between the microstructure evolution and the creep behavior was discussed. The findings of this study provide new insights into suppressing precipitation of TCP and optimizing alloy heat treatment processes to improve creep properties.

2. Materials and Methods

2.1. Materials and Heat Treatment

A low-density experimental nickel-based single crystal superalloy designed with high γ' volume fraction and Mo content was adopted in this work. It had relatively good high-temperature mechanical properties, although there is a certain tendency of TCP precipitation. The chemical composition (weight percent) of the experimental superalloy (Exp. Alloy) is listed in Table 1, and was determined and verified by inductively coupled plasma–mass spectrometry (ICP-MS).

Table 1. Chemical composition of the experimental superalloy, wt.%.

Element	Al	Mo	Re	Ta	Hf	Y	Ni
nominal	7.0~8.5	7.0~11.0	3.0	1.0~4.5	0.1	0.05	Bal.
measured	6.9~8.3	7.2~11.3	2.85	1.2~4.6	0.08	0.045	Bal.

The single-crystal cylindrical rods (about φ16 × 150 mm) were prepared by a high-rate solidification (HRS) Bridgman apparatus using the screw-selecting method with the withdraw rate of 75 μm/s, the temperature gradient was approximately 4 K/mm, and the rods were chosen according to the orientations only within 5° deviating from the [001] orientation determined with the Laue X-ray back reflection method. In addition, the dendrite structure had the same orientation, and the grain boundaries were not observed after macro-etching, which means that the cylindrical rods had a single crystal structure. In order to eliminate the primary phases and reduction in the segregation to produce a homogeneous microstructure, a solution heat treatment was applied to dissolve the precipitated phases for subsequent reprecipitates in an optimized morphology and size. A heat treatment (HT) regime included a multi-stage solution treatment (1310 °C/2 h + 1320 °C/4 h + 1330 °C/4 h + 1340 °C/6 h + 1350 °C/6 h) and two-step aging treatment (1040 °C/2 h + 870 °C/32 h) was carried out in a tubular resistance furnace. Different cooling rates after ST were obtained by two cooling methods. One is to put the sample directly into water (20 °C) after removing it from the furnace (labeled as WQ), which has a cooling rate of about 1000–1200 K/min; the other (labeled as AC) is to cool the sample in flowing air at a cooling rate of 150~300 K/min. The detailed heat treatment process is listed in Table 2. To observe the microstructure evolution during high-temperature thermal exposure, the samples were subjected to an isothermal exposure of 1100 °C and rapidly water quenched to maintain the situation at high temperatures.

Table 2. Heat treatment schedule of experimental alloy under different cooling rates.

Sample	Heat Treatment Schedule	Cooling Rate after ST (K/min)
AC	1310 °C/2 h + 1320 °C/4 h + 1330 °C/4 h + 1340 °C/6 h + 1350 °C/6 h, air cooling	150~300
WQ	1310 °C/2 h + 1320 °C/4 h + 1330 °C/4 h + 1340 °C/6 h + 1350 °C/6 h, water cooling	1000~1200
HT	1310 °C/2 h + 1320 °C/4 h + 1330 °C/4 h + 1340 °C/6 h + 1350 °C/6 h, air cooling, 1040 °C/2 h, air cooling, 870 °C/32 h, air cooling	150~300

Note: AC represents air cooling after solution treatment, WQ represents water cooling after solution treatment, HT represents solution treatment + aging treatment.

2.2. Creep Test

Creep tests were performed at 1100 °C/137 MPa on rods with orientation within 5° deviating from [001] and with the gauge length of 25 mm and diameter of 5 mm. The tests were interrupted after creep deformation for 10 h and cooled down to room temperature before removing the load to study the dislocation structure formed during creep. The strain was measured by a displacement sensor with the accuracy of 1×10^{-3} mm. At least 3 specimens were tested at each condition.

2.3. Microstructural Characterization

The microstructures of the specimens were characterized by a scanning electron microscopy (SEM, ZEISS EVO10, Oberkochen, Germany). Measurements of the γ' phase area fraction were performed by image analysis on black and white images of samples that were quenched after heat treatment and creep. A JEM-2100 transmission electron microscope (TEM) with an auxiliary energy-dispersive spectroscopy (EDS) detector was used to observe the γ–γ' phase morphology and elemental distribution of the heat-treated samples and measure the dislocation structure after creep. The TEM samples were cut from cross-sections parallel to (001) of the experimental alloys and electrochemically thinned in a solution of 15 mL perchloric acid and 85 mL alcohol at −20 °C.

2.4. Lattice Misfit Determination

The lattice parameters of two phases at room temperature after different heat treatment are measured by using Rigaku SmartLab X-ray diffractometer (CuKα: 40 kV, 200 mA) with a scanning speed of 0.5°/min. The (200) peak of the nickel-based superalloy, which is a combination of the overlapping (200) peak of the γ matrix and the corresponding peak of the γ' phase, was measured. Bragg's law states that when an X-ray beam impinges on a crystal lattice, the maximum intensity of the diffracted beam occurs when the angle between the incident and the diffracted beam $2\theta_{hkl}$ the wavelength of the radiation, λ, and the distance between lattice planes, d_{hkl} are related by Equation (1):

$$\lambda = 2d_{hkl}\sin\theta_{hkl} \tag{1}$$

where, *hkl* denotes the Miller indices for the specific family of lattice planes, and in this study *hkl* = 200. Moreover, the lattice misfit δ was determined from the lattice parameters of the γ- and γ' phases (a_γ and $a_{\gamma'}$) according to Equation (2):

$$\delta = 2(a_{\gamma'} - a_\gamma)/(a_{\gamma'} + a_\gamma). \tag{2}$$

The measured X-ray profiles of the (200) reflections were then split up into three Gaussian peak profiles using Origin 9.0 Software.

3. Results

3.1. Microstructure of the As-Cast and Heat-Treatmented Alloy

The as-cast microstructure is shown in Figure 1. It has a distinct "cross-flowered" dendritic structure arranged in the same direction, and no obvious grain boundaries are observed after macro-etching using optical microscope (OM), as shown in Figure 1a, which means that it was a single crystal structure. The interdendritic region was further examined with SEM, where the large bulky γ' phase (primary γ') and (Mo, Re)-rich phase were observed, as shown in Figure 1b, c. However, after ST treatment, the SEM backscattered electrons (BSE) morphology of alloy and elemental distribution map are shown in Figure 2. The bulky γ' phase and (Mo, Re)-rich phase at interdendrites are completely dissolved, and the elements are basically uniformly distributed, except for the slight segregation of Re in the cores of the dendrites. Thus, it is believed that the adopted solid solution regimen is capable of achieving the goal of solid solution completely.

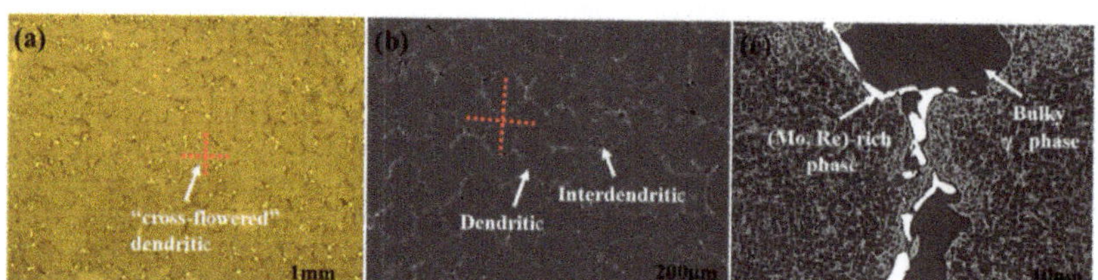

Figure 1. The microstructure of as-cast experimental alloy: (**a**) OM image of dendritic structure; (**b**) SEM of dendritic structure; (**c**) interdendritic region of (**b**).

The SEM secondary electrons (SE) morphology of γ' reprecipitation after solution treatment under different cooling rates is displayed in Figure 3. The reprecipitated γ' phase was uniformly distributed overall and embedded in the γ matrix channel. Nevertheless, the microstructure and size of the γ' phase was significantly affected by the cooling conditions. With the decrease in cooling rate, the size of γ' phase was bigger. After being cooled down by WQ and AC, the size of secondary γ' precipitate was measured to have the statistical mean diameters of 0.359 and 0.491 μm, respectively, as shown in Figure 4a,b. Meanwhile, the γ-channel was transformed from a serrated to a straight one with the increasing the cooling rate. This came from the result of the growth of the γ' phase and the increased coherent strain energy. It is not unnoticeable that the lower the cooling rate is, the relatively larger the area fraction of γ' phase, which increased from 75.6% for the WQ sample to 79.7% for the AC sample. The detailed statistics analyses are presented in Table 3. It can be assumed that the lower cooling rate provided for the precipitation and growth of the γ' phase. The cooling process after solution treatment was equivalent to undergoing a transient aging treatment, and this is more clearly confirmed by comparing the results of the HT samples, as seen in Figure 3c. After two-step aging treatment, the size of the γ' phase grew to 0.621 μm and its area fraction reached 82.3%, as listed in Table 3. However, the number density of the γ' phase for the HT sample was about 6.4/μm^2, which was much lower than that of 12.7/μm^2 under the WQ cooling condition. Under slow-cooling conditions, the number density of γ' phase is lower. This leads to a decrease in the total coherent strain energy and results in a coarsening of the γ' phase [7]. Indeed, the secondary γ' precipitates are transformed from sphere to cube with the slow-cooling rate [25].

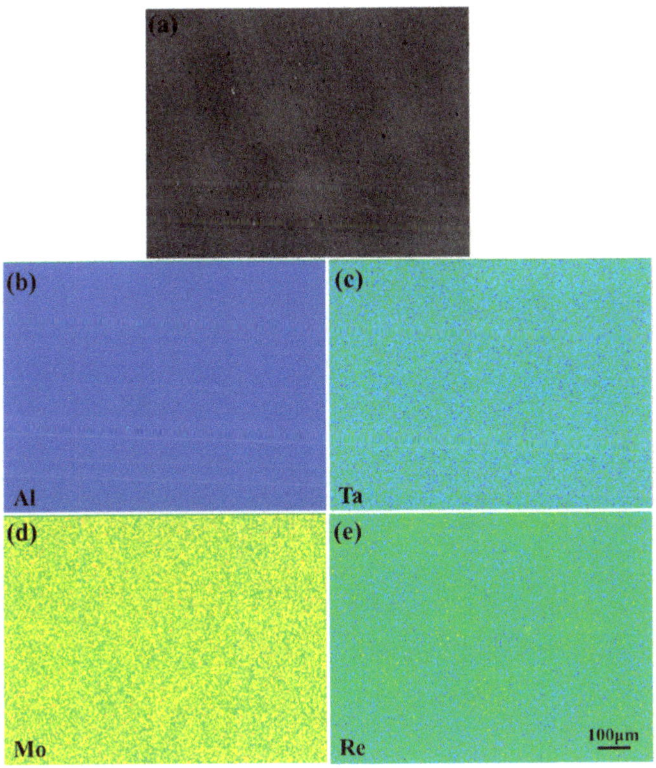

Figure 2. (**a**) The SEM-BSE morphology of alloy after ST treatment and elemental distribution map: (**b**) Al, (**c**) Ta, (**d**) Mo and (**e**) Re.

The microstructure of γ' phases under different cooling conditions are shown in Figure 5. It is found that the finer γ' phases are distributed orderly under WQ cooling condition, and the four sides are concave, as marked with a green dashed line in Figure 5a. This is due to the fact that the γ' phase particles have the smallest elastic modulus along the [001] orientation; it will preferentially grow along the direction of body diagonals under the interaction of coherent strain. Meanwhile, the growth of cube corners will be enhanced due to the larger potential rate of supply of solute to these regions [30]. These γ' phases are unstable, and as adjacent γ' precipitates grow and collide with each other, the concave edges tend to be straightened due to the coherent strain energy [31]. In contrast, when the cooling condition is AC, a large number of polygonal shape γ' phase exist. Some vanishing γ-channels were located in the γ' phase, which indicates that the growth of γ' precipitates itself by merging adjacent to each other. In addition, the tertiary γ' phases appeared in the γ-channel of the AC sample with a size of about 30~55 nm. After examining the composition of the tertiary γ' phase, it is found that its Al, Ta content was lower compared with the secondary γ' phase, but its Mo and Re contents were higher. It typically results that multiple nucleation events occurred at different undercooling degrees below the γ' solvus due to a complex interaction between the increasing thermodynamic driving force of nucleation. This results from the temperature drop (increased undercooling) and the decreasing diffusivity of alloying elements and previous nucleation events resulting in a decrease in this driving force; this is similar to the results reported by Singh [27]. Surprisingly, for the HT sample, aside from the further coarsening of the γ' precipitates, a dislocation network was found to be formed at the γ–γ' interface. This is most likely due to a high amount of Mo and Re addition, causing a large lattice misfit. Even the spontaneous formation of dislocation networks to relaxing the interfacial misfit stress without an external stress.

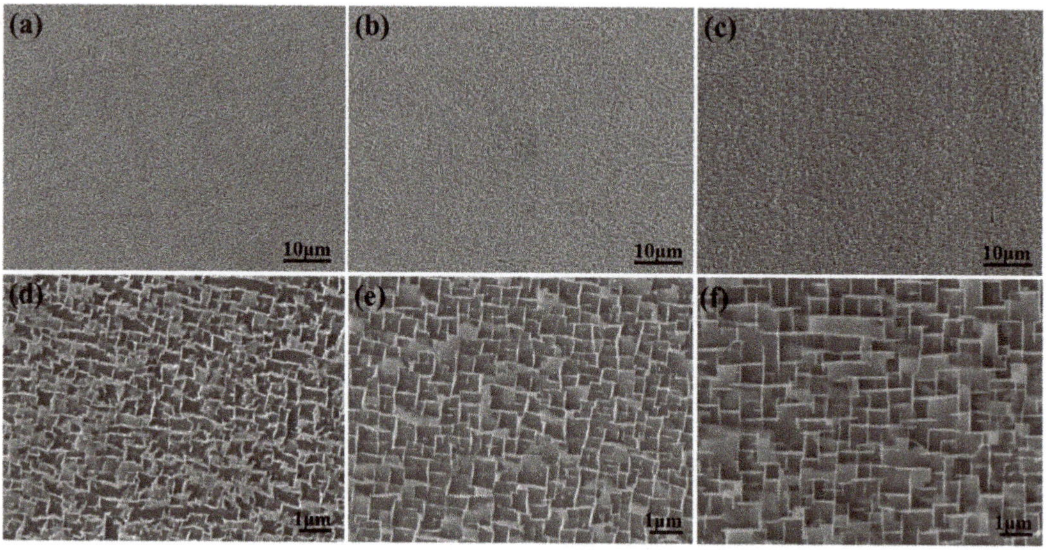

Figure 3. The SEM-SE morphology of secondary γ' phases after heat treatment under different cooling rates: (**a**,**b**) WQ, (**d**,**e**) AC and (**c**,**f**) HT.

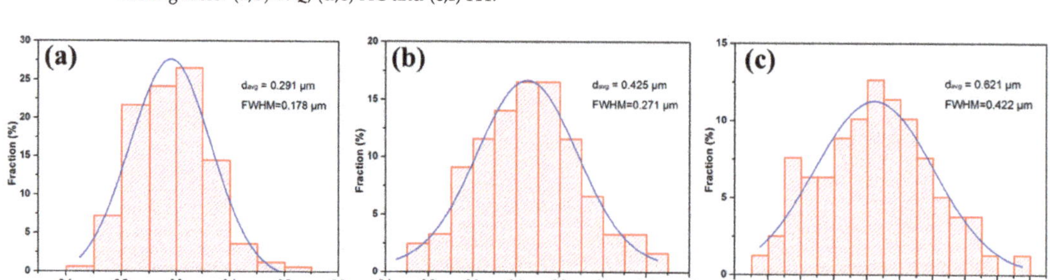

Figure 4. The size distribution of secondary γ' precipitates after heat treatment under different cooling rates: (**a**) WQ, (**b**) AC and (**c**) HT.

Table 3. Size and area fraction of γ' phase after heat treatment under different cooling rates.

Sample	Size of γ' Phase (μm)	Area Fraction of γ' Phase (%)	Number Density of γ' Phase (μm^{-2})
HT	0.621	82.3 ± 2.4	4.53
AC	0.425	79.2 ± 2.8	6.40
WQ	0.291	76.6 ± 3.2	12.78

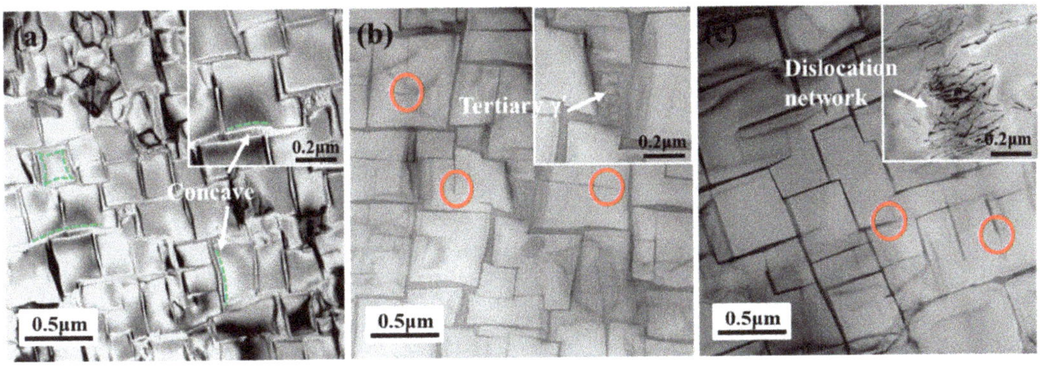

Figure 5. The TEM microstructure of γ' phases after different heat treatment schedule: (**a**) WQ; (**b**) AC and (**c**) HT.

3.2. Element Partitioning and Lattice Misfit of γ–γ' Phase

The compositions of γ- and γ' phases under different cooling conditions and full heat treatment was measured by TEM equipped with EDX spectra. The results are listed in Table 4. It is evident that the reprecipitated γ' precipitates with a lower Al and Ta contents while the γ-phase matrix with a lower Mo and Re contents in WQ condition compared to the AC condition. This was probably due to the fact of the formation of γ' precipitates at higher temperatures during the slow-cooling condition, where the faster diffusion rates and longer diffusion time allowed these precipitates to achieve a near-equilibrium composition [32]. This result was enhanced after the two-step aging treatment in HT sample. For the quantitative assessment of the elemental distribution behavior, the elemental partitioning coefficient k_i is introduced:

$$k_i = C_i^{\gamma'} / C_i^{\gamma} \tag{3}$$

where $C_i^{\gamma'}$ and C_i^{γ} are the atomic fractions of an element i in the γ' and γ-phases, respectively. From the calculation results of k_i in Table 4, the elements of Mo and Re partition preferentially to the γ matrix with $k_i < 1$, while the elements Al and Ta partition preferentially to the γ' precipitates with $k_i > 1$. It is clear that with the decrease in cooling rate, the partitioning of Mo and Re to the γ matrix and Al amd Ta to the γ' precipitates is simultaneously enhanced. Therefore, those elements are soluble in γ matrix, Mo and Re should diffuse away, while elements Al and Ta should diffuse into the γ' precipitate to accomplish the γ' coarsening.

Figure 6 shows the fitted X-ray profiles of the $(002)_{\gamma,\ \gamma'}$ planes of alloy after ST under different cooling rate and HT at room temperature. It is clear that the peaks from γ- and γ' phases of the AC sample are more spaced apart, and the diffraction angles shifted to lower values compared to the WQ sample, as seen in Figure 6a, b, which indicated that it has a larger absolute value of lattice misfit. However, the mismatch of the sample becomes smaller after aging, which is different from the Vegard Law calculation [33], as seen in Figure 6d, probably due to the coarsening of the γ' phase and the release of the mismatch stress by the formation of the dislocation network.

Table 4. The compositions of γ- and γ′ phase under different cooling conditions and fully heat treatment (at.%).

Condition		Al	Mo	Re	Ta	Ni
WQ	γ	7.82	11.53	2.36	1.31	76.98
	γ'	11.96	4.28	0.56	2.25	80.95
	$k = C_{\gamma'}/C_{\gamma}$	1.53	0.37	0.24	1.71	1.05
AC	γ	4.26	13.46	3.26	1.19	77.82
	γ'	12.59	4.05	0.50	2.37	80.49
	$k = C_{\gamma'}/C_{\gamma}$	2.96	0.30	0.15	1.98	1.03
HT	γ	3.65	13.17	4.65	1.17	77.48
	γ'	13.70	4.35	0.53	2.32	79.10
	$k = C_{\gamma'}/C_{\gamma}$	3.75	0.33	0.11	1.99	1.02

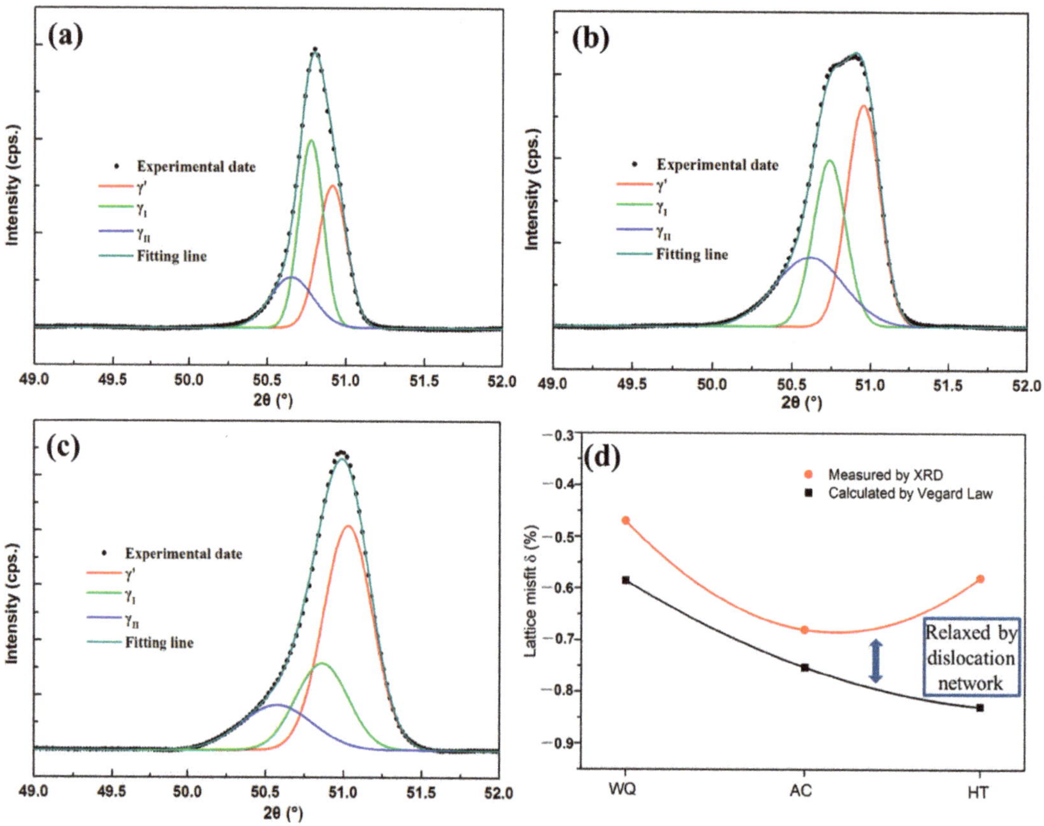

Figure 6. Diffractometer scans of (002) γ, γ' peaks of experimental alloy after different heat treatment at room temperature: (**a**) WQ, (**b**) AC, (**c**) HT and (**d**) the lattice misfit measured by XRD and calculated by Vegard Law (the phase compositions in Table 4 were used).

3.3. Microstructure Evolution during Thermal Exposure at 1100 °C

Figure 7 illustrates the microstructure of γ′ and γ-phases in the alloy after different heat treatment during thermal exposure at 1100 °C for 1 h, 10 h and 50 h. With the prolonged thermal exposure time, the γ′ phase underwent undirected coarsening and the morphology transforms from cubic to irregular. It can be seen that the γ′ precipitates are uniformly distributed, and their morphology remains mostly cubic after 1 h of thermal exposure in the WQ and AC samples. However, at the same time, the γ' phase in the HT samples clearly underwent an undirected coarsening, forming irregular shapes by merging with each other. When thermally exposed for over 10 h, the γ' of the WQ and AC samples also gradually coarsened and lost its cubic shape. However, for the HT samples, it precipitated the TCP phase which surrounded by the γ' envelope. Subsequently, the γ' precipitates continued to coarsen and topological inversion was observed after 50 h of thermal exposure for all samples.

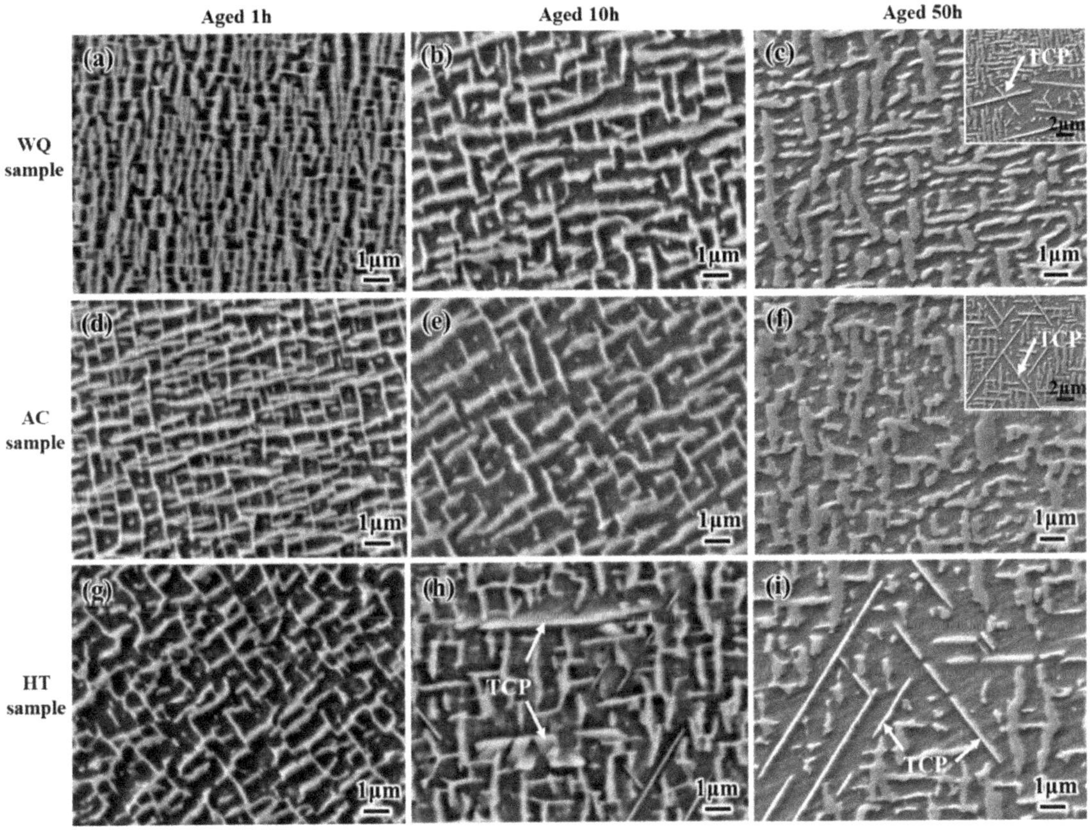

Figure 7. The SEM-SE microstructure evolution of γ' phase after different heat treatment during thermal exposure at 1100 °C: (**a–c**) WQ samples; (**d–f**) AC samples and (**g–i**) HT samples.

The size of γ' precipitates as a function of time is plotted in Figure 8a. It should be noted that the size of γ' precipitates is not measurable after 50 h of thermal exposure due to the "labyrinth-like" shape. It can be seen that the size of the γ' phase increased rapidly at first and then slowed down with the prolongation of the thermal exposure time. This was probably because the interfacial area and lattice mismatch strain of γ/γ' phase, which is the thermodynamic driving force for the coarsening of the γ' phase, was gradually consumed, so that the coarsening rate gradually decreased. Secondly, the WQ sample had the smallest γ' phase size after thermal exposure for the same time, which can be explained by comparing the lower dominant coherent strain of γ/γ' phase of the WQ sample to the other samples; in addition, during the coarsening process, more Re with low diffusion coefficients was repelled from the γ' phase, which was beneficial to delaying the coarsening rate. Meanwhile, the coarsening of the γ' phase broadened the spacing of the γ matrix, and the γ matrix width of the WQ sample increased the least, as shown in Figure 8b. In addition, no significant tertiary γ′ phase was found in the γ-channels of all samples after 50 h of long-term thermal exposure, which means that the tertiary γ′ phase was dissolved back into the γ matrix as the γ-phase became coarsened and the elemental saturation decreased. After the long-term thermal exposure of 50 h, the area fraction of γ′ phase decreased and tended to be consistent for all samples, as shown in Figure 8c. However, at the initial stage of thermal exposure, both WQ and AC samples showed a transient increase in their γ′ phase area fraction rather than a single decrease for HT sample. This is because the initial stage of the thermal exposure process is similar to the aging process and allowed the γ′ phase to grow and reach the maximum area fraction.

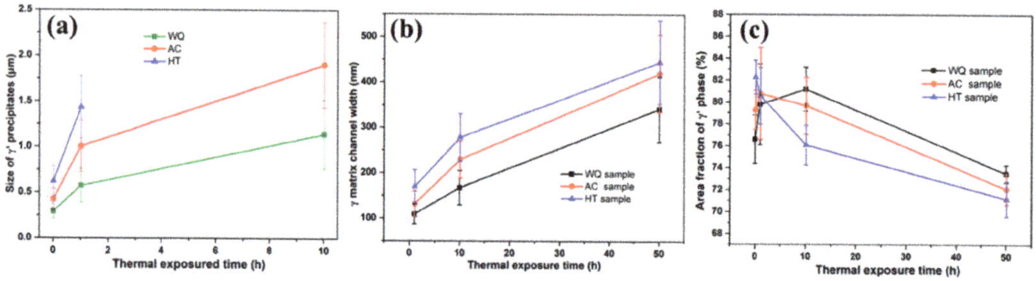

Figure 8. The Variation in the size of γ′ precipitates (**a**), width of γ matrix channel (**b**), and the area fraction of γ′ phase (**c**) in the alloys during thermal exposure at 1100 °C.

To illustrate the precipitation behavior of TCP during thermal exposure, firstly, the composition and structure of the TCP phase were analyzed, it was rich in Mo and Re elementsand identified as σ-phase [34], as presented in Figure 9. Then, the area fraction and length of TCP phases of the samples after different thermal exposure times were measured, as seen in Figure 10. It is clear that despite the as-cast samples undergoing the same solid solution heat process, the cooling rate after ST still significantly affected the precipitation behavior of the TCP phases. The area fraction of TCP phases in WQ sample after 50 h of thermal exposure was remarkably smaller than that in AC and HT samples, which was due to the fact that HT samples have the highest content of Mo and Re in their γ matrix, as listed in the previous Table 4. However, the length of the TCP phase in the WQ sample after 50 h of thermal exposure was higher than that in AC and HT samples, and the reasons for this will be discussed in detail in the next section. In summary, the faster cooling rate after ST not only slowed down the coarsening of the γ′ phase but also reduced the precipitation of the TCP phase, i.e., the fast-cooling rate was to some extent beneficial to the microstructure stabilization.

3.4. Creep Behavior under 1100 °C/137 MPa

The typical creep curves of the experimental alloy after different heat treatment are shown in Figure 11a. It can be seen that the creep process includes three stages, namely a primary stage, a steady state stage and an accelerated stage. The HT samples have the shortest rupture life of only 49.8 h. However, by increasing the cooling rate after ST, the rupture life of the WQ sample increased significantly from 101.2 h for the AC sample to 184.5 h, which was about four times longer than that of the HT sample. In addition, there was a slight increase in elongation of the HT sample compared to the WQ and AC samples. In order to better analyze the intrinsic mechanisms of the reduction in rupture life, quantitative features of creep behavior corresponding to different creep stages were researched, as illustrated in Table 5 and Figure 11b. The lowest steady state creep rate of 0.37×10^{-4} h^{-1} can be found for the WQ sample, which is about one-fifteenth of that of the HT sample; this is one of the reasons why it has the longest fracture life. It is noteworthy that the WQ sample has the highest strain and the longest time of the primary stage and tertiary stage, while the primary stage creep is almost invisible for the HT sample. Thus, this suggested that increasing the cooling rate after ST not only affects the reprecipitation of γ', but also influences the deformation mechanism of creep and significantly improves the creep properties of the alloy.

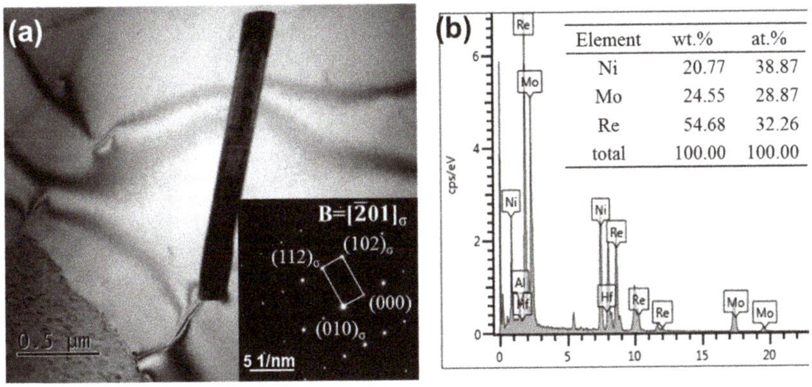

Figure 9. Typical TEM images and SAD patterns (**a**) and the compositional result by EDS (**b**) of σ phases for HT samples after thermal exposure at 1100 °C for 50 h.

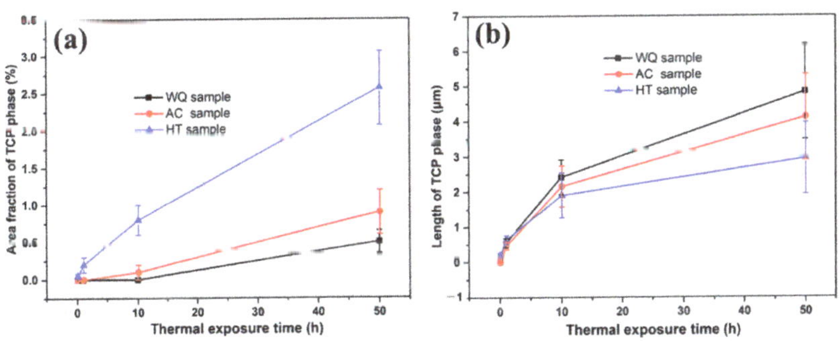

Figure 10. Area fraction (**a**) and length (**b**) of TCP phases of samples after different thermal exposure times.

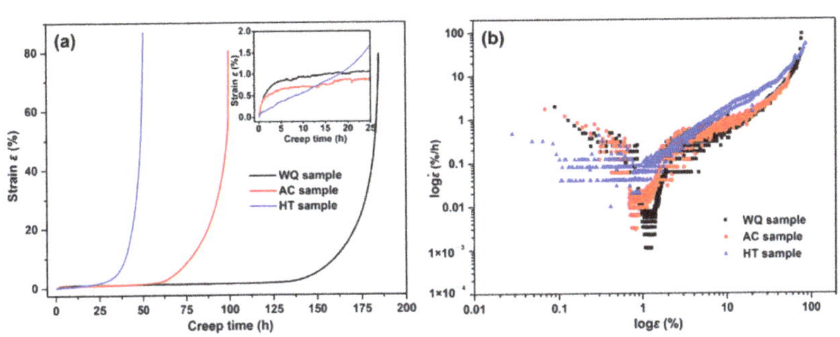

Figure 11. (**a**) Creep strain–time curves (The inset shows the primary stage of creep); (**b**) strain rate with respect to strain of the different heat treatment sample at 1100 °C/137 MPa.

Table 5. Creep properties of the different heat treatment sample at 1100 °C/137 MPa.

Condition	Life (h)	Elongation (%)	Steady state Creep Rate $\dot{\varepsilon}_{ss}(\times 10^{-8}\ s^{-1})$	Time of the Primary Stage (h)	Time of the Tertiary Stage (h)	Strain of the Primary Stage (%)
HT	49.8 ± 4.6	80.0 ± 3.3	14.89	0.9	21.1	0.15
AC	101.2 ± 7.9	84.1 ± 4.5	4.02	8.9	36.7	0.71
WQ	184.5 ± 10.2	87.9 ± 5.2	1.03	15.4	57.4	0.98

The microstructures of samples after creep for 10 h and rupture at 1100 °C and 137 MPa are shown in Figure 12. There were significant differences in microstructure after 10 h of creep. The rafting was perpendicular (N-type rafts) to the loading direction and had been basically completed in the WQ sample, as shown in the Figure 12a. However, only part of the regions was rafted, and the morphology of the γ' phase mostly was irregular in the AC sample. For the HT sample, its γ' morphology is little different from that of the AC sample, but visible TCP phase precipitations can be seen. The WQ sample had a higher rafting rate and raft integrity compared to the other two samples due to its higher fraction of finer regular γ' phase and the more negative lattice misfit obtained during the primary stage creep at a high temperature. In addition, more γ matrix, which seem like a "small island" and was embedded in the γ' phase, were observed in AC and HT samplesed; this topological inversion microstructure restricted the motion of dislocations in the γ-phase and accounted for the lower strain in the primary stage creep.

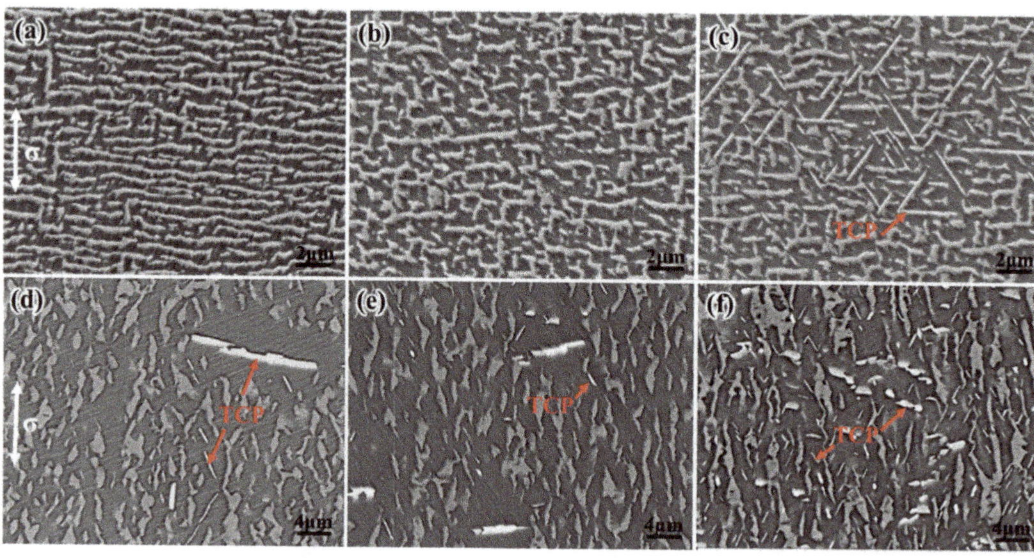

Figure 12. The microstructure of different samples after creep testing under 1100 °C/137 MPa: (**a**–**c**) interrupted for 10 h, (**d**–**f**) ruptured; (**a**,**d**) WQ sample, (**b**,**e**) AC sample and (**c**,**f**) HT sample (the loading direction is shown by the arrow).

The γ–γ' interfacial dislocation network after crept interrupted for 10 h was observed, as shown in Figure 13. It can be seen that the dislocation network of the WQ sample is denser with the smallest spacing of about 22.3 nm, while the spacing of the AC sample and HT sample are about 33.4 nm and 40.6 nm, respectively. The order of magnitude relationship between them was consistent with the calculated results by Vegard Law, as shown in Figure 14. This is reasonable because for the WQ samples at the beginning of creep, the γ' phase content increases under the thermal effect, and the elemental distribution between the two phases is aggravated. Particularly, the differences in Ta element content were most pronounced (see in Table 6), which in turn makes it have a more negative mismatch degree and thus form a denser dislocation network. The dense dislocation network can effectively prevent the dislocations cutting into the γ' phase, which is beneficial to improve the creep performance [35]. Therefore, increasing the cooling rate after ST is conducive to promoting the formation of rafts and forming a denser dislocation network during the primary stage of creep. After ruptured, the γ–γ' phases microstructure of all samples undergoes more pronounced coarsening and loss of N-type rafts. The coarsened rattan shape γ' phase is to some extent parallel to the stress axis due to the huge accumulation of deformation. In addition, the TCP phase presented in all samples, but the amount of TCP was significantly lower in the WQ samples compared to the HT, this coincides with the results of thermal exposure.

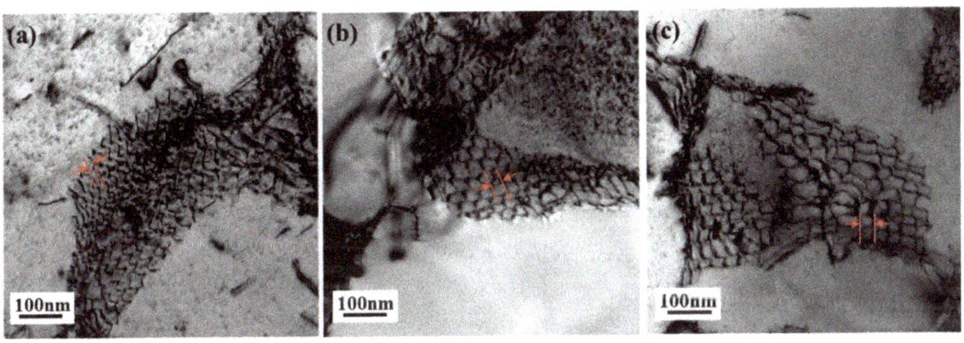

Figure 13. The dislocation network formed in samples interrupted by creep 1100 °C/137 MPa for 10 h: (**a**) WQ sample, (**b**) AC sample and (**c**) HT sample. (Beam = [001], the spacing of the dislocation network is marked by red arrows).

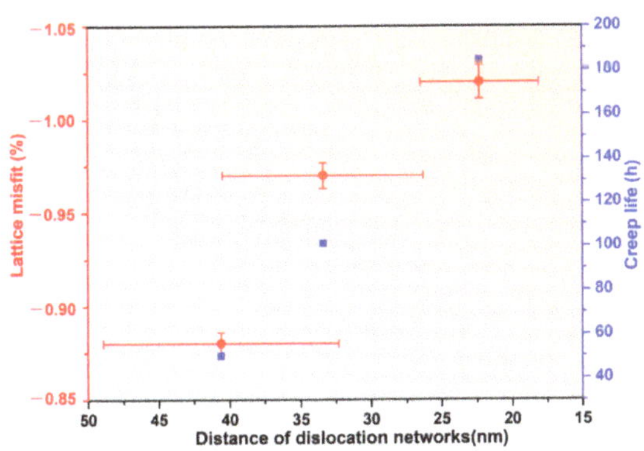

Figure 14. The lattice misfit and dislocation network spacing after 10 h of creep interruption at 1100 °C/137 MPa, and denser dislocation networks showed longer creep life.

Table 6. γ- and γ' phase compositions after interruption of crept 10 h (at.%).

Condition		Al	Mo	Re	Ta	Ni
WQ	γ	3.57	13.84	4.03	2.36	76.19
	γ'	12.62	4.55	0.36	2.70	79.78
AC	γ	3.60	14.25	4.26	1.21	76.68
	γ'	13.11	4.62	0.47	2.17	79.63
HT	γ	3.68	14.06	4.35	1.13	76.79
	γ'	13.02	4.70	0.50	2.25	79.55

Figure 15 shows the morphology in the longitudinal section of the AC and HT samples after creep deformation at 1100 °C/137 MPa. It can be seen that there were numerous micropores formed inside the fractured samples, and they decreased rapidly with the increase in the distance from the fracture surface, as shown in Figure 15a,b, and the quantitative statistical results are shown in Figure 16a. Micropores in SX superalloys generally include solidification pores (S pores), homogenization pores (H pores) and creep deformation pores (D pores). S pores and H pores are generally irregular or ellipsoidal (see Figure 15c), and the H pores are caused by the Kirkendall–Frenkel effect; meanwhile, the D pores are square- or rhombus-shaped, because its shape depends on the slip of dislocations on the octahedral slip system (see Figure 15d,e), and the long sides of the square is are parallel to the [001] direction, and its facets are lay on {110} planes. In this work, D pores accounted for the main part. Due to the formation of micropores, the true stress increased significantly, which in turn exacerbated the deformation of the nearby matrix to form more micropores. This is amongst the reasons why the creep rate increased rapidly at the end of creep.

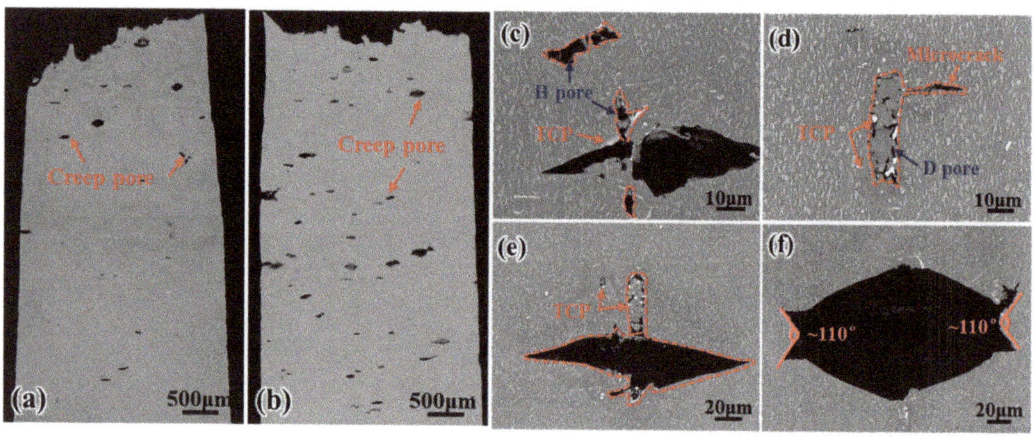

Figure 15. SEM micrographs of different samples ruptured after creep deformation at 1100 °C/137 MPa: (**a**) WQ sample, (**b**) HT sample, (**c**) TCP phases near homogenization pores, (**d**) TCP phases near the creep deformation pores and microcracks and (**e**,**f**) growth of pores and microcracks.

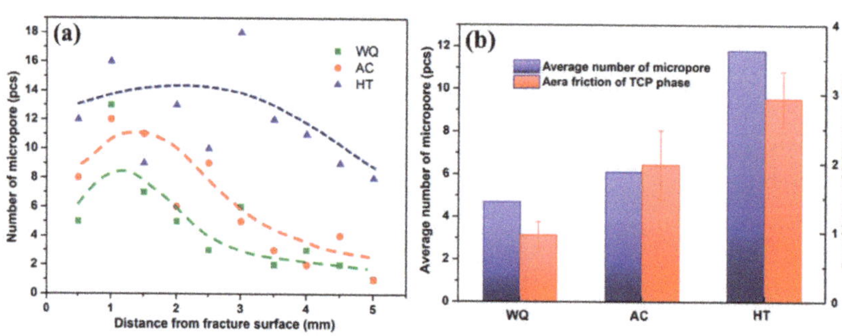

Figure 16. (**a**) number of micropores varies with the distance from the fracture surface and (**b**) histogram of average number of micropores and TCP phase area fraction.

Compared with HT samples, the number of micropores in WQ samples was significantly less, as shown in Figure 16a. Further observation of the microstructure around the micropores and microcracks revealed that a large number of TCP phases are accompanied near them, as shown in Figure 15c–f. This implied that the micropores or microcracks were nucleated around the TCP phase and gradually grown with the accumulation of deformation. Actually, the area fraction of TCP phase of fractured WQ sample was about 0.9%, which was lower than 1.9% and 2.9% for the AC and HT samples, respectively. Thus, the average number of micropores was essentially proportional to the area fraction of the TCP phase after the ruptured samples is shown in Figure 16b. This explained why the WQ sample had the lowest number of micropores. In the early stage of creep, dislocations mainly moved in γ–γ' phases microstructure, especially filled in the γ-channel. As the creep progressed, the γ–γ' phases microstructure underwent directional coarsening, and the TCP phases gradually precipitated from the supersaturated γ-phase and grew up gradually. The TCP phase was brittle and semi-coherent with the γ matrix. If dislocations encounter the TCP phases when they are slipping or climbing in γ–γ' phases microstructure, dislocations will accumulate at the interface of TCP/γ or TCP/γ' and to generate vacancies. Because the easily movable dislocations are located in the <110> {111} of the octahedral slip system, it gradually grew into cuboid micropores along the [001] direction. Creep was continued, and the microcracks were easily initiated at the corners of the micropores due to stress concentration and propagated on the {111} planes which had the largest Schmid factor, as shown in Figure 15f. The microcracks and micropores grow continuously under the action of applied stress and connected with each other to form large cracks until fracture occurred. Thus, it was obvious that the initiation and propagation of these micropores and microcracks near the TCP phase accelerated the fracture of the SX superalloy.

4. Discussion

4.1. Effect of Cooling Rate on the Reprecipitation and Coarsening of γ' Phase

In the previous section, the experimental results showed that the cooling rate after ST has a significant effect on the size distribution, morphology and phase composition of γ' reprecipitation. In this research, upon solution treatment at γ' super-solvus temperatures, the primary phase of alloy was completely dissolved and obtained a single γ solid solution, and the secondary γ' phase precipitated during its subsequent cooling. A classical theory proposed by Ricks et al. [30] suggests that the morphological development of the γ' reprecipitation from a single γ-phase solid solution occurs in the sequence spheres, cubes, arrays of cubes and eventually solid-state dendrites as coarsening is promoted by ageing, and this process is influenced by the lattice misfit [16,36]. For the experimental alloy, it has a high γ' volume fraction (over 80 vol.%) and with a negative lattice misfit, so that it precipitates and transforms into a cubic secondary γ' phase rapidly during cooling process after ST. When γ' phases get coarsened, the coherent strain energy was increased and the γ' phases were transformed to cubic with concave feature.

The difference in the nucleation and growth of γ' reprecipitates caused by cooling rates cannot be ignored. The observed density value for the γ' precipitates increased with the cooling rate, which indicated that the decomposition of the γ-phase occurred under large undercooling. Under large undercooling below the equilibrium instability temperature, the driving force for the nucleation of the γ' phase is expected to increase rapidly, and thus the nucleation rate of the γ' precipitate per unit volume will increase. The homogenous nucleation rate ($\dot{N}$) of the γ' phase from the γ-phase was calculated from [37]:

$$\dot{N} = Aexp\{\frac{-\Delta G^*}{kT}\} \exp\{\frac{-Q}{kT}\} \quad (4)$$

where A is a pre-exponential factor, T is the temperature (K), ΔG^* is the activation energy for nucleation and Q is the activation energy for self-diffusion. The activation energy for nucleation is calculated from:

$$\Delta G^* = \frac{16\pi\sigma^3}{3(\Delta G_v)^2} \quad (5)$$

where σ is the interfacial energy between γ- and γ', ΔG_v is the driving force for γ' precipitation. Babu et al. [24] calculated and summarized that the nucleation rate increases rapidly with large undercooling below the equilibrium instability temperature. However, below a certain temperature, the nucleation rate decreases slightly due to the reduction in atomic mobility. For the WQ condition, the density of the γ' reprecipitates are 2 times higher than that of AC, as listed in Table 3. In addition, the shorter the diffusion time, the higher the particle number density, and the overlapping of precipitation diffusion fields limits the growth rate of γ' precipitates under WQ conditions compared with AC conditions, resulting in the formation of finer size γ' precipitates. Also, due to the limited diffusion rate, coupled with the superimposed fast cooling rate, there was only a very limited time for partitioning of the alloying elements between the γ' and γ-phases. Therefore, the composition of γ' precipitates was far from the equilibrium, as shown in Table 4. The high cooling rate during WQ prevented any further nucleation events despite the non-equilibrium conditions; thus, a monomodal size distribution of γ' precipitates is observed. However, the relatively slower cooling for AC samples, the secondary γ' precipitates nucleated at relatively higher temperatures (lower undercooling) with lower nucleation rates, resulting in a lower density of the precipitates, and the diffusion rate was fast enough to form a phase closer to the equilibrium composition. However, the γ matrix region between the secondary γ' precipitates, away from the growing γ'/γ interfaces, retained a far-from equilibrium composition. As the temperature decreased during successive cooling, the driving force for γ' phase nucleation increased, and eventually, re-nucleation at lower temperatures resulted in the formation of very fine tertiary γ' precipitates in the region between the secondary γ' precipitates.

The (directional) coarsening of the γ' phase is a typical feature of the microstructure evolution of the superalloy under high-temperature thermal exposure, which have a significant effect on the high-temperature creep properties. Therefore, the coarsening rate of the γ' phase in the alloy under different cooling conditions needs to be investigated. The size of γ' and γ-phases continued to increase during thermal exposure at 1100 °C; the topological inversion phenomenon appeared even after 50 h due to the high γ' phase fraction. The γ' precipitates coarsening usually obeys the LSW theory based on matrix diffusion, the description for calculation is as follows [38,39]:

$$r_t^n - r_0^n = Kt \tag{6}$$

where r_t is the average radius at the thermal exposure time t, r_0 is the average radius at t = 0, n is the temporal exponent and K is coarsening rate constant. Accordingly, the coarsening rate constants of γ' precipitates in experimental alloys are presented in Figure 17. Obviously, the experimental data appeared to match perfectly to the classical LSW model when n = 3 according to Equation (6) for all samples. The K values was 0.16 $\mu m^3/h$ for WQ sample were calculated by fitting the slopes of the line connected by these points, which was much lower than the values for the AC and HT samples. So, the γ' coarsening rate was significantly reduced by increasing the cooling rate after ST.

The coarsening of the γ' phase is an important reason for the decline of the creep performance. In order to strengthen the high-temperature creep performance of the superalloy, it is necessary to slow down the coarsening process of the γ' phase as much as possible. In general, the coarsening of γ' precipitates depends on the reduction in the interfacial energy and coherent strain energy of the γ–γ' phases. Under the condition that the volume fraction of the γ' phase is basically unchanged, the interfacial energy of the γ–γ' phases decreases with the increase in the size of the γ' precipitate. Furthermore, the coherent strain energy is related to the distribution of alloying elements in the γ- and γ' phases; the lower the microsegregation of the γ/γ' phase is, the smaller the coherent strain energy is. Because the interfacial energy is difficult to tune by considering the formation of fine and cubic γ' precipitates to sufficiently hinder the movement of dislocations, the coherent strain energy can be achieved by reducing the microsegregation of the γ/γ' phase. From the results in Figures 7, 8 and 17, it can be determined that by increasing the cooling rate after solution treatment, the microsegregation of the two phases was decreased (see Table 4), and the coherent strain energy was also lowered. Although the interface energy of γ/γ' phase increased somewhat due to the reduction in the size of the γ' phase, the overall driving force for coarsening of the γ' precipitate was decreased. In addition, in the coarsening process, more rhenium with a low diffusion coefficient needed to be repelled from the γ' phase, which together slowed down the coarsening rate of its γ' phase.

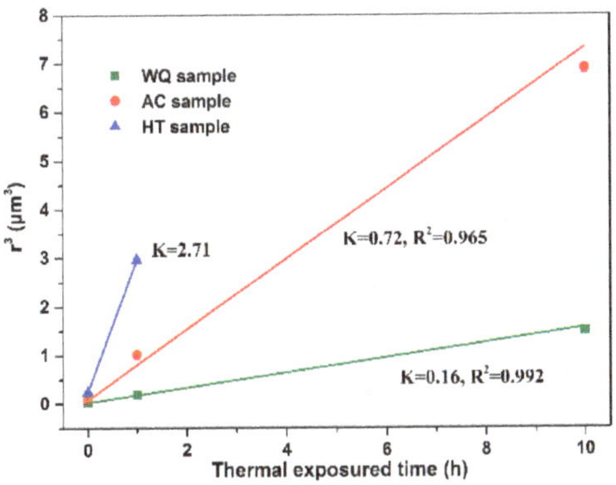

Figure 17. Plots of precipitates size (r^3) vs. time (t) for γ' phases during thermal exposure at 1100 °C, the coefficient of determination (R^2) were also labeled.

4.2. Effect of Cooling Rate on Precipitation of the TCP Phase

As has been established, the TCP phase precipitates from the supersaturated γ-phase during thermal exposure [13,40] and causes severe degradation of the alloy properties [9,41]. On the one hand, the precipitation of the TCP phase consumes a large amount of solid solution elements, such as Mo and Re, leading to a decrease in the strength of the γ matrix; on the other hand, TCP as a brittle phase causes stress concentration and becomes the origin of micro-cracks [34]. Therefore, the supersaturation of alloying elements in γ-phase of heat-treated specimen determined the nucleation and growth behavior of the σ-phase. As mentioned above, the Mo and Re concentrations of the γ-phase in the WQ samples under rapid cooling are lower than those in the AC samples under slow cooling, as shown in Table 4. So, a lower nucleation rate of the σ-phase is observed in the WQ specimens than in the AC specimens during the initial period of thermal exposure, which is consistent with the lowest TCP phase area fraction of the WQ sample in Figure 10a. However, for the HT samples, which under a slow cooling rate and having undergone two-step aging, the γ' phase adequately grew and expelled Mo and Re elements from the γ' phase into the γ-phase. This further increased the supersaturation of alloying elements in the γ-phase and thus rapidly precipitated a large amount of σ-phase during the initial period of thermal exposure. Nevertheless, with the growth of the σ phase, the Mo and Re concentrations of the γ-phase in HT samples decreased significantly after the initial period of thermal exposure due to the remarkable consumption of Mo and Re elements by σ phase, while the growth rate of the TCP phase is proportional to the supersaturation degree of the γ-phase during thermal exposure [40]. Therefore, there were lower Mo and Re concentrations of γ-phase in the HT samples compared to the WQ samples, which resulted in a reduction in growth driving force of σ-phase and thus shorter σ phase. Altogether, the cooling rate after ST changes the supersaturation degree of the γ-phase and thus affects the nucleation and growth behavior of the TCP phase. This phenomenon was probably attributed to the fact as follows: first, with the temperature decreased from upon the γ' dissolution temperature, the γ' phase precipitated from the supersaturated γ-phase and it's a diffusion-type phase transformation, so the composition of the γ- and γ' phases is influenced by the cooling rate. Increasing the cooling rate after ST, the time and temperature for diffusion of alloying elements are reduced and the elements are 'frozen' in γ- and γ' phases. Therefore, the compositional difference between the γ- and γ′ phases in the WQ sample is smaller, i.e., the Mo and Re content (saturation) of the γ-phase is lower.

4.3. Effect of γ′ Reprecipitation and TCP Phase on Creep Properties

It has been mentioned above that the creep properties of the experimental alloy were substantially improved by increasing the cooling rate after solid solution. It is essential to investigate the relationship between the microstructural evolution (γ–γ′ phases and TCP phase) and the stress-rupture property of the alloy. In general, the main strengthening mechanisms of Ni-based single crystal superalloy include solid solution strengthening [42,43], precipitation phase strengthening [44] and interfacial dislocation network strengthening [45]. At high temperatures, the mechanical properties of SX superalloys are strongly dependent on the morphology, size and volume fraction of the γ′ phase. A classical work by Nathal [46] showed that in a Re-free Ni-based single crystal superalloys with a negative mismatch, the creep life shows a peak at a γ′ phase size of about 450~500 nm, and the optimal size range of γ′ phase decreases as the lattice misfit becomes more negative. Murakumo [5] suggested that the highest creep life was obtained with a γ′ volume fraction of about 70% at room temperature. It can also be demonstrated that the alloys containing spherical precipitates had lower creep strain rates than those containing cubic precipitates [7]. Generally, the strength increments in critically resolved shear stress (CRSSs) for the precipitates shearing ($\Delta\tau_c$) is calculated using followings:

$$\Delta\tau_c = \frac{1}{2}\left(\frac{Gb}{\lambda}\right)\frac{2w}{\pi}\left(\frac{2\pi\gamma_{APB}r}{wGb^2} - 1\right)^{0.5} \tag{7}$$

and the stress σ_{OR} required for a dislocation to slip through a narrow matrix channel is given by equation:

$$\sigma_{OR} = \sqrt{\frac{2}{3}}\left(\frac{Gb}{hS}\right) \tag{8}$$

where γ_{APB} is the antiphase boundary energy of γ′ phase, b is the Burgers vector, r is the γ′ mean size, λ is the average interparticle spacing, G is the shear modulus, h is the width of the γ-channel, w is the fitting parameter and S is the Schmid factor. In the current study, the experimental alloys used water cooling after solution treatment, which had the smallest γ′ phase size and γ-channel width. In the early stage of creep, σ_{OR} is the dominant due to the dislocations move mainly in the γ-channel, thereby the WQ sample has the strongest creep strength at this stage. After that, the γ and γ′ phases are coarsened to a certain extent (about 550~700 nm), and its γ′ volume fraction increased (about 80%), as seen in Figure 8. At this time, the strength increment $\Delta\tau_c$ brought by the γ′ phase is dominant. Therefore, the WQ sample always has the highest strength compared to the other samples.

Furthermore, it can be seen that the faster cooling rate samples have a larger strain of primary creep stage. Rae [47] proposed that the primary creep rate is controlled principally by the dislocation activity and density accumulating of <112>{111} slip systems in the γ-channels, and the greater primary creep is due entirely to a more rapid creep rate. During the primary creep stage, for the WQ sample, a regular and cubic γ′ phase was enveloped by γ-channels due to the faster cooling rate after ST, whose γ-channels are interconnected and dislocation-depleted state; the dislocation of <112>{11} slip systems is easily activated and accumulated, and coupled with a longer primary creep stage can accumulate a higher strain. However, for AC and HT samples, its γ′ phase is coarser and irregular, and there are tertiary γ′ phases or pre-formed dislocation networks in the γ-channel. The presence of fine tertiary γ ′ particles impede propagation of the perfect matrix dislocations which are forced to cut the γ ′ precipitates much earlier in some localized regions [48]. The strain of primary creep is particularly influenced by tertiary γ′ precipitation in the γ-channel because of these particles may increase the resistance of the normal dislocation bowing out and dislocation motion is limited [49], thus ultimately leading to a low strain. However, it will undergo dissolution during elevated temperature thermal exposure and therefore affects more the primary creep behavior rather than the whole creep process. This is also in agreement with the fact that no significant tertiary γ' was found in the microstructure of thermally exposed and creep-interrupted samples.

Under elevated temperature and low stress, the original cubic-shaped γ' phase undergoes directional coarsening and the higher the degree of lattice misfit between γ- and γ' phases, a denser dislocation network is formed at the interface of the two phases, which prevented the dislocations cutting into the γ' rafts, thus improving the creep lifetime [10]. The microstructure turns into a more complete rafts perpendicular to the stress for the WQ sample compared to the AC and HT sample. In addition, a denser dislocation network formed in the WQ sample can effectively prevent dislocations from penetrating into the γ' phase; the stability of dislocation network helps to correspondingly stabilize the lamellar γ/γ' structure during the stable creep stage. Thus, the WQ sample has the lowest steady state creep rate. Furthermore, when the creep enters the tertiary stage of creep, the grown TCP consumes a large amount of Re and Mo and reduces the solid solution strength of the matrix, and the TCP phase becomes the nucleation site for micropores and microcracks because it is a brittle phase and semi-coherent with the matrix, which accelerates the damage accumulation at tertiary stage. Compared with the HT and AC samples, the rapidly cooled sample (WQ) had a smaller amount of TCP and delayed its precipitation, which not only delayed the onset of entry into the tertiary stage, but increased the time of the tertiary stage. These are representative of the reasons as to why faster cooling rates lead to longer creep life of the superalloy.

5. Conclusions

1. The cooling rate after solid solution treatment significantly affected the size distribution and morphology of the γ' reprecipitates (secondary γ' phase), and with the increasing of the cooling rate, the size of γ' precipitates decreases while its number density increases. The morphology of γ' phase also transforms from cubic to complex shape.
2. The size of γ' reprecipitates under fast cooling rate showed a monomodal size distribution, while the tertiary γ' phase precipitated in the γ-channel under slow-cooling rate, and the faster cooling rate leads to lower Mo and Re content in the γ-phase (i.e., lower supersaturation degree).
3. During the thermal exposure at 1100 °C, the coarsening rate of γ' phase under fast cooling rate is slower, and the area fraction of the precipitated TCP phase is lower due to lower supersaturation degree of the γ-phase, but the length of the TCP is longer compared to the slow-cooled sample.
4. The creep life of the alloy significantly improved by increasing the cooling rate after solution treatment. On the one hand, this comes from the better homogeneity and thermal stability of the microstructure under high cooling rate after solution heat treatment; On the other hand, The finer cubic γ' precipitation facilitated rafting, which, combined with the reduction in the TCP phase as the origin of microcracks, resulted in better high-temperature creep properties of the alloy.

Author Contributions: Methodology, J.H.; validation, Y.P.; formal analysis, H.Z. and C.A.; investigation, J.H.; writing—original draft preparation, J.H.; writing—review and editing, C.A., Y.R. and J.H.; supervision, S.L. and S.G.; project administration, S.G.; funding acquisition, Y.S., S.G. and H.Z. All authors have read and agreed to the published version of the manuscript.

Funding: This research was funded by National Science and Technology Major Project of China [Grant numbers: 2017-VI-0016-0088 (S. Gong), 2019-VI-0016 (Y. Shang)]; the National Natural Science Foundation of China (NSFC) [Grant number: 52101117 (H. Zhang)].

Institutional Review Board Statement: Not applicable.

Informed Consent Statement: Not applicable.

Data Availability Statement: Not applicable.

Conflicts of Interest: The authors declare no conflict of interest.

References

1. Reed, R.C. *The Superalloys: Fundamentals and Applications*; Cambridge University Press: Cambridge, UK, 2006; Chapters 1 and 3.
2. Pollock, T.M.; Tin, S. Nickel-Based Superalloys for Advanced Turbine Engines: Chemistry, Microstructure and Properties. *J. Propul. Power* **2006**, *22*, 361–374. [CrossRef]
3. Nembach, E.; Schänzer, S.; Schröer, W.; Trinckauf, K. Hardening of nickel-base superalloys by high volume fractions of γ'-precipitates. *Acta Metall.* **1988**, *36*, 1471–1479. [CrossRef]
4. Long, H.; Mao, S.; Liu, Y.; Zhang, Z.; Han, X. Microstructural and compositional design of Ni-based single crystalline superalloys—A review. *J. Alloys Compd.* **2018**, *743*, 203–220. [CrossRef]
5. Murakumo, T.; Kobayashi, T.; Koizumi, Y.; Harada, H. Creep behaviour of Ni-base single-crystal superalloys with various γ' volume fraction. *Acta Mater.* **2004**, *52*, 3737–3744. [CrossRef]
6. Wang, T.; Wang, X.; Zhao, Z.; Zhang, Z. Dissolution behaviour of the γ' precipitates in two kinds of Ni-based superalloys. *Mater. High Temp.* **2016**, *33*, 51–57. [CrossRef]
7. Bhowal, P.R.; Wright, E.F.; Raymond, E.L. Effects of cooling rate and γ' morphology on creep and stress-rupture properties of a powder metallurgy superalloy. *Metall. Trans. A* **1990**, *21*, 1709–1717. [CrossRef]
8. Li, Y.; Wang, L.; He, Y.; Zheng, W.; Lou, L.; Zhang, J. Role of interfacial dislocation networks during secondary creep at elevated temperatures in a single crystal Ni-based superalloy. *Scr. Mater.* **2022**, *217*, 114769–114773. [CrossRef]
9. Huang, Y.S.; Wang, X.G.; Cui, C.Y.; Li, J.G.; Ye, L.H.; Hou, G.C.; Yang, Y.H.; Liu, J.L.; Liu, J.D.; Zhou, Y.Z.; et al. The effect of coarsening of γ' precipitate on creep properties of Ni-based single crystal superalloys during long-term aging. *Mater. Sci. Eng. A* **2020**, *773*, 138886. [CrossRef]
10. Pollock, T.M.; Argon, A.S. Directional coarsening in nickel-base single crystals with high volume fractions of coherent precipitates. *Acta Metall. Mater.* **1994**, *42*, 1859–1874. [CrossRef]
11. Long, H.; Mao, S.; Liu, Y.; Yang, H.; Wei, H.; Deng, Q.; Chen, Y.; Li, A.; Zhang, Z.; Han, X. Structural evolution of topologically closed packed phase in a Ni-based single crystal superalloy. *Acta Mater.* **2020**, *185*, 233–244. [CrossRef]
12. Tang, S.; Ning, L.K.; Xin, T.Z.; Zheng, Z. Coarsening Behavior of Gamma Prime Precipitates in a Nickel Based Single Crystal Superalloy. *J. Mater. Sci. Technol.* **2016**, *32*, 172–176. [CrossRef]
13. Matuszewski, K.; Rettig, R.; Matysiak, H.; Peng, Z.; Povstugar, I.; Choi, P.; Müller, J.; Raabe, D.; Spiecker, E.; Kurzydłowski, K.J.; et al. Effect of ruthenium on the precipitation of topologically close packed phases in Ni-based superalloys of 3rd and 4th generation. *Acta Mater.* **2015**, *95*, 274–283. [CrossRef]
14. Lv, X.; Zhang, J.; Feng, Q. The promotion of Ru on topologically close-packed phase precipitation in the high Cr-containing (∼9wt.%) nickel-base single crystal superalloy. *J. Alloys Compd.* **2015**, *648*, 853–857. [CrossRef]
15. Fuchs, G.E. Solution heat treatment response of a third-generation single crystal Ni-base superalloy. *Mater. Sci. Eng. A* **2001**, *300*, 52–60. [CrossRef]
16. van Sluytman, J.S.; Pollock, T.M. Optimal precipitate shapes in nickel-base γ-γ' alloys. *Acta Mater.* **2012**, *60*, 1771–1783. [CrossRef]
17. Caron, P.; Khan, T. Improvement of Creep strength in a nickel-base single-crystal superalloy by heat treatment. *Mater. Sci. Eng. A* **1983**, *61*, 173–184. [CrossRef]
18. Jia, C.; Zhang, F.; Wei, K.; Lv, S. Effective solution treatment can result in improved creep performance of superalloys. *J. Alloys Compd.* **2019**, *770*, 166–174. [CrossRef]
19. Sun, N.; Zhang, L.; Li, Z.; Shan, A. Effect of heat-treatment on microstructure and high-temperature deformation behavior of a low rhenium-containing single crystal nickel-based superalloy. *Mater. Sci. Eng. A* **2014**, *606*, 417–425. [CrossRef]
20. Du, Y.; Yang, Y.; Diao, A.; Li, Y.; Wang, X.; Zhou, Y.; Li, J.; Sun, X. Effect of solution heat treatment on creep properties of a nickel-based single crystal superalloy. *J. Mater. Res. Technol.* **2021**, *15*, 4702–4713. [CrossRef]
21. Epishin, A.; Link, T.; Svetlov, I.L.; Nolze, G.; Neumann, R.S.; Lucas, H. Mechanism of porosity growth during homogenisation in single crystal nickel-based superalloys. *Int. J. Mater. Res.* **2013**, *104*, 776–782. [CrossRef]
22. Hegde, S.R.; Kearsey, R.M.; Beddoes, J.C. Designing homogenization-solution heat treatments for single crystal superalloys. *Mater. Sci. Eng. A* **2010**, *527*, 5528–5538. [CrossRef]
23. Karunaratne, M.S.A.; Cox, D.C.; Carter, P.; Reed, R.C. *Modelling of the Microsegregation in CMSX-4 Superalloy and its Homogenisation during Heat Treatment*; Superalloy 2000; TMS: Warrendale, PA, USA, 2000; pp. 263–272. [CrossRef]
24. Babu, S.S.; Miller, M.K.; Vitek, J.M.; David, S.A. Characterization of the microstructure evolution in a nickel base superalloy during continuous cooling conditions. *Acta Metall.* **2001**, *49*, 4149–4160. [CrossRef]
25. Yu, H.; Wang, Z.; Zhang, B.; Ning, Y.; Fu, M.W. Re-precipitation mechanisms of the γ' phase with sphere, near-sphere, cubic, octets and finally-dendrite in as-cast Ni-based superalloys. *J. Alloys Compd.* **2021**, *876*, 160104. [CrossRef]
26. Gabb, T.P.; Gayda, J.; Telesman, J.; Garg, A. *The Effects of Heat Treatment and Microstructure Variations on Disk Superalloy Properties at High Temperature*; Superalloy 2008; TMS: Warrendale, PA, USA, 2008; pp. 121–130. [CrossRef]
27. Singh, A.R.P.; Nag, S.; Hwang, J.Y.; Viswanathan, G.B.; Tiley, J. Influence of cooling rate on the development of multiple generations of γ' precipitates in a commercial nickel base superalloy. *Mater. Charact.* **2011**, *62*, 878–886. [CrossRef]

28. Hardy, M.C.; Argyrakis, C.; Kitaguchi, H.S.; Wilson, A.S.; Buckingham, R.C.; Severs, K.; Yu, S.; Jackson, C.; Pickering, E.J.; Llewelyn, S.C.H.; et al. *Developing Alloy Compositions for Future High Temperature Disk Rotors*; Superalloy 2020; TMS: Warrendale, PA, USA, 2020; pp. 19–30. [CrossRef]
29. Mitchell, R.J.; Preuss, M.; Tin, S.; Hardy, M.C. The influence of cooling rate from temperatures above the γ' solvus on morphology, mismatch and hardness in advanced polycrystalline nickel-base superalloys. *Mater. Sci. Eng. A* **2008**, *473*, 158–165. [CrossRef]
30. Ricks, R.A.; Porter, A.J.; Ecob, R.C. The growth of γ' precipitates in nickel-base superalloy. *Acta Met.* **1983**, *75*, 1354–1361. [CrossRef]
31. Cosentino, F.; Warnken, N.; Gebelin, J.; Reed, R.C. Numerical and experimental study of post-heat treatment gas quenching and its impact on microstructure and creep in CMSX-10 superalloy. *J. Mater. Process. Technol.* **2013**, *213*, 2350–2360. [CrossRef]
32. Rojhirunsakool, T.; Meher, S.; Hwang, J.Y.; Nag, S.; Tiley, J.; Banerjee, R. Influence of composition on monomodal versus multimodal γ' precipitation in Ni–Al–Cr alloys. *J. Mater. Sci.* **2013**, *48*, 825–831. [CrossRef]
33. Caron, P. *High γ' Solvus New Generation Nickel-Based Superalloys for Single Crystal Turbine Blade Applications*; Superalloy 2000; TMS: Warrendale, PA, USA, 2000; pp. 737–746. [CrossRef]
34. Rae, C.M.F.; Reed, R.C. The precipitation of topologically close-packed phases in rhenium-containing superalloys. *Acta Mater.* **2001**, *49*, 4113–4125. [CrossRef]
35. Zhang, J.X.; Koizumi, Y.; Kobayshi, T. Strengthening by γ/γ' interfacial dislocation networks in TMS-162—Toward a fifth-generation single-crystal superalloy. *Metall. Mater. Trans. A* **2004**, *35*, 1911–1915. [CrossRef]
36. Xia, W.; Zhao, X.; Yue, L.; Zhang, Z. A review of composition evolution in Ni-based single crystal superalloys. *J. Mater. Sci. Technol.* **2020**, *44*, 76–95. [CrossRef]
37. Russell, K.C. Nucleation in solids: The induction and steady state effects. *Adv. Colloid Interface Sci.* **1980**, *13*, 205–318. [CrossRef]
38. Zhang, J.; Huang, T.; Lu, F.; Cao, K.; Wang, D.; Zhang, J.; Zhang, J.; Su, H.; Liu, L. The effect of rhenium on the microstructure stability and γ/γ' interfacial characteristics of Ni-based single crystal superalloys during long-term aging. *J. Alloys Compd.* **2021**, *876*, 160114. [CrossRef]
39. Guan, Y.; Liu, Y.; Ma, Z.; Li, H.; Yu, H. Precipitation and coarsening behavior of γ' phase in CoNi base superalloy under different aging treatments. *Vacuum* **2020**, *175*, 109247. [CrossRef]
40. Tan, X.P.; Hong, H.U.; Choi, B.G.; Kim, I.S.; Jo, C.Y.; Jin, T.; Hu, Z.Q. Characterization of topologically close-packed phases in secondary reaction zone in a coated CMSX-4 single crystal Ni-based superalloy. *J. Mater. Sci.* **2012**, *48*, 1085–1089. [CrossRef]
41. Sugui, T.; Minggang, W.; Tang, L.; Benjiang, Q.; Jun, X. Influence of TCP phase and its morphology on creep properties of single crystal nickel-based superalloys. *Mater. Sci. Eng. A* **2010**, *527*, 5444–5451. [CrossRef]
42. Roth, H.A.; Davis, C.L.; Thomson, R.C. Modeling solid solution strengthening in nickel alloys. *Metall. Mater. Trans. A* **1997**, *28*, 1329–1335. [CrossRef]
43. Heckl, A.; Neumeier, S.; Göken, M.; Singer, R.F. The effect of Re and Ru on γ/γ' microstructure, γ-solid solution strengthening and creep strength in nickel base superalloys. *Mater. Sci. Eng. A* **2011**, *528*, 3435–3444. [CrossRef]
44. Raynor, D.K.; Silcock, J. Strengthening mechanisms in γ' precipitating alloys. *Met. Sci. J.* **1970**, *4*, 121–130. [CrossRef]
45. Yue, Q.; Liu, L.; Yang, W.; Huang, T.; Zhang, J.; Fu, H. Stress dependence of dislocation networks in elevated temperature creep of a Ni-based single crystal superalloy. *Mater. Sci. Eng. A* **2019**, *742*, 132–137. [CrossRef]
46. Nathal, M.V. Effect of initial gamma prime size on the elevated temperature creep properties of single crystal nickel base superalloys. *Metall. Trans. A* **1987**, *18*, 1961–1970. [CrossRef]
47. Rae, C.M.F.; Zhang, L. Primary creep in single crystal superalloys: Some comments on effects of composition and micro-structure. *Mater. Sci. Technol.* **2009**, *25*, 228–235. [CrossRef]
48. Locq, D.; Caron, P.; Raujol, S.; Pettinari-Sturmel, F.; Coujou, A.; Clément, N. *On the Role of Tertiary γ' Precipitates in the Creep Behaviour at 700 °C of a PM Disk Superalloy*; Superalloy 2004; TMS: Warrendale, PA, USA, 2004; pp. 179–187. [CrossRef]
49. Wilson, B.C.; Fuchs, G.E. *The Effect of Composition, Misfit, and Heat Treatment on the Primary Creep Behavior of Single Crystal Nickel Base Superalloys PWA 1480 and PWA 1484*; Superalloy 2008; TMS: Warrendale, PA, USA, 2008; pp. 149–158. [CrossRef]

crystals

MDPI

Article

Effect of Abnormal Grains on the Mechanical Properties of FGH96 Solid-State Diffusion Bonding Joint

Jingqing Zhang [1], Yong Shang [2,*], Qiaomu Liu [2,*], Junwu Wang [3], Yanling Pei [2], Shusuo Li [3] and Shengkai Gong [2]

1 School of Materials Science and Engineering, Beihang University, Beijing 100191, China; zhangjingqing0320@126.com
2 Research Institute for Frontier Science, Beihang University, Beijing 100191, China; peiyanling@buaa.edu.cn (Y.P.); gongsk@buaa.edu.cn (S.G.)
3 Institute of Aero Engine Research, Beihang University, No. 37 Xueyuan Road, Beijing 100191, China; wangjunwu916@163.com (J.W.); lishs@buaa.edu.cn (S.L.)
* Correspondence: cs881013@buaa.edu.cn (Y.S.); lqiaomu@163.com (Q.L.)

Abstract: The hollow twin-web disk is designed to improve the thrust-to-weight ratio of the aero engine, where the welding joint microstructures determine the disk's mechanical properties. This study aimed to elucidate the effect of abnormal grains formed in the welding region on the mechanical properties of FGH96 solid-state diffusion bonding joints. Digital image correlation using images captured by scanning electron microscopy (SEM-DIC) and electron backscattering diffraction (EBSD) technologies were applied. The results show that abnormally large grains (2.5 times that of the matrix), with preferred orientation in the bonding region, were detrimental to the joint mechanical properties. The yield and tensile strengths were 995.85 MPa and 1456.67 MPa, respectively, and the corresponding relative (ratio to the matrix) ones were 92.54% and 88.81%. After modifying the bonding process, the grain size in the bonding region was tailored to close to that of the matrix, and considerable twin boundaries (TBs) formed, leading to the relative tensile and yield strength reaching 98.86% and 99.37%. Furthermore, the failure mode changed to intragranular type from intergranular type. It demonstrates that tailoring the newborn grain size, introducing TBs inside, and eliminating preferred orientation during the welding process can be an efficient way to improve the joint mechanical properties.

Keywords: FGH96 joint; welding; abnormal grain; grain orientation; twin boundary; failure

1. Introduction

The powder metallurgy (PM) Ni-based superalloys exhibit many excellent performances compared to the conventional wrought superalloys, such as the uniformity of composition, high damage tolerance, and oxidation resistance [1,2]. As a typical 2nd-generation PM Ni-based superalloy, FGH96 is widely used to manufacture turbine disks [3,4]. In order to improve the thrust-to-weight ratio, the traditional single-web turbine disk was supposed to be substituted by hollow twin-web turbine disks (TWD), which are conducive to weight reduction and cooling efficiency [5–7]. The welding techniques were applied to produce the hollow profiles, among which the solid-state diffusion bonding (SSDB) process was considered a prevailing method, since it can avoid the formation of adverse phases in the bonding regions, such as blocky brittle phases or intermetallic compounds, which are inescapable during the transient liquid phase bonding and braze welding [8–10]. Due to the microstructure discrepancy between the welding areas and the matrix regions, the welding region was usually the weak zone of the joint and determined the mechanical properties of the TWD. Therefore, it is important to study the microstructures formed in different welding processes and their effects on the mechanical properties of bonding joints.

The microstructure features in the welding zone, such as the grain sizes, orientation distribution, and the grain boundary characterization distribution (GBCD), were decided by the welding processes, for example, the bonding temperature and pressures, the initial material states, and the pure Ni interlayer application [11–13]. All the above microstructure features can strongly influence the material properties, including the physical and chemical properties [14–17], and mechanical properties [18–22], which are widely studied in different based materials (BMs). However, few studies were accessible for the SSDB joints.

It is well known that grain sizes influence mechanical properties and failure mode. For example, the yield strength, tensile strength, and fracture elongation decreased with increasing the grain size in nickel-based superalloy deformed at room temperature [23]. While in the studies of Maowen Liu and F.K. Yan [24,25], excellent strength ductility synergy was accomplished in the recrystallized 316 stainless steel by tailoring grain size into the nanoscale. Similar studies were carried out on magnesium [26], and a simultaneous increase in strength and ductility were achieved by tailoring the grain size from 125 μm to 51 and 5.5 μm, due to the activation of non-basal slip systems and the formation of nano-spaced stacking faults, where the activation of more dislocations helped to accommodate strain and improve the uniform elongation, and the high density of nano-spaced stacking faults acted as an additional strengthening mechanism. The grain size also influenced the failure mode. Tim P. Gabb [27,28] revealed that the specimens with a fine grain failed mostly from internal inclusions, while those with coarse grains always failed from crystallographic facets.

In addition to the grain size, the grain orientations also have an impact on the mechanical properties, which are significantly outstanding in the single crystal superalloys, excluding the effect of high-angle grain boundaries (HAGB) and twin boundaries (TBs) [29–32]. Yifei Li [29] found that the [111] orientated specimens displayed the longest creep life at 850 °C for a 3rd generation single crystal superalloy, the [11] one showed the shortest creep life and longest elongation, and the [1] one presented the intermediate performance. This phenomenon was related to the different activated slip systems and their interactions at different stages for the specimens with different orientations. Other studies [33,34] also revealed that the activation of different slip systems (cube slip or octahedral slip systems) was mainly affected by the crystal orientation at intermediate or low temperatures, and then affected the fatigue properties. Shiqi Zhang [35] figured out that the geometric necessary dislocations (GNDs) density had a strong orientation dependency during the monotonic deformation of aluminum alloy: <111> orientated grains with a higher Taylor factor accumulated more GNDs than <100> orientated grains, which was attributed to the fact that higher Taylor factor grains required larger stress to realize uniform geometrical change.

Moreover, TBs play a vital role in adjusting the mechanical properties. Numerous studies [36–38] demonstrated that twinning could produce a much improved strength without sacrificing resistance to fracture due to the coherent nature of TBs. Depending on its characterization, this kind of boundary can block or transmit the slip and thus provide strength and ductility [37]. Shiteng Zhao [38] showed a bulk nanostructuring method to make a pure Ti achieve an ultimate tensile strength of almost 2 GPa and a true failure strain close to 100% at 77 K by introducing a multiscale, hierarchical twin architecture into the coarse-grained titanium, which diminished the trade-off between the strength and ductility. The pre-twinning strategy, based on stacking fault energy (SFE) controlling in medium Mn steel, provided continuous hardening capacity after yield; consequently, the tensile strength increased by 1.7 times with an acceptable ductility via alleviating shear strain accumulation and retarding crack initiation [39].

Up to now, many studies [21,38,40,41] have indicated an inner relationship among grain size, grain orientation, and TBs numbers, which comprehensively affect the material properties. Bingshu Wang [40] reported that although higher yield strength was produced in the small grains, deformation twinning was favored in larger grains and affected by the grain orientation. Finally, twin–twin interactions in large grains also promote hardening. It is also proposed that too large or too small grains are not conducive to the TBs formation [38]. M. Sarkari Khorrami [42] showed that the formation of abnormally grown grains is concomitant with the development of $\{001\}\langle 100\rangle$ cube and $\{110\}\langle 001\rangle$ Goss texture components in deformed aluminum alloy. Furthermore, the pre-existing preferred orientation in the deformed alloy can, in turn, enhance the incubation of abnormal grain growth [43]. R.T. Ott [41] studied the dependence of the strength and ductility on the twin density and orientations of ultra-fine grained Ag, which presented that the untwinned grains provided decreased strength compared with twinned grains due to relatively low resistance to slip, and the twinned grains without <111> orientation were softer than those with <111> orientation.

The formers' studies suggest that the microstructures correlated with grain size, orientation, and TBs can offer crucial information for the strengthening and toughing mechanism, and provide consults for reinforcement in metal alloys. Therefore, it can be deduced that these factors and mechanisms may also be suitable for PM superalloy SSDB joints. However, up to now, the accessible information on the research was still poor, and no detailed analysis was carried out on the PM superalloy SSDB joints.

In the present study, the relationship among the three factors (grain size, orientation, and TBs) and their effects on the mechanical properties of FGH96 SSDB joints were studied, and then the microscopic mechanism was analyzed, which could lend sight into tailor grain microstructures and improve the mechanical properties of the SSDB joint.

2. Materials and Methods

2.1. Materials

The chemical composition of the BMs (a PM superalloy FGH96) is summarized in Table 1. PM FGH96 alloy cylinders with a diameter of 40 mm and a height of 40 mm were welded through the SSDB technique using a 5–10 μm pure Ni interlayer by electroplating. The cylinders were bonded at 1140 °C under 8–10 MPa for 1 h in a vacuum less than 7×10^{-3} Pa and cooled in the furnace. The bonding temperature and time were chosen according to the solution treatment of FGH96 carried out at 1127 °C~1150 °C for 2 h. Two bonding processes were designed, as shown in Figure 1, which were carried out by the Beijing Institute of Aeronautical Materials. For the first process, the initial condition of the FGH96 for bonding was a supersolvus solid solution state. After the bonding process, the joint was aged at 760 °C for 16 h to adjust the morphology of γ', which was named the original bonding process. The other bonding process was named the modified bonding process, where the initial condition of the FGH96 for bonding was a hot forging state (with a total 60% deformation and a 0.1 mm/s reduction rate at 1050 °C), then the joint was treated through the standard supersolvus solid solution heat treatment (1150 °C for 2 h) and aging heat treatment (760 °C for 16 h).

Table 1. Chemical composition of base material (BM), i.e., FGH 96 superalloy, in this study.

Composition (wt.%)										
Co	Cr	Mo	W	Al	Ti	Nb	Zr	C	B	Ni
12.5~13.5	15.5~16.5	3.8~4.2	3.8~4.2	2.0~2.4	3.5~3.9	0.6~1.0	0.025~0.05	0.02~0.05	0.006~0.015	Bal.

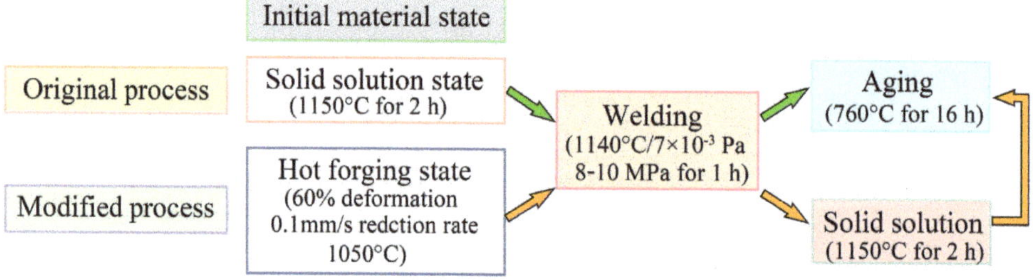

Figure 1. The flowchart for welding processes with two different initial material states.

2.2. Methods and Characterization

Dog-bone-shaped, sheet-type tensile specimens with a gauge length of 25 mm, gauge width of 3 mm, thickness of 1 mm, and with the bonding region sited in the middle of the gage length, were cut from the bonded cylinders, which were used for the uniaxial tensile test at room temperature with a strain rate of $4.2 \times 10^{-4}\ s^{-1}$. As a comparison, the BMs that followed the same welding thermal cycle were also made into tensile specimens with the same dimensions. The quasi in situ tensile experiments [44] were performed and the specimens were tensile-deformed to different strains of 4%, 9%, and 15%. The microscopic strain distributions in the bonding region and neighboring matrix zone were analyzed by the digital image correlation (DIC) technique using secondary electron (SE) images captured by scanning electron microscopy (SEM), i.e., the SEM-DIC technique. The Vic-2D software (version 2009.1.0, Correlated Solutions Inc., Columbia, DC, USA) was applied as the postprocessing tool for the strain calculation. Secondary γ' with a size of 100–200 nm in FGH 96 was chosen as a speckle pattern to achieve a strain field at a sub-micron resolution. Furthermore, the evolutions of crystallography messages during the quasi in situ tensile experiments were analyzed by the electron backscattering diffraction (EBSD) technique. All the microstructure characterizations were conducted by SEM (Apreo S LoVac, FEI, Czech) equipped with an EBSD system operated at 25 kV. In order to track the microstructure evolution of the joint, tensile testing was interrupted for EBSD scans and taking images for DIC on the same area of interest (AOI) between successive steps. The detailed operations can be referred to the article [44]. The dislocation morphologies in deformed samples were identified by a transmission electron microscope (TEM, JEM2100, Tokyo, Japan) operated at 200 kV.

3. Results

3.1. Microstructural Characterization of FGH96 SSDB Joints

Figure 2 showed the microstructures of the FGH96 SSDB joints with different bonding processes. The EBSD orientation image microscopy (OIM) maps, where colors indicate the crystallographic orientation parallel to the normal direction of the bonding interface, revealed that most newborn grains in the bonding region of the joint bonded by the original process (named the original joint in the following text) were rendered by violet color, suggesting the grains were with a preferential crystallographic texture, as shown in Figure 2a,b. Notably, these messages were sampled from at least three different specimens in different areas, making the observation statistically sound. In contrast, various colors were randomly distributed in different grains in the bonding region of the joint bonded by the modified bonding process (named the modified joint), and the grains of the BM followed the same welding thermal cycle (named the BM), which indicated no preferential crystallographic texture, as shown in Figure 2c,d. Furthermore, the standard stereographic orientation triangles (Figure 2e–h) for the grains in the bonding regions and BM verified that the grain orientation in the X-direction (the external stress) was mainly located near <111> polar, with fewer at <001> corner, and little at <110> corner for the original joint, while it was spread all over the triangle for the modified one and the BM.

Regarding the joints bonded with different processes, the grain sizes and GBCD for the grains in the bonding regions are shown in Figure 2i,j, accompanied by the same messages for the BM. The size of the newborn grains in the bonding region of the original joint was the largest (60.12 μm), almost three times that of the BM (24.06 μm). While the modified joint displayed a smaller newborn grain size (28.44 μm), which was equivalent to that of the BM. Identifying from the GBCD in Figure 2j, little TBs (only 1.98%) were obtained in the bonding region of the original joint. When the modified process was operated, the TBs in the bonding regions increased to 50.82%, which was the same amount as that of the BM.

The morphologies of γ' in different areas, from the bonding regions to the matrix zone, were shown in Figure 3, which indicates that the size and shapes of γ' were different for different regions. This discrepancy can be used to identify the failure location for tensile specimens.

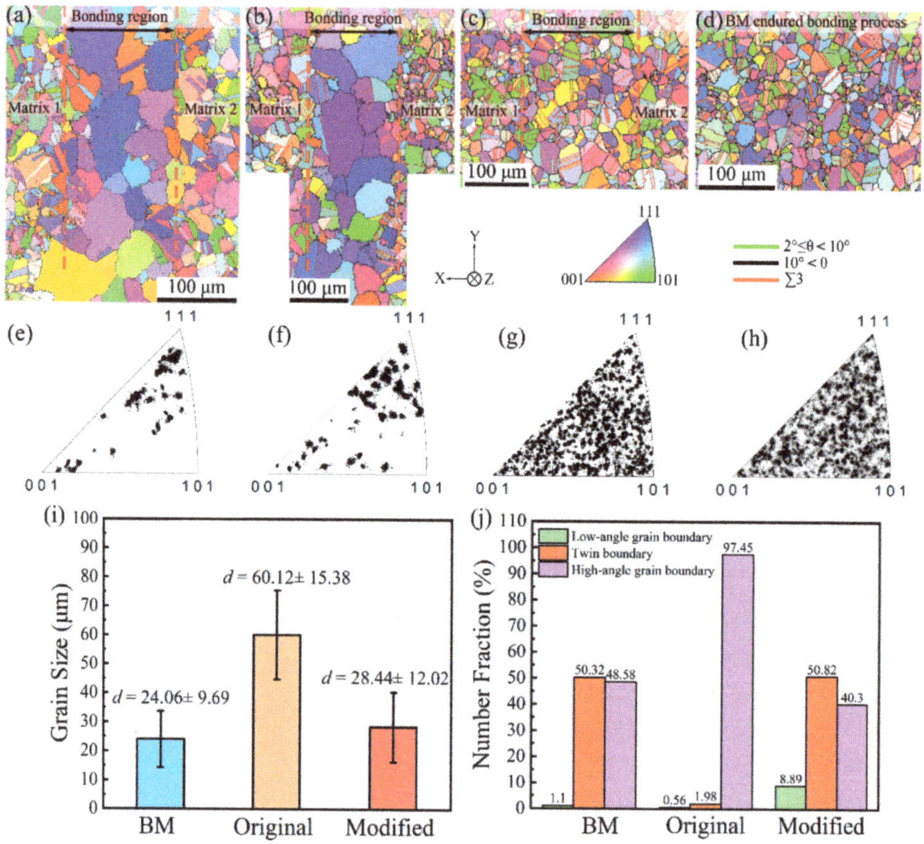

Figure 2. EBSD patterns of FGH96 SSDB joints with different bonding processes and the BM endured the bonding thermal cycle. (**a**,**b**) Orientation image microscopy (OIM) maps in the X-direction (the normal direction of the bonding interface) of the joint bonded by the original bonding process. (**c**) The OIM map in the X-direction of the joint bonded by the modified bonding process. (**d**) The OIM map for the BM endured the welding thermal cycle. (**e**–**h**) The corresponding orientation distribution for the grains in the bonding region in (**a**–**c**), and the grains in the BM in (**d**). The grain size (**i**) and grain boundary character distribution (GBCD) (**j**) for the grains in the bonding region and BM.

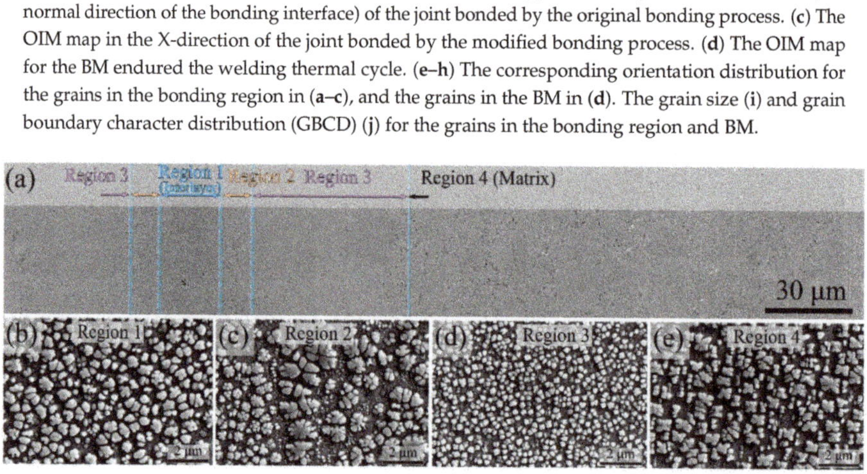

Figure 3. (**a**) Backscattered electron (BSE) images of FGH96 SSDB joint from the bonding region to the matrix region, and the γ' morphology in different regions of (**a**): (**b**) region 1, (**c**) region 2, (**d**) region 3, and (**e**) region 4.

3.2. Mechanical Properties

Tensile strength, yield strength, and elongation of the different joints are displayed in Figure 4a, together with that of the BM. Furthermore, the relative strength and elongation, i.e., the ratio between the joint and the BM, are shown in Figure 4b. Moreover, the fracture morphologies of different samples are shown in Figure 4c–e. The tensile strength and yield strength of the original joint reached 1465.67 MPa and 995.85 MPa, which were 92.54% and 88.81% of that of the BM, respectively. Unexpectedly, the relative elongation reached 116.11%. When the bonding process was modified, the joint exhibited a tensile strength of 1583.86 MPa and yield strength of 1121.27 MPa, with a relative tensile strength of 98.86% and yield strength of 99.37%. Obviously, these values were improved largely, compared with the original joint. However, the relative elongation decreased to 95.25%.

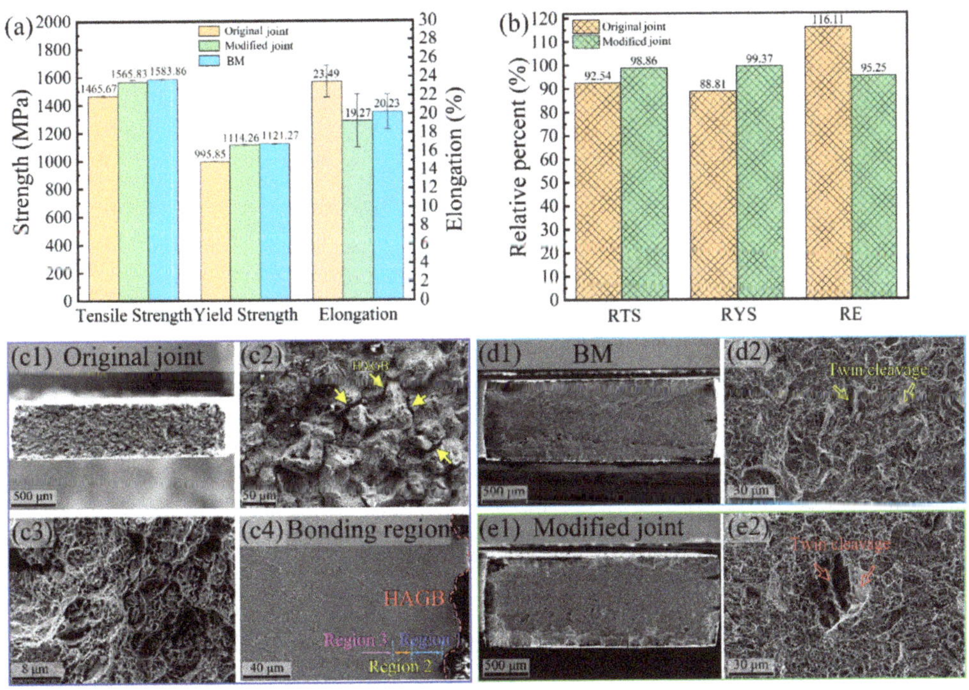

Figure 4. Tensile strength, yield strength, and elongation of the SSDB joints and BM endured with the same bonding process (**a**), and the relative strength and elongation for different joints (**b**). Fracture morphology of SSDB joint with different bonding processes (**c1–c4**,**e1**,**e2**) and BM (**d1**,**d2**).

The fracture morphologies (Figure 4c) showed that the fracture surfaces were rock candy-shaped and distributed with dimples, implying the typical ductile and intergranular fracture characteristics for the original joint. Identifying from the section profile (Figure 4(c4)), the fracture site of the joint was in the bonding region according to the joint microstructure (Figure 3). The relative position between the primary crack line and the high-angle grain boundaries (HAGB) displayed that the primary crack line coincided with the HAGB of the abnormally large grain, suggesting the crack propagated along the HAGB. However, the fracture morphologies of the modified joint and the BM were planar and distributed with dimples, implying the fracture type transferred into a ductile intragranular type. It is worth noting that some small planes arising from twin cleavage were distributed on the fracture surface, as shown in Figure 4(d2,e2), suggesting that the TBs played an important role in the deformation behavior.

4. Discussion

The results of this work show that abnormal large grains with preferred grain orientations and a small number of TBs formed in the bonding region of the FGH96 SSDB joint bonded by the original process, leading to relatively poor mechanical properties. After the bonding process was modified, the grain size in the bonding region was tailored to be similar to that of the BMs, accompanied by the same fraction of TBs, and the preferred grain orientation vanished. Then, the tensile mechanical properties were improved largely. Moreover, the fracture type transferred into the intergranular type from the intragranular type.

4.1. The Origin of Abnormal Grain Growth and Its Correlation with Preferred Grain Orientation and Twin Boundaries for the Newly Formed Grains in the Bonding Region

The grain growth during welding is not only related to the strain energy caused by the imposed external bonding stress but also to the material initial states before being bonded, such as the initial grain size, the secondary phases, and the reserved strain energy in the materials depending on the heat treatments. In order to qualitatively and quantitively identify this information for the two different initial BMs used in this work, EBSD and SEM were applied. The obtained results are shown in Figure 5. It can be seen that many large primary γ' and smaller secondary ones precipitated at the grain boundaries or in the grain interior of the BM with a hot forging state, as shown in Figure 5c,d, while no γ' were found in the BM with a solid solution state, as presented in Figure 5a,b. Furthermore, the grain sizes were much different for the two BMs (See Figure 5i).

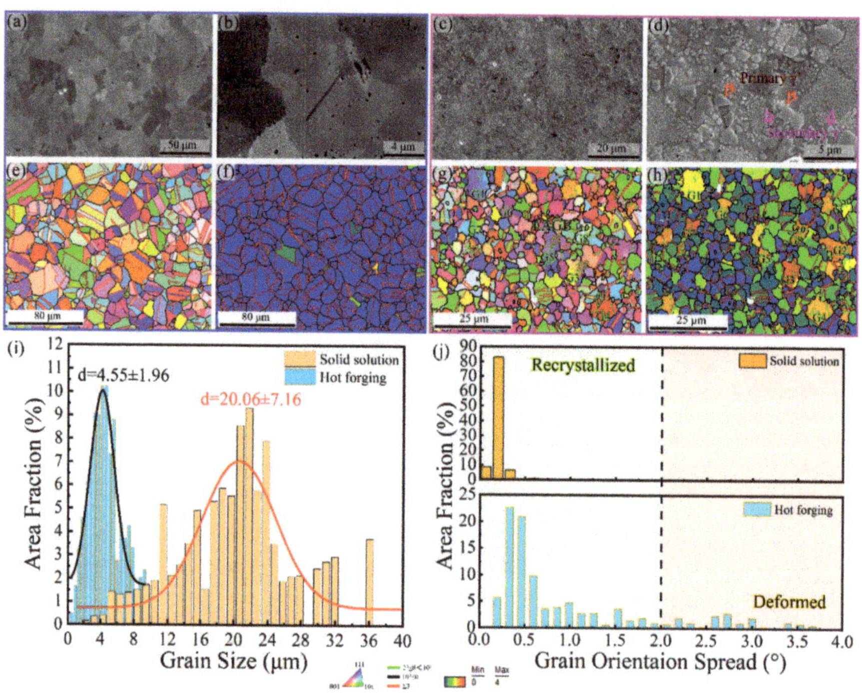

Figure 5. The microstructure characterization of the FGH96 base materials with different heat treatments. (**a**) Secondary electron (SE) images for solid solution (SS) treated state, and high magnification (**b**), (**c**) SE images for hot forging (HF) state, and high magnification (**d**). (**e–h**) are, respectively, the OIM map, grain orientation spread (GOS) map for SS state (**e**,**f**), and HF state (**g**,**h**). The grain size distribution (**i**) and the area fraction of grains with a specified GOS (**j**) for the two specimens are also statistically displayed.

The grain orientation spread (GOS) measures the orientation deviation between all the points within a grain relative to the average orientation for that grain and is commonly used to characterize recrystallization [45]. A critical of GOS < 2° for recrystallization is commonly used [45–48]. As a result, the GOS can be used as a credible index for identifying grain inhomogeneous deformation. In order to qualitatively identify the pre-existing strain in the initial materials before being bonded, the GOS was statistically analyzed, which is shown in Figure 5j. Furthermore, the visual GOS maps and the OIM maps are shown in Figure 5e–h for the two initial BMs with different heat treatments.

From the statistical results of GOS, it can be seen that all the GOS values for the grains in the BM with a solid solution state were less than 2°. Moreover, the orientation colors in the OIM map (Figure 5e) were homogeneously distributed, and no color gradients were presented within a single grain, suggesting that no deformed grains exist and the recrystallization is completed, i.e., negligible strain energy existed in the initial material. In contrast, grains with a GOS > 2° occupied a certain area fraction for the BM with a hot forging state. Furthermore, orientation gradients can be seen in many grains, such as the G1–G8 grains in Figure 5g, as inhomogeneous distributions of colors were within these grains in the OIM map. Moreover, these grains with inhomogeneous orientations presented larger GOS values and grain sizes, as revealed in Figure 5h, implying that the specimen was mostly, but not completely, recrystallized after the hot forging and some deformed grains were reserved [48], i.e., pre-existing nonnegligible strains reserved in the initial material. Furthermore, the remaining deformation and unfinished recrystallization can be reinforced by the tangled low-angle grain boundaries (LAGB) in the grains with larger GOS, as indexed by the arrows in Figure 5g. It can be supposed that all the differences in the initial microstructures of the BMs can lead to differences in the microstructure of the welding zone.

The BMs with a solid solution state were used as the initial materials when the original bonding process was carried out. As a result, the kinetics for the grain growth in the bonding process mainly come from the strain energy caused by the imposed bonding pressure, since negligible strain energy existed in the initial material due to the completed recrystallization. The imposed pressure (8–10 MPa for 1 h) brings out a larger strain in the pure Ni interlayer than that in the BMs due to solution strengthening; that is, more strain energy is stored in the pure Ni interlayer. In view of the fact that there was no prior strain energy in the BMs and a weak one was caused by the external stress in the bonding process, the grain growth mostly concentrates in the grains surrounding the pure Ni interlayer due to the strain-induced grain boundary migration [49], and this explains the result that the grain size (24 μm in Figure 2i) in the matrix region of the original joint is close to that (20 μm in Figure 5i) of the initial BM. The supersolvus heat temperature (1140 °C) applied in the bonding process provides the thermodynamic condition for the grain growth. Driven by the thermodynamic and kinetic conditions, the grain boundaries on either side of the pure Ni interlayer would migrate, leading to the growth and coalescence of grains, and the grain growth path goes through the pure Ni interlayer to consume the higher strain energy [50,51]. This is one aspect that leads to the formation of abnormally large grains in the bonding regions of the original joint, as shown in Figure 2a,b.

On the other aspect, there is no obstacle to the grain boundary migration due to the absence of γ' in the BM, as shown in Figure 5a,b. On the third aspect, the application of Ni interlayer in the welding process promotes atom diffusion [12,52], which accelerates the grain boundaries mobility and grain coalescence. It can be deduced that the formation of abnormal grains in the bonding region is the result of integrating the above three effects, leading to the grain size increase largely from 20.06 μm on average to 60.12 μm.

Apart from the abnormally large grain size, a notable characterization, i.e., most of the large grains with a near <111> preferred orientation in the X direction (the external stress direction or the normal direction to the bonding interface) and less with a near <001> orientation, while none with a <101> orientation was displayed in the bonding region of the original joint, as presented in Figure 2a,b,e,f. Many studies [53,54] illustrated that the abnormal grain growth was accompanied by the formation of a preferred orientation texture, typically a low-energy, high-symmetry plane. According to the theory, the {111} planes, the close-packed planes of atoms with the lowest surface energy in FCC, satisfy the condition to be the favored orientation, which is consistent with our results for the larger grains in the bonding regions, i.e., the {111}//bonding interface. It can be speculated that the large grains, with the orientation near the {111}//bonding interface, grow much faster than the surrounding grains with other orientations, and even consume other grains by grain boundary migration during the bonding process; as a result, the preferred orientation is produced at last. A similar phenomenon was observed in the in situ annealing process for pure Ni and Cu [51]. In the study, the grains with a special orientation had the priority to grow and consumed the surrounding grains with other orientations, leading to the formation of orientation texture at the stage of abnormal grain growth, where the area fraction of {111} grains rose steeply even from 0%, {001} grain increased during the initial stage, then decreased at the final one, while the {101} grain decreased all the way.

Other studies [55] demonstrated the favored {100}-orientated grains in the abnormal grain growth in FCC films formed after annealing, attributed to the minimization of the strain energy since the <100>-oriented grains have the lowest and equal plane stress ($\sigma1$ and $\sigma2$) and the lowest strain energy density. Alejandro Barrios [56] also revealed that the abnormal grain growth occurred predominantly in the family of grains with <100> orientation along the loading direction during high-cycle loading at room temperature in ultra-fine grained Ni, due to the lowest strain energy density of <100> orientated grains, since the grain elastic anisotropy dictated the thermodynamic driving force of abnormal grain growth at room temperature. In the present work, the study object is a Ni-based alloy block instead of pure Ni film and experiences low static stress and high solid solution temperature, where the capillary effects of GB energy and surface energy play a dominant role in driving grain growth [56]. As a result, in order to balance the surface energy and elastic strain energy, the most abnormal grains with preferred orientation {111}//bonding surface, and fewer with {001}//bonding surface, are formed in the bonding region.

It is reported that oversized grains are not conducive to the TBs formation inside due to the extremely high energy required to introduce multiscale twin architecture [38]. Additionally, the TBs in the grains with small grain sizes or unfavored orientations are consumed, as these grains are swallowed during the abnormal grain growth [57,58], which is the main factor that decreases the TBs density. Eventually, the TBs exhibited extremely fewer number fractions (only 1.98%) in the newly formed large grains of the original joint, compared with that (as high as 50.32%) of the BMs (see Figure 2j).

When the bonding process was modified, the hot forging alloy acted as the initial material before being bonded. The large primary γ' and smaller secondary ones in the BM can provide a pinning force for the grain boundary migration [48,59,60]. Although the γ' can solubilize at the supersolvus temperature (1140 °C for 1 h) in the bonding process, the solution at this condition is a time-consuming process, and the primary γ' perhaps can partly remain, since the solution treatment of FGH96 was carried out at 1150 °C for 2 h in general operation. Hence, the γ' in the material can prohibit effectively the abnormal grain growth during the bonding process.

Identifying the EBSD patterns of the initial material with a hot forging state, the average grain size was about 4.55 μm (Figure 5i), which was much smaller than that both in the matrix region (24 μm) and in the bonding regions (28 μm) of the modified joint, as presented in Figure 2i, indicating that the grains in both the bonding and matrix regions grew during the bonding process. The remaining deformed grains in the BM provide strain energy to support the pre-existing recrystallized grains (with a small GOS value < 2°) to grow or to support the deformed grains to continue recrystallization in the whole volume of the material, not restricted within the regions surrounding the pure Ni interlayer during the bonding process. Finally, the deformed grains are consumed to reduce the overall free energy present in the system [61]. As a result, the grains in the matrix region of the modified joint grew from 4.55 μm to 24.06 μm. As to the grains in the bonding region, the driven force for the grain growth comes from not only the prior deformed grains but also the strain energy in the pure Ni interlayer, leading to relatively larger grains with 28.44 μm. No abnormal grain growth was found in the bonding region, which is different from the case in the original bonding process, as presented in Figure 2c,i, mainly due to the retarding effect of the primary and secondary γ' on the grain boundaries migration, and partly due to the strain energy from the deformed grains, which drive the overall grain growth in the material instead of being limited in the local region surrounding the pure Ni interlayer. Since no abnormal grain formed in the bonding regions and obtained a similar grain size to that of the matrix region, no preferred grain orientation appeared. Furthermore, the number fractions of TBs in both regions are similar.

It can be concluded that abnormal grain growth is the essential prerequisite for the preferred grain orientation formation and decreased TBs. The abnormal large grains, preferred grain orientation, and the TB amount in the bonding regions have a critical role in the mechanical properties of the bonding joint, which will be discussed in Section 4.2.

4.2. The Influence of Abnormal Grains on the Mechanical Properties

The original joint with abnormally large and preferred orientated grains showed weak yield and tensile strengths, as well as high elongation compared with that of the modified joint, as shown in Figure 4. In addition, the fracture types were different, that is, intergranular fracture or intragranular fracture. All the phenomena are related to the different microstructures of joints, hence, the mechanisms of mechanical properties are clarified and checked out below, in aspects of the discrepancy in microstructural characters, including grain size, preferred orientation, and TBs amounts.

Grain refinement is considered an effective hardening route to significantly improve strength based on the Hall–Petch relationship [62], where the yield stress, σ_y, is related to the grain size, d, through the equation: $\sigma_y = \sigma_0 + k_y d^{-1/2}$, in which σ_0 is a lattice friction stress, and k_y is a constant of yielding. According to this expression, it is easily comprehensible that the modified joint gave rise to a higher yield strength compared to the original one, since the grain size in the bonding region of the modified joint is almost half of that of the original, as statistically displayed in Figure 2i. Furthermore, the large number fraction (50.82%) of TBs in the bonding region of the modified joint effectively subdivides the grains, in other words, refines the grains further. As for the original joint, most of the newly formed grains in the bonding regions presented a preferred near <111>-orientation, hence, the number of grains with obviously different grain orientations that need to be coordinated decreased, which reduces the resistance of metal plastic deformation and joint strength. As a result, the modified joint exhibits a yield strength of 1114.26 MPa and relative yield strength of 99.37%. The value is improved by 10% compared with the original joint.

Figure 6 shows the microscopic strain evolution with increased global strain for the original joint calculated by SEM-DIC. It can be seen that the strain value in the bonding region was higher than that in the neighboring matrix regions and the discrepancy became increasingly larger with the global strain proceeding, as shown in Figure 6c, indicating that the strain was more and more accumulated in the newly formed large grains and led to fracture at this region, as shown in Figure 4(c4). In detailed observation, the strain was revealed to be mainly concentrated along with the slip bands and intermitted by the HAGBs, suggesting that the abnormal grains are favorable for slip activation and no obstacles for slips exist in the interior of the grain, as presented in Figure 6a,b,d.

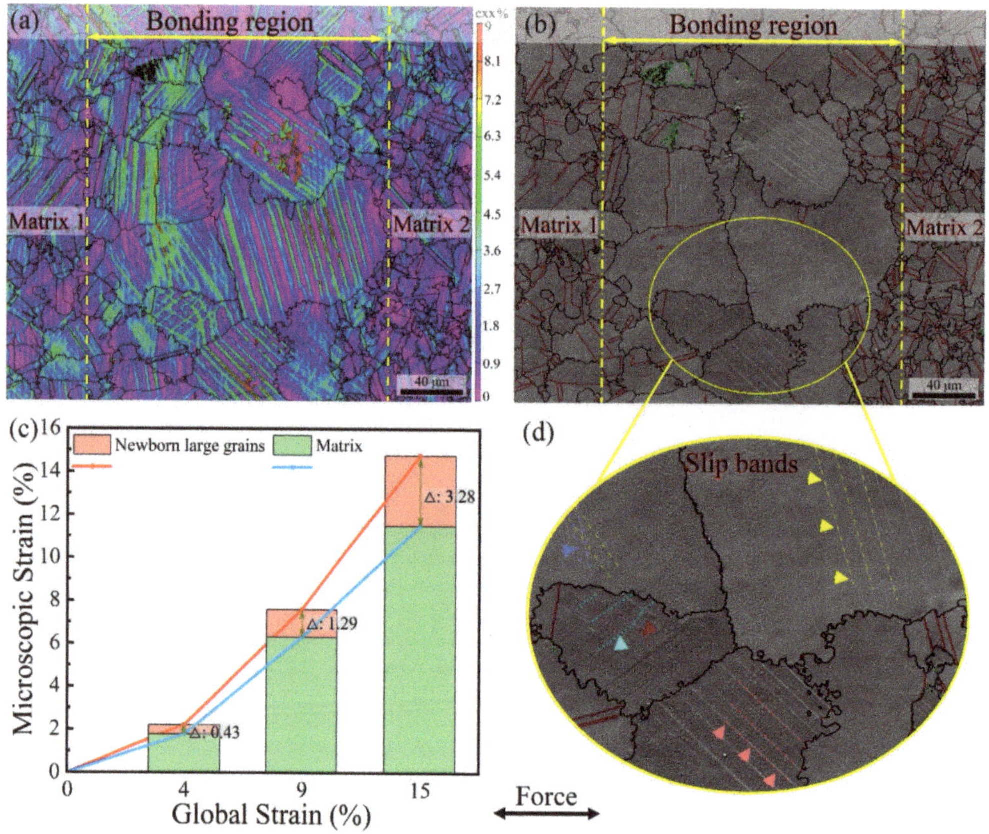

Figure 6. The microscopic strain distribution at 4% global strain by SEM-DIC (**a**), and the SEM images (**b**) with a higher magnification (**d**). The microscopic strain discrepancy between the bonding region and the neighboring matrix region with increased global strain (**c**).

The tensile strength or strain-hardening ability and the ductility are strongly controlled by the blocking of dislocation motion and the number of activated slip systems in the deformed process. According to Kocks [63], work hardening is a consequence of the fact that some fraction of mobile dislocations are stored in the crystals or react with other dislocations to form new obstacles (obstacle dislocations) and then impede the continued slips, which is linked to the change in obstacle dislocation density during plastic deformation, i.e., $d\rho = d\rho_{STOR} - d\rho_{RECOV}$, where $d\rho_{RECOV}$ is related to the recovery of dislocations already stored, which decreases the work-hardening rate, and $d\rho_{STOR}$ is related to dislocation storage and enhances the work-hardening rate due to increasing obstacle density. $d\rho_{STOR}$ is inversely proportional to the mean free path for the mobile dislocation. In the original joint, the abnormal grains provide a larger mean free path for the mobile dislocation, and most of the mobile dislocations exit through the specimen surface without any obstacles in the interior of the grain, and the only obstacle resource is the HAGBs, hence, the obstacle dislocation density is low in the abnormal grains, leading to adverse work-hardening ability. In order to support the speculation, TEM observations for the dislocation at different sites of the bonding region were carried out when the original joint deformed to 20% global strain, as shown in Figures 7 and 8. The specimens were prepared by the focused ion beam (FIB) technique combined with EBSD in order to identify the sites of specimen extraction. Figure 7a showed the dislocation morphology in the interior of the abnormal grain, displaying that the dislocations lined regularly in the slip bands and escaped from the specimen surface without any obstacles, and no dislocation tangles formed. It can be indicated that rare obstacle dislocations are stored in the interior of abnormal grain and induce work hardening. Turn sight to the HAGB in the bonding region, abundant dislocations were effectively impeded and stacked (in Figure 7c,f,g), suggesting that the work-hardening effect mainly comes from the HAGB for the abnormal grains. The phenomenon of the dislocations proved the Kocks theory in our case. When the bonding process was modified, the smaller grain sizes reduced the mean free path of dislocations, rendering a much higher work-hardening ability. Additionally, a large concentration of TBs present in the microstructure can serve to effectively resist dislocation motion [25,49,64] and give rise to nonuniform plastic microstrain due to the local strain accommodation, so as to raise the resistance ability of the alloy to plastic deformation [38,44]. The blocking interaction between the TB and dislocations was presented in Figure 7d,e, which confirms the contribution of TBs to the strain hardening ability.

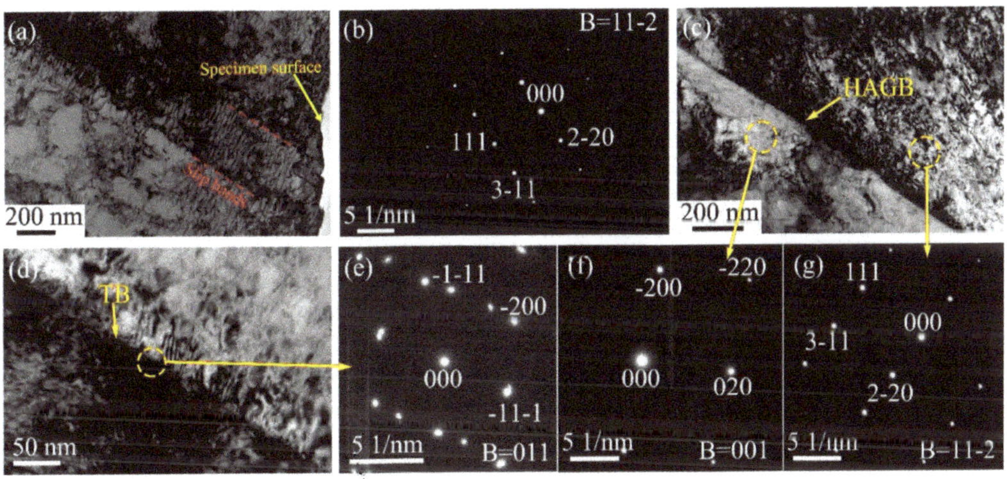

Figure 7. The bright-field images of the dislocation in the abnormal grain interior of the original joint at 20% global strain (**a**) and the corresponding selected area electron diffraction (SAED) of the matrix via **B** = 11-2 (**b**). The dislocation morphology at the HAGB (**c**), the twin boundary (**d**), and corresponding SAED patterns (**e**–**g**).

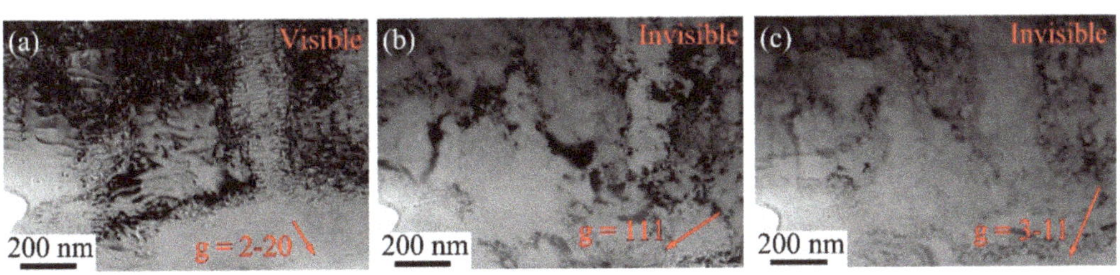

Figure 8. The bright-field images of dislocation under two-beam diffraction conditions for Figure 7a: (**a**) **g** = 2–20, (**b**) **g** = 111, and (**c**) **g** = 3–11.

The preferred orientated morphologies usually lead to anisotropic strengthening and deformation behaviors [31,65]. In order to clarify the relationship between the preferred grain orientation and microscopic deformation evolution, quasi in situ tensile tests combined with EBSD analyses for the same region were carried out on the original joint with incremental degrees of global strains, and the obtained results are shown in Figure 9. Several abnormal grains (G1U-G5D) in the bonding region were taken into analysis. According to the two-beam electron diffraction analysis and the judge criterion of the dislocation burger vector, i.e., $\vec{g} \cdot \vec{b} = 0$, {1–11} <-112> dislocations were identified to be activated, as presented in Figure 8, and then the Schmid factors (SF) evolution for this kind of dislocation are shown in Figure 9b. It can be seen that the SFs of the abnormal grains were lower than those of smaller grains in the surrounding matrix regions and became lower all the way with the increasing global strain and orientation rotations, as presented in Table 2, indicating that the abnormal grains with preferred near <111>-orientations were not favorable for slip activation and movements, that is, the <111>-orientated grains should have more plastic strain resistance and lead to higher alloy strength, however, it is inconsistent with the experimental results shown in Figure 6. Consequently, it can be inferred that the softening effects coming from the abnormal grain size and the absence of TBs surpass the hardening effect of orientation. In conclusion, the strengths of the bonding joint are not determined by a single factor, but by a comprehensive consideration. Finally, the modified joint triggered a higher tensile strength (1565.83 MPa) than that of the original one (1465.67 MPa).

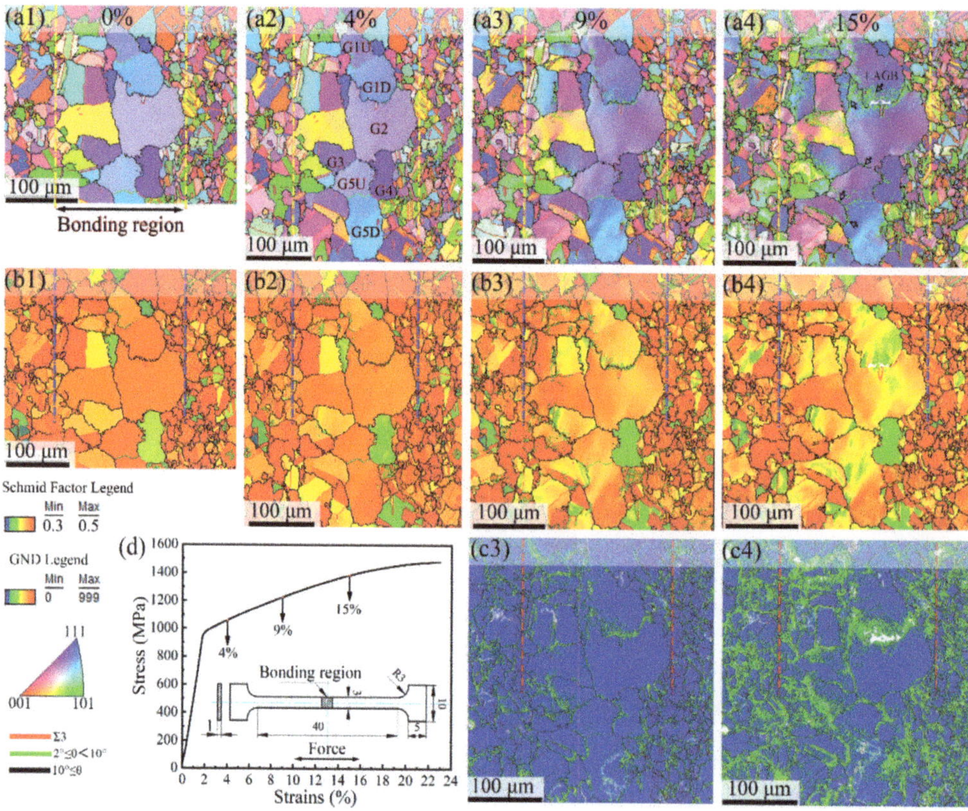

Figure 9. The EBSD patterns evolution of the original joint at different global strains. Orientation image microscopy maps (OIMs) with corresponding inverse polar figure (IPF)//X-axis (the stress direction) (**a1–a4**), Schmid Factor for {111}<11-2> slips systems (**b1–b4**), and GND (**c3**,**c4**), (**d**) the preset engineering strain values for quasi in situ EBSD observation, and the dimensions of the tensile specimen with the stress direction (the inserted figure).

Table 2. The Schmid factors for several abnormal grains in Figure 8 at different global strains.

Global Strain / Slip System / Grain	0%	4%	9%	15%
	{111} <11-2>	{111} <11-2>	{111} <11-2>	{111} <11-2>
G1U	0.45	0.44	0.41~0.45	0.38~0.45
G1D	0.46	0.45	0.41~0.44	0.38~0.42
G2	0.46	0.45	0.42~0.46	0.39~0.45
G3	0.42	0.42	0.38~0.44	0.36~0.44
G4	0.39	0.38	0.36~0.38	0.34~0.38
G5U	0.47	0.46	0.43~0.45	0.39~0.44
G5D	0.47	0.46	0.42~0.46	0.38~0.47

Traditionally, the strength and ductility of alloy often exhibit the opposite behavior, i.e., higher tensile strength with lower ductility or lower tensile strength with higher ductility, which is known as a strength–ductility trade-off [66]. In our case, the bonding joints also obeyed this rule. The original joint with lower strength exhibited a higher elongation and a relative one (116%) because the abundant dislocations can be easily activated and move in the abnormal grains without obstacles, leading to more plastic deformation, while the modified joint with higher strengths showed a lower elongation due to the fact that the much more microscopic plastic strain needed to be accommodated, resulting from the orientation diversity of fine grains with TBs [44]. It is notable that TBs as a low-energy boundary can improve the tensile strength without sacrificing ductility attributed to their coherent nature [36,67], which can block or transmit incoming dislocations, depending on their characterizations, thus providing strength and ductility, respectively [37]. As a result, although the elongation of the modified joint decreased compared with the original one, the relative elongation still reached 95.25%.

Different fracture types, i.e., intergranular or intragranular types, were found in the original and modified joint. It is suggested that the formation of intergranular cracks (IGCs) strongly depends on the interaction of slip bands with HAGBs, i.e., the piling up of dislocation at the HAGBs, and strain incompatibilities caused by a Schmid or Taylor factor mismatch between neighboring grains [68]. When dislocation carried by the slip bands cannot transfer through a HAGB, localized grain boundary sliding occurs and results in intergranular cracking [69]. For the original joint, the HAGBs in the bonding region are the only obstacle to the slips resulting from the absence of TBs, as revealed in Figure 6. Furthermore, the neighboring grains have similar orientations and Schmid factors, leading to the slips not being able to transmit and abundant dislocations piling up at the HAGB, as shown in Figure 7c. Finally, the lattice curvature and stress concentration are attained at HAGB with increasing global strain, and then the grain boundary crack is promoted and propagated due to the deformation incompatibility between adjacent grains [22,70]. The geometric necessary dislocations (GNDs) evolution with increased global strain, shown in Figure 9c, manifested that the GNDs mainly accumulated at the HAGB, while the GND density in the interior of the abnormal grain was kept lower all the way, demonstrating that the lattice curvature or the change in geometric shape mainly developed at the HAGB. Moreover, the LAGB mainly formed around the HAGB with increasing global strain, as shown in Figure 9a, and provides additional support.

In addition to the effect of dislocation piling up at the HAGB on the IGCs, it is also found that IGCs are related to the inclination of the grain boundary plane to the tensile axis and Schmid factors of the grains adjacent to these grain boundaries. The preferential formation of IGCs is along grain boundaries perpendicular to the tensile axis and adjacent to grains with low Schmid factors. The IGCs are then driven by the normal stresses acting on the grain boundaries [68,71]. For the abnormal grains of the original joint, a higher fraction of HAGBs are normal to the tensile stress (X direction) due to the grain shape adjustment during the bonding process; furthermore, the abnormal grains exhibited lower SFs due to the preferred near <111> orientation, as displayed in Figure 9. As a result, parts of the IGCs are caused by normal stress exerted on the grain boundaries when the tensile processes proceed. Figure 10 shows that grain reference (referred to grain average orientation) orientation (GROD) for the selected grains in Figure 9 at 15% global strain. The GRODs in the interior of the grains were smaller than 5° (Figure 10g), suggesting a smaller change in orientations. It is noted that the GROD values at the edges reached the highest for every grain, as presented in Figure 10a–f, indicating that higher local misorientation and local strain incompatibility developed at HAGB, and that these locations act as the source and propagation path for cracks. In conclusion, the original joints exhibit an intergranular fracture type due to the comprehensive effect of grain orientation and size, grain shape, and TBs.

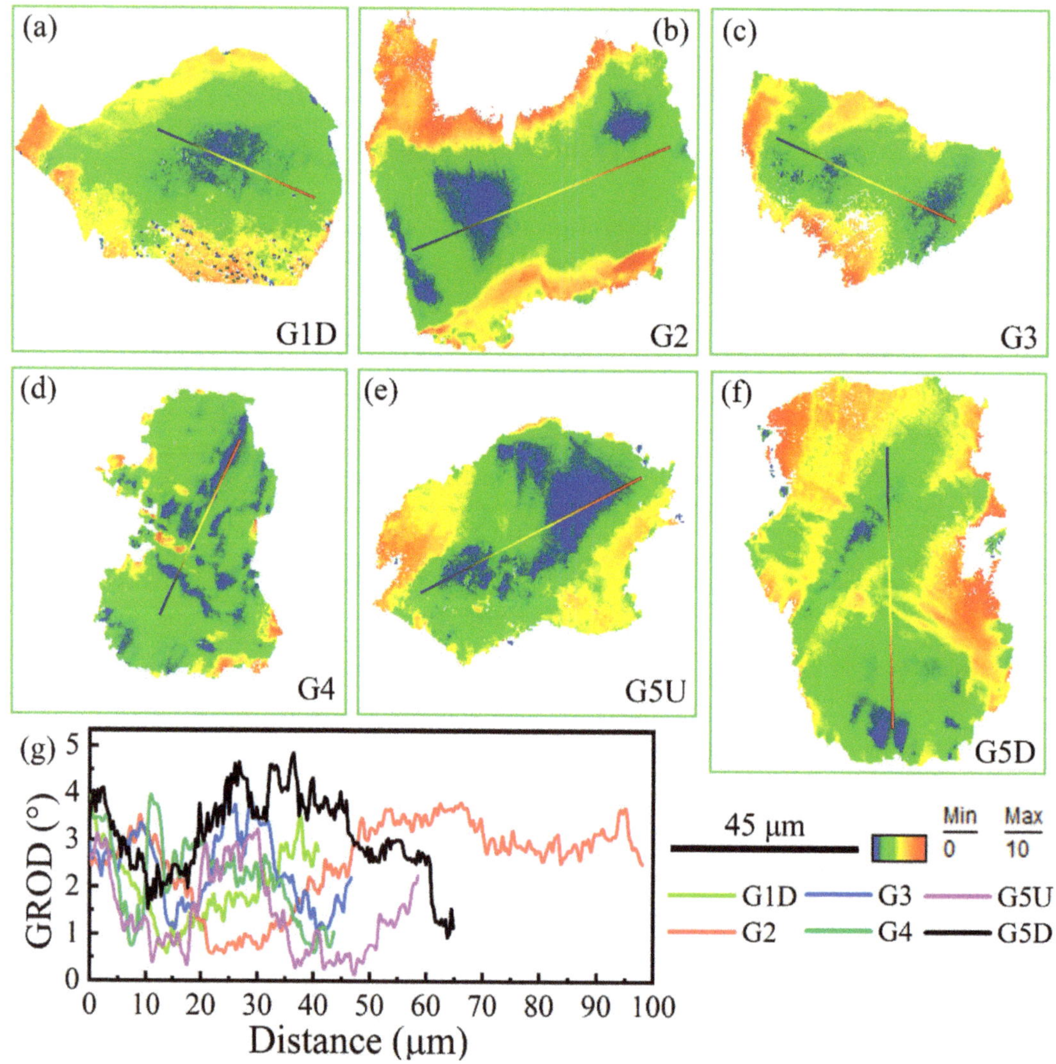

Figure 10. The maps of grain reference (referred to grain average orientation) orientation deviation (GROD) for several grains in Figure 8 at 15% global strain (**a**–**f**), and the orientation deviation profile along specific lines in the interior of the grain (**g**).

After the bonding process was modified, grain orientation diversity and the amount of TBs were introduced to the refined grains in the bonding region. The TBs can either deflect or block crack propagation, which leads to a meandering zigzag propagation path in the interior of the grain [38]. As shown in Figure 4(d2,e2), the twin cleavage planes presented in the fracture surface of BM and the modified joint. More fracture surfaces are created by such a mechanism to dissipate more imposed strain energy, which is helpful to gain better fracture resistance. Due to the strain compatibility between grains with different orientations, and local strain development in the interior of grains under the effect of TBs, new HAGBs are finally formed in the interior of the grains and develop into cracks; finally, the intragranular fracture is developed. This mechanism was detailly explained and discussed in our previous work [44].

Our present work suggests that tailoring newly formed grain size and introducing twin boundaries, along with eliminating the preferred orientation in the bonding region, can be an efficient way to improve the mechanical properties of the bonding joint. Furthermore, integrating TBs and HAGBs could be promising in the development of strong yet ductile bonding joints.

5. Conclusions

The influence of abnormal grains on the mechanical properties of the FGH96 solid-state diffusion bonding joint was investigated by SEM-DIC combined with EBSD. Based on the obtained results, the major conclusions are as follows:

(1) The joint characterized by abnormally large grains with preferred orientation in the bonding region has low relative (ratio to the matrix) yield strength (88.81%) and tensile strength (92.54%), but high relative elongation (116.11%). This is attributed to the easier activated slip systems in the large grains and the absent resistance from the twin boundaries.

(2) The micro-strain, which accumulates at slip bands, escalates in the bonding region with larger grains (2.5 times that of the matrix), leading to failure located at the bonding region. Due to the marginal amount of twin boundaries in this region, the slip systems are mainly retarded by the high-angle grain boundaries, where concentrated stress and lattice curvature would occur, leading to the intergranular fracture

(3) After modifying the welding process, the grains in the bonding region are tailored to be close to that of the matrix, along with twin boundaries forming inside. The tensile and yield strength are increased by 100 MPa and 118 MPa, respectively, and the relative tensile and yield strength reach 98.86% and 99.37%, which results from the effect of fine-grained strengthening and twin boundaries on the micro-strain distribution. Furthermore, the fracture mode changes to the intragranular type.

(4) Tailoring the newborn grain size in the bonding region along with introducing twin boundaries into the grain is an efficient way to improve the mechanical properties of the bonding joint.

Author Contributions: J.Z. formal analysis, software, data curation, investigation, writing—original draft, writing—review and editing; Y.S. methodology, project administration, writing—review and editing, validation; Q.L. methodology, investigation; J.W. methodology, investigation; Y.P. investigation, formal analysis, supervision; S.L. investigation, formal analysis, supervision; S.G. methodology, formal analysis, supervision, funding acquisition, conceptualization, validation. All authors have read and agreed to the published version of the manuscript.

Funding: This research was funded by the National Science and Technology Major Project, China (2017-VI-0016-0088).

Institutional Review Board Statement: Not applicable.

Informed Consent Statement: Not applicable.

Data Availability Statement: Not applicable.

Conflicts of Interest: The authors declare that they have no known competing financial interest or personal relationship that could have appeared to influence the work reported in this paper.

References

1. Peng, Z.; Zou, J.; Wang, X. Microstructural characterization of dislocation movement during creep in powder metallurgy FGH96 superalloy. *Mater. Today Commun.* **2020**, *25*, 101361. [CrossRef]
2. Zhang, C.; Zhang, L.; Li, M.; Shen, W.; Gu, S. Effects of microstructure and γ' distribution on the hot deformation behavior for a powder metallurgy superalloy FGH96. *J. Mater. Res.* **2014**, *29*, 2799–2808. [CrossRef]
3. Qiao, S.; Wang, Y.; Lv, L.; Huang, Z.; Tan, G. Normal and abnormal grain growth in a FGH96 superalloy during thermomechanical treatment. *J. Mater. Res. Technol.* **2021**, *15*, 7033–7049. [CrossRef]
4. Yuli, G.Y.H.S. Thermo-mechanical fatigue behavior of nickel-base powder metallurgy superalloy FGH96 under tension-tension loading. *Acta Metall. Sin. Eng. Lett.* **2010**, *23*, 147–153.
5. Cairo, R.R.; Sargent, K.A. Twin Web Disk-A Step Beyond Convention. *J. Eng. Gas. Turb. Power* **2002**, *124*, 298–302. [CrossRef]
6. Li, L.; Tang, Z.; Li, H.; Gao, W.; Yue, Z.; Xie, G. Convective heat transfer characteristics of twin-web turbine disk with pin fins in the inner cavity. *Int. J. Therm. Sci.* **2020**, *152*, 106303. [CrossRef]
7. Zhang, M.; Yao, Q.; Sun, S.; Li, L.; Hou, X. An efficient strategy for reliability-based multidisciplinary design optimization of twin-web disk with non-probabilistic model. *Appl. Math. Model.* **2020**, *82*, 546–572. [CrossRef]
8. Pouranvari, M.; Ekrami, A.; Kokabi, A. Microstructure evolution mechanism during post-bond heat treatment of transient liquid phase bonded wrought IN718 superalloy: An approach to fabricate boride-free joints. *J. Alloys Compd.* **2017**, *723*, 84–91. [CrossRef]
9. Arhami, F.; Mirsalehi, S.E.; Sadeghian, A.; Johar, M.H. The joint properties of a high-chromium Ni-based superalloy made by diffusion brazing: Microstructural evolution, corrosion resistance and mechanical behavior. *J. Manuf. Process.* **2019**, *37*, 203–211. [CrossRef]
10. Xue, H.; Li, T.; Guo, W.; Chen, C.; Zhao, J.; Ding, Z. Effect of graphite content on microstructure and properties of Al_2O_3 ceramic and 304 stainless steel brazed joints. *Mater. Lett.* **2022**, *307*, 131050. [CrossRef]
11. Xiong, J.; Yuan, L.; Zhu, Y.; Zhang, H.; Li, J. Diffusion bonding of nickel-based superalloy GH4099 with pure nickel interlayer. *J. Mater. Sci.* **2019**, *54*, 6552–6564. [CrossRef]
12. Zhong, Y.; Xie, J.; Chen, Y.; Yin, L.; He, P.; Lu, W. Microstructure and mechanical properties of micro laser welding NiTiNb/Ti6Al4V dissimilar alloys lap joints with nickel interlayer. *Mater. Lett.* **2022**, *306*, 130896. [CrossRef]
13. Xu, X.; Ma, X.; Zhao, G.; Chen, X.; Wang, Y. Abnormal grain growth of 2196 Al-Cu-Li alloy weld seams during extrusion and heat treatment. *J. Alloys Compd.* **2021**, *867*, 159043. [CrossRef]
14. Wei, H.; Tang, J.; Xu, D. Effect of abnormal grain growth on thermoelectric properties of hot-pressed Bi0.5Sb1.5Te3 alloys. *J. Alloys Compd.* **2020**, *817*, 153284. [CrossRef]
15. Baure, G.; Zhou, H.; Chung, C.-C.; Stozhkova, M.A.; Jones, J.L.; Nino, J.C. Grain orientation effects on the ionic conductivity of neodymia doped ceria thin films. *Acta Mater.* **2017**, *133*, 81–89. [CrossRef]
16. Zhang, F.; Zheng, L.; Wang, F.; Zhang, H. Grain orientation dependence of ω phase precipitation in ordered body-centered cubic NiTi based alloys. *Intermetallics* **2019**, *108*, 77–80. [CrossRef]
17. Wang, Y.; Zhang, Y.; Jiang, H. Effect of grain size uniformity and crystallographic orientation on the corrosion behavior of Mg-2Zn-1Al bar. *Mater. Charact.* **2021**, *179*, 111374. [CrossRef]
18. Jeng, Y.; Tsai, P.; Chiang, S. Effects of grain size and orientation on mechanical and tribological characterizations of nanocrystalline nickel films. *Wear* **2013**, *303*, 262–268. [CrossRef]
19. Pushkareva, M.; Sket, F.; Segurado, J.; Llorca, J.; Yandouzi, M.; Weck, A. Effect of grain orientation and local strains on void growth and coalescence in titanium. *Mater. Sci. Eng. A* **2019**, *760*, 258–266. [CrossRef]
20. Zhao, Z.; Wang, Y.; Safaei, B.; Long, H.; Chu, F.; Wei, Y. Orientation effect on intergranular fracture behaviors along symmetrical tilt grain boundaries in bcc iron. *Mater. Today Commun.* **2021**, *29*, 102981. [CrossRef]
21. Blochwitz, C.; Jacob, S.; Tirschler, W. Grain orientation effects on the growth of short fatigue cracks in austenitic stainless steel. *Mater. Sci. Eng. A* **2008**, *496*, 59–66. [CrossRef]
22. Masoumi, M.; Tavares, S.S.M.; Pardal, J.M.; Martins, T.R.B.; da Silva, M.J.G.; de Abreu, H.F.G. The role of microstructure and grain orientations on intergranular cracking susceptibility of UNS 17400 martensitic stainless steel. *Eng. Fail. Anal.* **2017**, *79*, 198–207. [CrossRef]
23. Zhu, Q.; Wang, C.; Qin, H.; Chen, G.; Zhang, P. Effect of the grain size on the microtensile deformation and fracture behaviors of a nickel-based superalloy via EBSD and in-situ synchrotron radiation X-ray tomography. *Mater. Charact.* **2019**, *156*, 109875. [CrossRef]
24. Liu, M.; Gong, W.; Zheng, R.; Li, J.; Zhang, Z.; Gao, S.; Ma, C.; Tsuji, N. Achieving excellent mechanical properties in type 316 stainless steel by tailoring grain size in homogeneously recovered or recrystallized nanostructures. *Acta Mater.* **2022**, *226*, 117629. [CrossRef]
25. Yan, F.; Liu, G.; Tao, N.; Lu, K. Strength and ductility of 316L austenitic stainless steel strengthened by nano-scale twin bundles. *Acta Mater.* **2012**, *60*, 1059–1071. [CrossRef]
26. Wei, K.; Hu, R.; Yin, D.; Xiao, L.; Pang, S.; Cao, Y.; Zhou, H.; Zhao, Y.; Zhu, Y. Grain size effect on tensile properties and slip systems of pure magnesium. *Acta Mater.* **2021**, *206*, 116604. [CrossRef]
27. Gabb, T.P.; Kantzos, P.T.; Palsa, B.; Telesman, J.; Gayda, J.; Sudbrack, C.K. Fatigue failure modes of the grain size transition zone in a dual microstructure disk, the minerals, metals and materials society. In Proceedings of the 12th International Symposium on Superalloys, Seven Springs, PA, USA, 9–13 September 2012; pp. 63–72.

28. Gabb, T.; Kantzos, P.; Telesman, J.; Gayda, J.; Sudbrack, C.; Palsa, B. Fatigue resistance of the grain size transition zone in a dual microstructure superalloy disk. *Int. J. Fatigue* **2011**, *33*, 414–426. [CrossRef]
29. Li, Y.; Wang, L.; Zhang, G.; Zhang, J.; Lou, L. Creep anisotropy of a 3rd generation nickel-base single crystal superalloy at 850 °C. *Mater. Sci. Eng. A* **2019**, *760*, 26–36. [CrossRef]
30. Li, P.; Yao, W.; Jiang, W.; Han, Q.; Huang, J. Orientation-dependent low cycle fatigue performance of nickel-base single crystal superalloy at intermediate temperature range. *Mater. Today Commun.* **2021**, *26*, 101836. [CrossRef]
31. Wang, G.; Zhang, S.; Tian, S.; Tian, N.; Zhao, G.; Yan, H. Microstructure evolution and deformation mechanism of a [111]-oriented nickel-based single-crystal superalloy during high-temperature creep. *J. Mater. Res. Technol.* **2022**, *16*, 495–504. [CrossRef]
32. Li, Y.; Wang, L.; Zhang, G.; Zheng, W.; Qi, D.; Du, K.; Zhang, J.; Lou, L. Creep deformation related to γ' phase cutting at high temperature of a [111] oriented nickel-base single crystal superalloy. *Mater. Sci. Eng. A* **2019**, *763*, 138162. [CrossRef]
33. Gabb, T.P. The Low Cycle Fatigue Deformation Response of a Single-Crystal Superalioy at 650 °C. *Mat. Sci. Eng. A* **1989**, *108*, 189–202. [CrossRef]
34. Miner, R.V.; Gabb, T.P.; Gayda, J.; Hemker, K.J. Orientation and Temperature Dependence of Some Mechanical Properties of the Single-Crystal Nickel-Base Superalloy Ren6 N4: Part II1. Tension-Compression Anisotropy. *Metall. Trans. A* **1986**, *17*, 507–512. [CrossRef]
35. Zhang, S.; Liu, W.; Wan, J.; Misra, R.D.K.; Wang, Q.; Wang, C. The grain size and orientation dependence of geometrically necessary dislocations in polycrystalline aluminum during monotonic deformation: Relationship to mechanical behavior. *Mater. Sci. Eng. A* **2020**, *775*, 138939. [CrossRef]
36. Cooper, R.A.; Wang, Y.; Vignolle, B.; Lipscombe, O.J.; Hayden, S.M.; Tanabe, Y.; Adachi, T.; Koike, Y.; Nohara, M.; Takagi, H.; et al. Revealing the Maximum Strength in Nanotwinned Copper. *Science* **2009**, *323*, 603–607. [CrossRef]
37. Zhang, Z.; Sheng, H.; Wang, Z.; Gludovatz, B.; Zhang, Z.; George, E.; Yu, Q.; Mao, S.X.; Ritchie, R.O. Dislocation mechanisms and 3D twin architectures generate exceptional strength-ductility-toughness combination in CrCoNi medium-entropy alloy. *Nat. Commun.* **2017**, *8*, 14390. [CrossRef] [PubMed]
38. Zhao, S.; Zhang, R.; Yu, Q.; Ell, J.; Ritchie, R.O.; Minor, A.M. Cryoforged nanotwinned titanium with ultrahigh strength and ductility. *Science* **2021**, *373*, 1363–1368. [CrossRef]
39. Li, J.; Zhang, F. A simultaneously improved strength and ductility on medium Mn TRIP steel designed by pre-twinning strategy based on SFE controlling. *Mater. Lett.* **2022**, *316*, 132078. [CrossRef]
40. Wang, B.; Liu, H.; Zhang, Y.; Zhou, B.; Deng, L.; Wang, C.; Chen, J.; Zhang, Y. Effect of grain size on twinning behavior of pure titanium at room temperature. *Mater. Sci. Eng. A* **2021**, *827*, 142060. [CrossRef]
41. Ott, R.; Geng, J.; Besser, M.; Kramer, M.; Wang, Y.; Park, E.; LeSar, R.; King, A. Optimization of strength and ductility in nanotwinned ultra-fine grained Ag: Twin density and grain orientations. *Acta Mater.* **2015**, *96*, 378–389. [CrossRef]
42. Khorrami, M.S.; Saito, N.; Miyashita, Y. Texture and strain-induced abnormal grain growth in cryogenic friction stir processing of severely deformed aluminum alloy. *Mater. Charact.* **2019**, *151*, 378–389. [CrossRef]
43. Novikov, V. Texture development during grain growth in polycrystals with strong preferred orientation. *Acta Mater.* **1999**, *47*, 1935–1943. [CrossRef]
44. Zhang, J.; Shang, Y.; Dong, Y.; Pei, Y.; Li, S.; Gong, S. The crack initiation and strengthening mechanism in FGH96 solid-state diffusion bonding joint by quasi-in-situ SEM-DIC and EBSD. *Mater. Today Commun.* **2022**, *31*, 103689. [CrossRef]
45. Wright, S.I.; Nowell, M.M.; Field, D.P. A Review of Strain Analysis Using Electron Backscatter Diffraction. *Microsc. Microanal.* **2011**, *17*, 316–329. [CrossRef]
46. Malta, P.O.; Alves, D.S.; Ferreira, A.O.V.; Moutinho, I.D.; Dias, C.A.P.; Santos, D.B. Static Recrystallization Kinetics and Crystallographic Texture of Nb-Stabilized Ferritic Stainless Steel Based on Orientation Imaging Microscopy. *Metall. Mater. Trans. A* **2017**, *48*, 1288–1309. [CrossRef]
47. Schuessler, B.J.; Field, D.P.; Overman, N.R.; Joshi, V.V. The Effect of Homogenization Heat Treatment on the Texture Evolution in U-10Mo Alloy. *Metall. Mater. Trans. A* **2021**, *52*, 3871–3879. [CrossRef]
48. Reeve, J.I.; Schuessler, B.J.; Frazier, W.E.; Field, D.P.; Joshi, V.V. The role of second phase particles and grain boundaries on recrystallization: Quasi-in situ experiments and modeling in U-10Mo alloy system. *J. Nucl. Mater.* **2022**, *559*, 153445. [CrossRef]
49. McCarley, J.; Tin, S. Understanding the effects of recrystallization and strain induced boundary migration on $\Sigma 3$ twin boundary formation in Ni-base superalloys during iterative sub-solvus annealing. *Mater. Sci. Eng. A* **2019**, *740–741*, 427–438. [CrossRef]
50. Chen, Z.; Liu, F.; Wang, H.; Yang, W.; Yang, G.; Zhou, Y. A thermokinetic description for grain growth in nanocrystalline materials. *Acta Mater.* **2009**, *57*, 1466–1475. [CrossRef]
51. Brons, J.; Thompson, G. A comparison of grain boundary evolution during grain growth in fcc metals. *Acta Mater.* **2013**, *61*, 3936–3944. [CrossRef]
52. Gao, Q.; Jiang, X.; Sun, H.; Song, T.; Mo, D.; Li, X. Interfacial reaction and microstructure investigation of 4J36/Ni/Cu/V/TC4 diffusion-bonded joints. *Mater. Lett.* **2021**, *305*, 130809. [CrossRef]
53. Humphreys, F.J.; Hatherly, M. *Recrystallization and Related Annealing Phenomena*, 2nd ed.; Elsevier: Pergamon, Turkey, 2004. Available online: https://www.elsevier.com/books/recrystallization-and-related-annealing-phenomena/rollett/978-0-08-044164-1 (accessed on 22 June 2022).
54. Gottstein, B.; Shvindlerman, L.S. *Grain Boundary Migragation in Metals: Thermodynamics, Kinetics, Applications*, 2nd ed.; CRC Press: Boca Raton, FL, USA, 2009.

55. Zhang, J.-M.; Zhang, Y.; Xu, K.-W. Dependence of stresses and strain energies on grain orientations in FCC metal films. *J. Cryst. Growth* **2005**, *285*, 427–435. [CrossRef]
56. Barrios, A.; Zhang, Y.; Maeder, X.; Castelluccio, G.; Pierron, O.; Zhu, T. Abnormal grain growth in ultrafine grained Ni under high-cycle loading. *Scr. Mater.* **2022**, *209*, 114372. [CrossRef]
57. Jin, Y.; Lin, B.; Bernacki, M.; Rohrer, G.; Rollett, A.; Bozzolo, N. Annealing twin development during recrystallization and grain growth in pure nickel. *Mater. Sci. Eng. A* **2014**, *597*, 295–303. [CrossRef]
58. Chen, X.-M.; Lin, Y.; Wu, F. EBSD study of grain growth behavior and annealing twin evolution after full recrystallization in a nickel-based superalloy. *J. Alloys Compd.* **2017**, *724*, 198–207. [CrossRef]
59. Dennis, J.; Bate, P.S.; Humphreys, F.J. Abnormal grain growth in Al–3.5Cu. *Acta Mater.* **2009**, *57*, 4539–4547. [CrossRef]
60. Sun, Y.; Fujii, H. Effect of abnormal grain growth on microstructure and mechanical properties of friction stir welded SPCC steel plates. *Mater. Sci. Eng. A* **2017**, *694*, 81–92. [CrossRef]
61. Wang, X.; Guan, D. The evolution of coarse grains and its effects on weakened basal texture during annealing of a cold-rolled magnesium AZ31B alloy. *J. Magnes. Alloy.* **2022**, *10*, 1235–1241. [CrossRef]
62. Balasubramanian, N.; Langdon, T.G. The Strength–Grain Size Relationship in Ultrafine-Grained Metals. *Metall. Mater. Trans. A* **2016**, *47*, 5827–5838. [CrossRef]
63. Mock, F. Laws for Work-Hardening and Low- Temperature Creep. *J. Eng. Mater. T ASME* **1976**, *98*, 76–85.
64. Kvashin, N.; Anento, N.; Terentyev, D.; Serra, A. {111} tilt grain boundaries as barriers for slip transfer in bcc Fe. *Comp. Mater. Sci.* **2022**, *203*, 111044. [CrossRef]
65. Yang, W.-P.; Li, J.-R.; Liu, S.-Z.; Shi, Z.-X.; Zhao, J.-Q.; Wang, X.-G. Orientation dependence of transverse tensile properties of nickel-based third generation single crystal superalloy DD9 from 760 to 1100 °C. *Trans. Nonferrous Met. Soc. China* **2019**, *29*, 558–568. [CrossRef]
66. Wang, Y.M.; Voisin, T.; McKeown, J.T.; Ye, J.; Calta, N.P.; Li, Z.; Zeng, Z.; Zhang, Y.; Chen, W.; Roehling, T.T.; et al. Additively manufactured hierarchical stainless steels with high strength and ductility. *Nat. Mater.* **2018**, *17*, 63–71. [CrossRef]
67. Huang, Q.; Yu, D.; Xu, B.; Hu, W.; Ma, Y.; Wang, Y.; Zhao, Z.; Wen, B.; He, J.; Liu, Z.; et al. Nanotwinned diamond with unprecedented hardness and stability. *Nature* **2014**, *510*, 250–253. [CrossRef]
68. West, E.; Was, G. Strain incompatibilities and their role in intergranular cracking of irradiated 316L stainless steel. *J. Nucl. Mater.* **2013**, *441*, 623–632. [CrossRef]
69. Zhang, Z.; Wang, Z. Dependence of intergranular fatigue cracking on the interactions of persistent slip bands with grain boundaries. *Acta Mater.* **2003**, *51*, 347–364. [CrossRef]
70. Jamali, A.; Ma, A.; LLorca, J. Influence of grain size and grain boundary misorientation on the fatigue crack initiation mechanisms of textured AZ31 Mg alloy. *Scr. Mater.* **2022**, *207*, 114304. [CrossRef]
71. West, E.; Was, G. A model for the normal stress dependence of intergranular cracking of irradiated 316L stainless steel in supercritical water. *J. Nucl. Mater.* **2011**, *408*, 142–152. [CrossRef]

crystals

MDPI

Article

Microscopic Phase-Field Simulation of γ' Precipitation in Ni-Based Binary Alloys Coupled with CALPHAD Method

Zhenzhi Liu [1], Yan Zhao [1,*], Xuyu Zhang [1], Xiao-Gang Lu [1], Chuanjun Wang [2] and Yu Zhang [2]

1 School of Materials Science and Engineering, Shanghai University, Shanghai 200444, China; liuzhenzhi@shu.edu.cn (Z.L.); zhangxuyu@shu.edu.cn (X.Z.); xglu@shu.edu.cn (X.-G.L.)
2 Ansteel Beijing Research Institute, Beijing 102211, China; wangchuanjun@aliyun.com (C.W.); zhangyu@aliyun.com (Y.Z.)
* Correspondence: zhaoyan8626@shu.edu.cn

Abstract: In the present work, the first (1st) and second (2nd) nearest-neighbor interaction energies are calculated by coupling the microscopic phase-field kinetic model with the calculation of phase diagrams (CALPHAD) method. The morphological evolution of the γ' precipitate and the variation of its atomic ordering parameter for Ni–X (X = Al, Fe, Mn, Pt, or Si) alloys during aging are studied. The simulation results predict different occupation preferences for solute and solvent atoms in the γ' phase, i.e., solute atoms are inclined to occupy the corner sites and solvent atoms tend to occupy the face sites. In order to understand the precipitation process of the γ' phase systematically, the ordering and clustering behaviors of solute atoms are analyzed.

Keywords: microscopic phase-field kinetic model; CALPHAD; ordering behaviors; γ' precipitates

1. Introduction

The excellent mechanical properties of Ni-based superalloys, which are due to the precipitation hardening effect by γ' precipitates, have attracted considerable interest in the aerospace industry [1–3]. The coherently precipitated γ' (ordered Ni_3X, $L1_2$-type structure) from the disordered γ (face-centered cubic structure) matrix reduces dislocation motion [4]. Since the ordering and clustering processes in Ni-based alloys occur for a very short time during precipitation [5], it is not enough to obtain effective information only from experiments using methods such as transmission electron microscopy (TEM) and powder X-ray diffraction (XRD) [6]. Multi-scale simulation methods have been widely used to study the microstructures and mechanical behaviors of superalloys [7–9]. Mesoscale phase-field simulations are useful for describing the co-evolution of massive-phase microstructures and dislocations, while molecular dynamics and microscopic phase-field methods are useful for studying mechanisms which require individual-atom resolution. Compared with molecular dynamics, the microscopic phase-field method has advantages in obtaining the lattice occupation information based on reliable interatomic interaction energies [10]. The microscopic phase-field kinetic model was first proposed by Khachaturyan [11], based on the Önsager-type microscopic diffusion equations. Then, it was employed to simulate the precipitation morphological evolution, including the strain-induced morphological transformation of coherent precipitates [12], the precipitation mechanism in the ternary Ni–Al–V alloy [13], and the early precipitation of the $\delta'(Al_3Li)$ ordered phase [14]. In these studies, the atomic configurations and the morphologies of the alloys were described by single-site occupation probability functions $P_\alpha(r,t)$, which represent the probabilities of finding an atom α on a given lattice site r at a given time t. The initial state corresponds to the homogenous disordered phase described by $P_\alpha(r,t) = c_\alpha$, where c_α is the overall concentration. When the homogenous phase is quenched to a lower temperature, it becomes unstable with respect to atomic ordering or clustering, depending on the interatomic interaction energies in the system [15].

When simulating the ordering and clustering process in Ni-based superalloys, one difficulty in coupling the phase-field and calculation of phase diagrams (CALPHAD) methods [16] is the complexity of deriving the interatomic interaction energy, especially in multicomponent systems. Meanwhile, for the extension to multicomponent systems, the interaction energies of high components must be optimally obtained from low components; therefore, the interaction energy is a key factor that determines the simulation accuracy. To date, efforts to calculate interaction energies have focused primarily on atomic intercalation [17] and first-principles calculations [18]. However, the key challenge is to obtain the interaction energy change with temperature and to study the ordering behavior at high temperature. In order to deal with such problems, a coupling method for the microscopic phase-field method and the CALPHAD method is developed, which has the potential to be extended for multicomponent systems.

In the present study, the first (1st) and second (2nd) nearest-neighbor interaction energies at different temperatures are calculated, based on thermodynamic data obtained by the CALPHAD method, and the early stage of the γ' precipitation process is simulated. The coupling method is applied to predict different occupation probabilities between solute and solvent atoms in the γ' phase in Ni–X (X denotes the solute atom: Al, Fe, Mn, Pt, or Si) alloys. In addition, the ordering and clustering behaviors of the solute atoms are studied systematically, which enables understanding of the precipitation mechanism of the γ' phase. For simplicity, the effect of the elastic strain energy on the two-phase morphology is ignored.

2. Methodology

2.1. Concentration Wave Representation in γ Solid Solution

In order to deal with the order–disorder transition, a description of atomic occupancy probability is introduced. In this case, the function $n(r)$, which determines the solute atom distribution in an ordered phase, can be expanded into a Fourier series, i.e., expressed as a superposition of static concentration waves. Considering a binary Ni–X (X = Al, Fe, Mn, Pt, or Si) system, the occupancy probability of solute atoms on the lattice site of Ni_3X is [2]:

$$n(r) = c + \left(\eta_1 e^{i2\pi a_1^* r} + \eta_2 e^{i2\pi a_2^* r} + \eta_3 e^{i2\pi a_3^* r}\right) \quad (1)$$

or

$$n(x,y,z) = c + \left(\eta_1 e^{i2\pi x} + \eta_2 e^{i2\pi y} + \eta_3 e^{i2\pi z}\right) \quad (2)$$

where η_1, η_2, and η_3 are the long-range-order parameters that represent the amplitudes of the corresponding concentration waves $e^{i2\pi x}$, $e^{i2\pi y}$, and $e^{i2\pi z}$ and c is the solute concentration. There are different values for different lattice sites in the γ phase, i.e., $n_1 = c + 3\eta_1/4$ for all corners and $n_2 = c - \eta_1/4$ for all face centers. In addition, a_1^*, a_2^*, and a_3^* denote the reciprocal lattice vectors of the lattice sites along the [100], [010], and [001] directions, respectively, and $|a_1^*| = |a_2^*| = |a_3^*| = 1/a_0$, where a_0 is the lattice parameter.

2.2. Helmholtz Free Energy

The Helmholtz free energy of a system based on the mean-field approximation [19–21] can be written as:

$$F(T,c,\eta) = \frac{1}{2\left[V_{\alpha\beta}(0) + 3V_{\alpha\beta}(k_1)\eta^2\right]c^2} + \left(\frac{k_B T}{4}\right)\left\{\begin{array}{c} c(1+3\eta)ln(c(1+3\eta))+ \\ [1-c(1+3\eta)]ln[1-c(1+3\eta)]+ \\ 3c(1-\eta)ln(c(1-\eta))+ \\ 3[1-c(1-\eta)]ln[1-c(1-\eta)] \end{array}\right\} \quad (3)$$

where k_B is the Boltzmann constant, k_1 is the wave vector in the <100> direction, and $V_{\alpha\beta}(0)$ and $V_{\alpha\beta}(k_1)$ are the Fourier transforms of the interaction energy between solute atoms at $k = 0$ and $k = k_1$, respectively. The interaction energy in γ lattice sites is given by:

$$V_{\alpha\beta} = 4V_{\alpha\beta}^1(cos\pi h \cdot cos\pi k + cos\pi h \cdot cos\pi l + cos\pi l \cdot cos\pi k) + 2V_{\alpha\beta}^2(cos2\pi h + cos2\pi l + cos2\pi k) \quad (4)$$

where $V_{\alpha\beta}^1$ and $V_{\alpha\beta}^2$ are the 1st and 2nd nearest-neighbor interaction energies and h, k, and l relate to the reciprocal lattice:

$$k = (k_x, k_y, k_z) = 2\pi(ha_1^* + ka_2^* + la_3^*) \tag{5}$$

For the γ and γ' phases in Ni–X (X = Al, Fe, Mn, Pt, or Si) binary systems, the 1st and 2nd nearest-neighbor interaction energies ($V_{\alpha\beta}^1$ and $V_{\alpha\beta}^2$) are much larger than other parameters, and $V_{\alpha\beta}(0)$ and $V_{\alpha\beta}(k_1)$ can be described by:

$$V_{\alpha\beta}(0) = 12V_{\alpha\beta}^1 + 6V_{\alpha\beta}^2 \tag{6}$$

$$V_{\alpha\beta}(k_1) = -4V_{\alpha\beta}^1 + 6V_{\alpha\beta}^2$$

2.3. Order Parameter

The value of the order parameter η in Equation (3) should minimize the free energy of the system:

$$\frac{4c\eta|V_{\alpha\beta}(k_1)|}{k_B T} = ln\left\{\frac{(1+3\eta)[1-c(1-\eta)]}{(1-\eta)[1-c(1+3\eta)]}\right\} \tag{7}$$

where η is a function of temperature T. There is no analytical solution for this equation; it must be solved numerically. For a given T, the γ and γ' phases become stable at concentrations c_γ and $c_{\gamma'}$, respectively. The equilibrium concentrations c_γ and $c_{\gamma'}$ are determined by the common tangent:

$$\left[\frac{\partial f_\gamma}{\partial c_\gamma}\right]_T = \left[\frac{\partial f_{\gamma'}}{\partial c_{\gamma'}}\right]_T \tag{8}$$

Therefore, the relationship between the equilibrium concentrations and the nearest-neighbor interaction energies can be expressed as:

$$V_{\alpha\beta}(0)c_\gamma + 3\eta^2 V_{\alpha\beta}(k)c_{\gamma'} + \left(\frac{k_B T}{4}\right)\cdot\left\{\begin{array}{l}(1+3\eta)\,ln\left\{\frac{c_{\gamma'}(1+3\eta)}{[1-c_{\gamma'}(1+3\eta)]}\right\}\\ +3(1-\eta)\cdot ln\left\{\frac{c_{\gamma'}(1-\eta)}{[1-c_{\gamma'}(1-\eta)]}\right\}\end{array}\right\} - V_{\alpha\beta}(0)c_\gamma - k_B T\cdot ln\left[\frac{c_\gamma}{(1-c_\gamma)}\right] = 0 \tag{9}$$

2.4. Coupling with CALPHAD to Calculate Interaction Energies

The phase diagram of the binary Ni–Al system can be calculated using the Thermo-Calc software (Version 2015a. Created by Sundman, Jansson, Ågren et al. Royal Institute of Technology (KTH), Stockholm, Sweden) [22] with TCNI7, as shown in Figure 1. According to the phase diagram, for given temperatures T_1 and T_2, the equilibrium concentrations c_1^γ and c_2^γ of the γ phase and $c_1^{\gamma'}$ and $c_2^{\gamma'}$ of the γ' phase tie-lines can be obtained, respectively. Then the values of $V_{\alpha\beta}(0)$, $V_{\alpha\beta}(k)$, and η can be determined using Equation (9).

2.5. Kinetic Equations

Since for a binary alloy system the sum of the occupation probabilities is unity, i.e., $P_A(r,t) + P_B(r,t) = 1.0$, only one equation is independent for each lattice site [23]:

$$\frac{dP(r,t)}{dt} = \frac{c_0(1-c_0)}{k_B T}\sum_{r'} L(r-r')\frac{\partial F}{\partial P(r',t)} + \xi(r,t) \tag{10}$$

where $L(r-r')$ is the probability of elementary diffusion jumps from r to r'. F is the Helmholtz free energy. A Langevin noise term $\xi(r,t)$ that satisfies the fluctuation–dissipation theorem is added, to introduce nucleation.

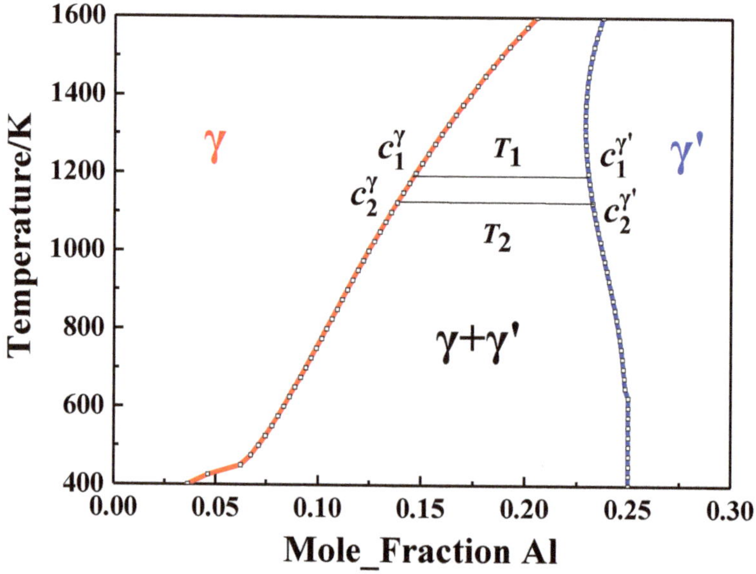

Figure 1. The Ni–Al partial binary phase diagram.

There are three assumptions in this methodology description. Firstly, a 3D crystal structure (fcc) is replaced by a 2D projection, and the influence on the lattice constants during the ordering transition can be taken into account. Secondly, the 1st and 2nd interaction energies in Equations (3) and (4) are used to approximate the intersection on the phase diagram, and the higher-order interactions are ignored. Thirdly, for simplicity, the lattice diffusion coefficient with respect to the kinetic parameter L is not considered in Equation (10).

3. Simulation Results and Discussion

3.1. 1st and 2nd Nearest-Neighbor Interaction Energies

The 1st and 2nd nearest-neighbor interaction energies ($V_{\alpha\beta}^1$ and $V_{\alpha\beta}^2$) of the Ni–X (X = Al, Fe, Mn, Pt, or Si) alloy are shown in Figure 2. It is obvious that $V_{\alpha\beta}^1$ and $V_{\alpha\beta}^2$ increase with temperature in the Ni–Al alloy, while showing the opposite trend in the Ni–Mn alloy. There is a small fluctuation in the $V_{\alpha\beta}^2$ curve of the Ni–Fe alloy between 620 K and 720 K. In the Ni–Pt alloy, as the temperature increases, $V_{\alpha\beta}^1$ and $V_{\alpha\beta}^2$ first increase and then decrease, with maxima at about 85 meV/atom for $V_{\alpha\beta}^1$ and −12 meV/atom for $V_{\alpha\beta}^2$ at 612 K. For the Ni–Si alloy, $V_{\alpha\beta}^1$ and $V_{\alpha\beta}^2$ are stable at lower temperatures then grow rapidly above 1000 K.

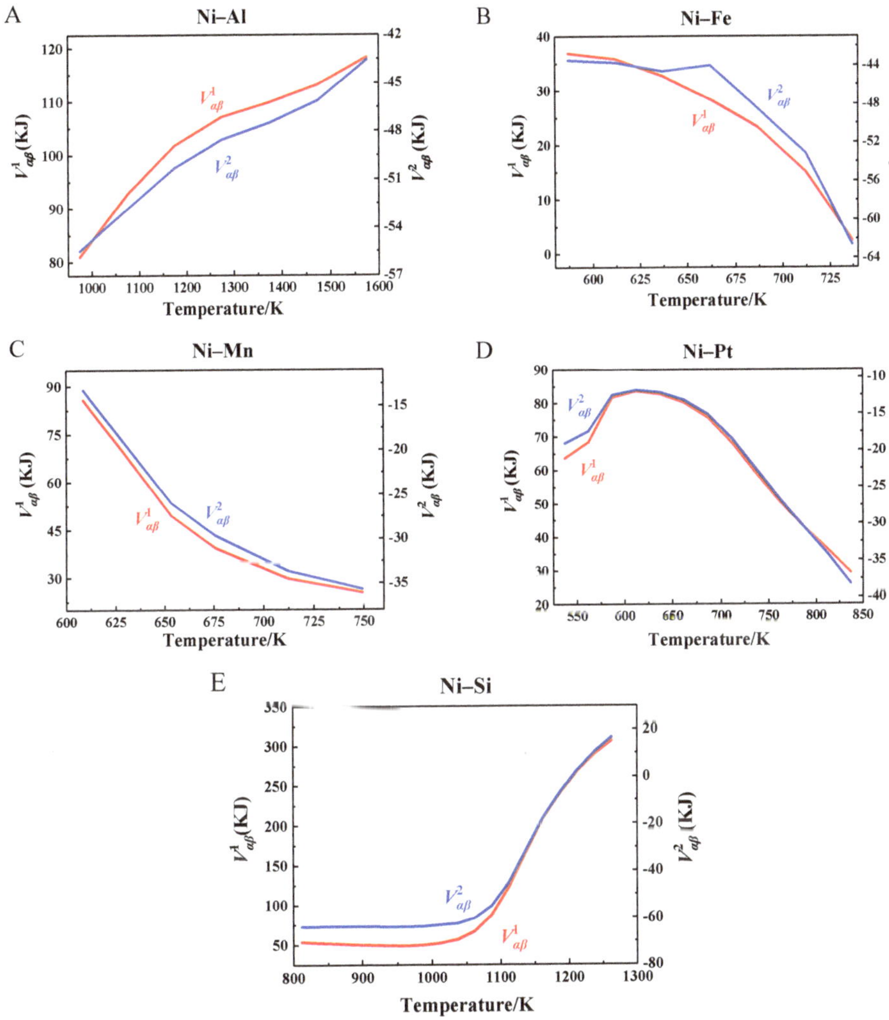

Figure 2. The 1st and 2nd nearest-neighbor interaction energies ($V^1_{\alpha\beta}$ and $V^2_{\alpha\beta}$) for: (**A**) Ni–Al; (**B**) Ni–Fe; (**C**) Ni–Mn; (**D**) Ni–Pt; (**E**) Ni–Si.

3.2. Morphological Evolution of γ' Precipitates

Although it is straightforward and desirable to perform three-dimensional (3D) simulations using the microscopic diffusion equations, a two-dimensional (2D) simulation is much less computationally intensive. In addition, its visualization and the analysis of the atomic configuration are much easier. Thus, all the results obtained in the present paper are reported using a 2D projection of a 3D system. This is equivalent to assuming that the occupation probabilities do not depend on the coordinate z along the [001] axis [12]. The γ' domain can be identified by the solute atoms arranged in lattice sites, which is consistent with the projection of the γ' phase, as shown in Figure 3.

This study focuses on the kinetic simulation of atomic ordering during the annealing process of the γ phase. The initial concentration of solute atoms in the alloy is $c_0 = 0.175$ atomic fraction, located in the equilibrium two-phase region, and the initial γ phase is generated by assigning the average concentration to an occupation probability function at each lattice site. The simulated supercell consists of 128 × 128 unit cells on the projected 2D square lattice, and the time step is 0.02. The color displayed in the simulation results is consistent with the occupancy probability. Thus, if the occupancy probability of a solute atom in any position is 1.0, then the position will be displayed as white; otherwise, it will be assigned the color blue, and so on.

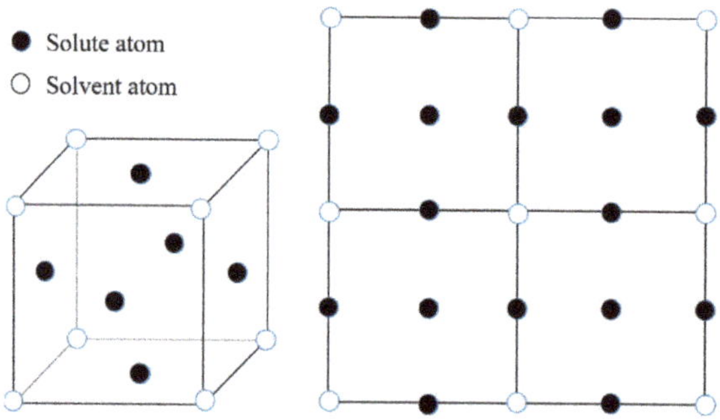

Figure 3. The γ'-phase structure and its projections.

Figure 4 shows the morphological evolution of the Ni–Al, Ni–Fe, Ni–Mn, Ni–Pt, and Ni–Si alloys versus time t^* (t^* is defined as $t/\Delta t$, where t is the simulation time and Δt is the time step) at 1574 K, 686 K, 618 K, 638 K, and 1162 K, respectively. In the initial aging stage, the atomic ordering process of the γ phase leads to atomic redistribution. As the segregation of solute atoms in the γ phase occurs, the γ' phase begins to precipitate from the matrix γ phase in a circular random distribution, as shown in Figure 4A1–E1, A2–E2. The interface between the γ and γ' domains is decentralized. Furthermore, the morphologies shown in Figure 4A3–E3 illustrate the process of γ'-particle growth, where the small γ' particles gradually merge with each other and grow, resulting in irregular shapes. Finally, the two-phase equilibrium of coexisting $\gamma + \gamma'$ is established, as shown in Figure 4A4–E4.

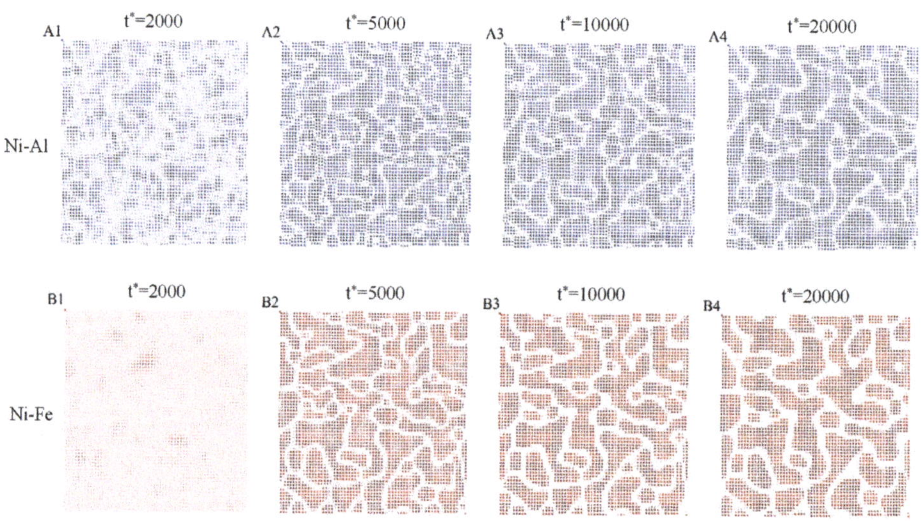

Figure 4. *Cont.*

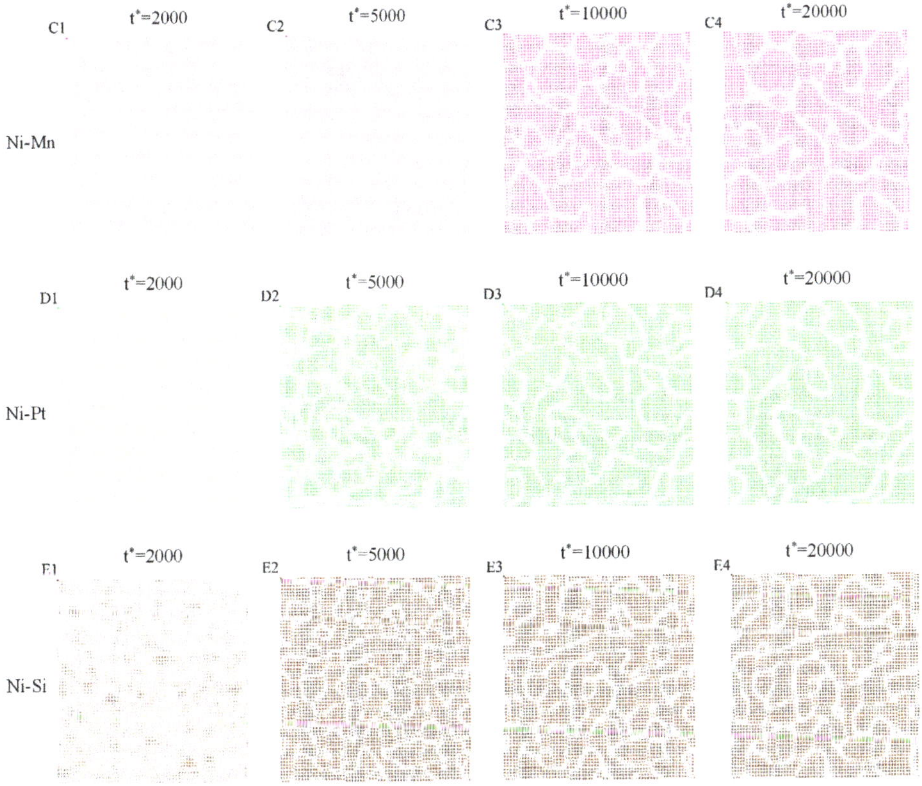

Figure 4. Microstructural evolution at simulation time t^* = 2000, 5000, 10,000, and 20,000 for: Ni–Al at 1574 K (**A1–A4**); Ni–Fe at 686 K (**B1–B4**); Ni–Mn at 618 K (**C1–C4**); Ni–Pt at 638 K (**D1–D4**); Ni–Si at 1162 K (**E1–E4**).

The process of solute-atom migration can be illustrated by the evolution of the solute concentration, as shown in Figure 5. In Figure 5, the horizontal axis ("Distance") denotes the length of a 1D line region assigned in the 2D images. The distribution of solute concentration in the line region evolves as the ordering proceeds. It can be observed that the solute atoms are enriched in the γ' phase and sparsely distributed in the γ phase boundary. The curves of solute concentration begin with a bulge, then gradually become stable. Finally, the uppermost domain is widened until the final equilibrium is established, which corresponds to the coarsening process.

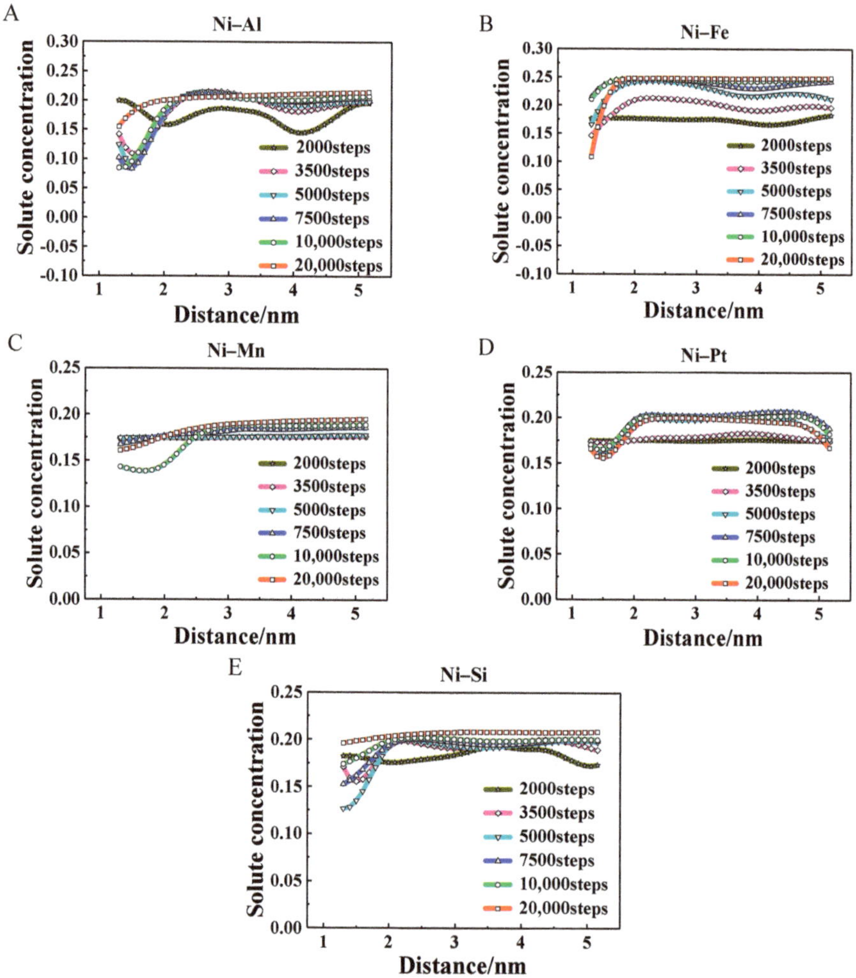

Figure 5. Variations of the solute concentration with distance for: (**A**) Ni–Al; (**B**) Ni–Fe; (**C**) Ni–Mn; (**D**) Ni–Pt; (**E**) Ni–Si.

3.3. *Evolution of Atomic Occupation*

Since it is difficult to quantitatively observe the occupancy probabilities of solute atoms in experiments, incorporating the sublattice models in CALPHAD has become an essential technique. Based on the equilibrium calculation, the sublattice models can present the lattice occupation, and the occupancy probabilities of solute atoms at corner and face sites as a function of aging time are predicted, as shown in Figure 6. At the beginning, there is no significant change in solute concentration in the incubation period, then the solute atoms tend to occupy corner sites, contributing to the ordering process of the alloys. In contrast, the solute concentration at face sites is almost zero, as these sites are occupied by the solvent atom Ni. Eventually, the solute concentration reaches the equilibrium value; the value for Al, Mn, Pt, and Si atoms is close to 0.8, while that for Fe atoms is close to 1.0.

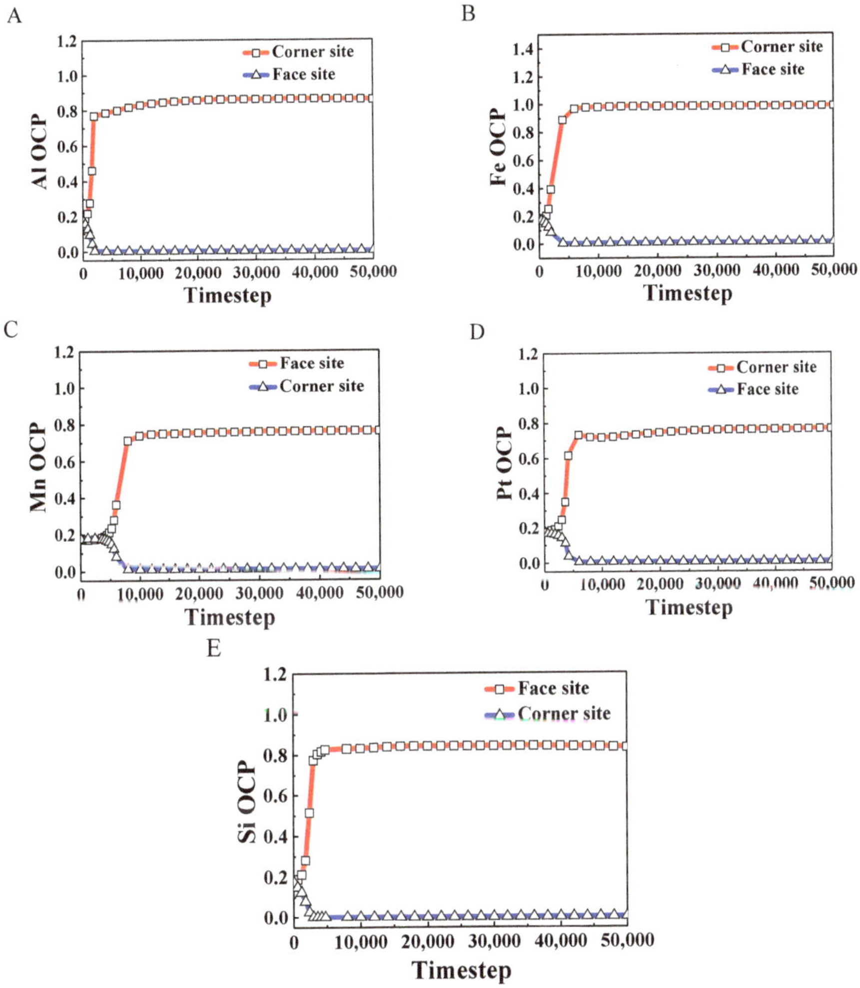

Figure 6. Occupancy probabilities (OCP) of solute atoms for: (**A**) Al; (**B**) Fe; (**C**) Mn; (**D**) Pt; (**E**) Si at corner and face sites as a function of timestep.

3.4. Evolution of Long-Range-Order Parameter and Solute Concentration

In order to study the precipitation mechanism of the γ' phase, the long-range-order parameter η_u is introduced [24]:

$$\eta_u(i,j) = 1 - \frac{\overline{P_u^{\alpha}}(i,j)}{\overline{P_u}(i,j)} \tag{11}$$

This describes the ordering degree with respect to the order parameter. Here, $\overline{P_u^{\alpha}}(i,j)$ and $\overline{P_u}(i,j)$ are the average occupation probabilities of the alloy element in the α site (face site) and in the unit cell u (including corner and face sites), respectively. When $\eta_u(i,j) = 1$, this means that alloy atoms are distributed equally at the lattice site (i,j) and around it. When $\eta_u(i,j) = 0$ or $\overline{P_u^{\alpha}}(i,j) = 0$, this means that alloy atoms in the unit cell occupy corner sites only, so that the lattice is in a completely ordered state. The temporal evolutions of the long-range parameter and the solute concentration are shown in Figure 7. There are two stages during aging. Firstly, corresponding to the transitional ordering stage, the long-rang-order parameter and the solute concentration rise rapidly, indicating that the disorder–order transition occurs over time. Then the two-phase equilibrium is established, and the long-range-order parameter remains stable. From Figure 7, it can be observed that the long-range-order parameter reaches a steady state earlier than the solute concentration in all alloys, which indicates that the ordering event of the order parameter occurs first and is completed within 10,000 timesteps. Interestingly, there is a bump in the solute concentration during the early stages. This indicates that the solute concentration decreases slightly during coarsening, then increases to a steady value through uphill diffusion. Finally, when the solute concentration reaches an equilibrium value, the stoichiometric Ni_3X (X = Al, Fe, Mn, Pt, or Si) precipitates are formed, which corresponds to the migration of solute atoms from the γ boundary to the γ' phase. Compared to other alloys, the clustering behavior of solute atoms in the Ni–Mn alloy (Figure 7C) lags significantly behind the order parameter, which reveals that the γ' precipitates formed in the early stage are supersaturated and unstable, resulting in the solute atom Mn migrating from the γ' phase to the boundary.

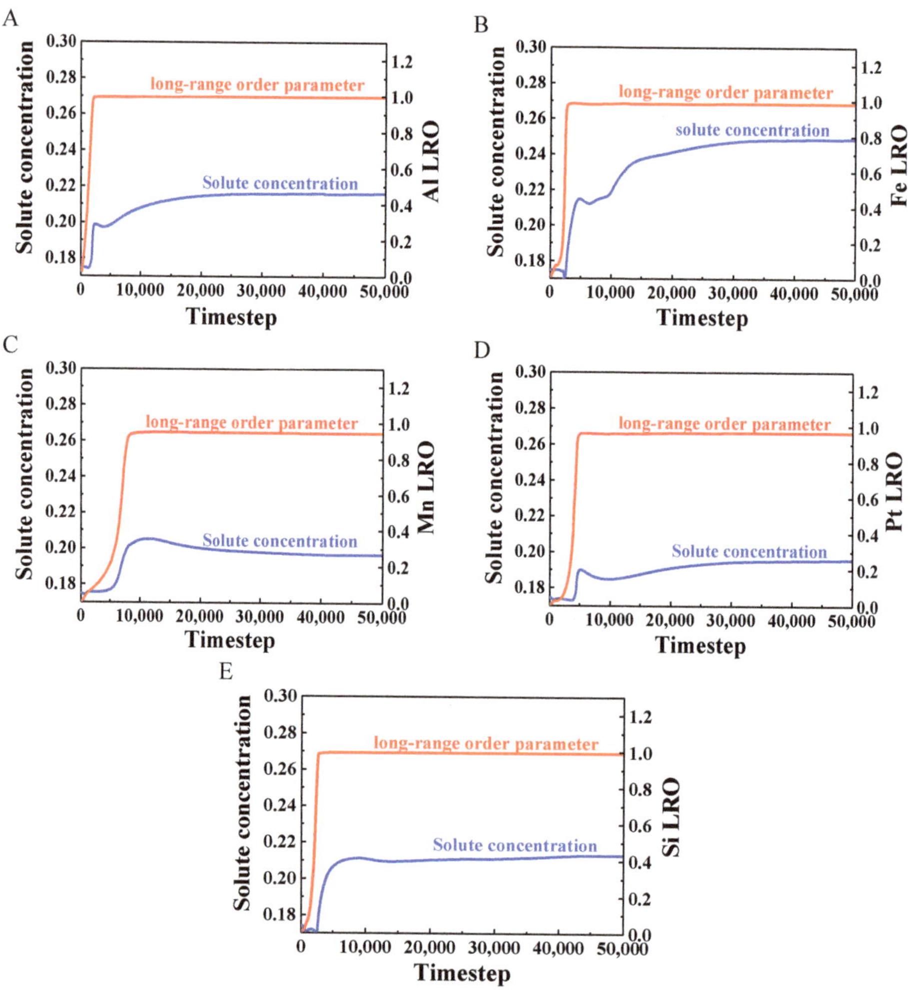

Figure 7. The temporal evolution of long-range-order parameter and solute concentration for: (**A**) Ni–Al; (**B**) Ni–Fe; (**C**) Ni–Mn; (**D**) Ni–Pt; (**E**) Ni–Si.

4. Conclusions

The microscopic phase-field kinetic model was used to simulate γ' precipitation from the γ matrix phase, and the first and second nearest-neighbor interaction energies were successfully obtained by employing the CALPHAD method. The following conclusions are drawn from this work:

1. There were different trends for the first and second nearest-neighbor interaction energies ($V^1_{\alpha\beta}$ and $V^2_{\alpha\beta}$) in Ni–X (X = Al, Fe, Mn, Pt, or Si) alloys. The $V^1_{\alpha\beta}$ and $V^2_{\alpha\beta}$ values increased with temperature in the Ni–Al and Ni–Si alloys, while the opposite trend was seen in the Ni–Fe and Ni–Mn alloys. In the Ni–Pt alloy, the interaction energies first increased, with maxima at about 85 meV/atom for $V^1_{\alpha\beta}$ and -12 meV/atom for $V^2_{\alpha\beta}$ at 612 K, and then decreased with temperature.
2. The morphological evolutions of the Ni–X alloys were simulated. The atomic ordering contributed to the γ'-phase precipitation from the γ phase, and the segregation and aggregation behavior of solute atoms in the γ phase greatly influenced the coarsening and growth process of the γ' phase.
3. The different occupation probabilities between solute and solvent atoms in the γ' precipitates were predicted in the binary alloys. The solute atoms tend to occupy corner sites and the solvent atoms prefer to occupy the face sites. The equilibrium occupation probability values of Al, Mn, Pt, and Si atoms were close to 0.8, while the value for Fe atoms was close to 1.0.
4. The temporal evolutions of the long-range parameter and the solute concentration were simulated to study the precipitation mechanism of the γ' phase. The results showed that the long-range-order parameter (nearly 5000 timesteps) reached a steady state before the solute concentration (nearly 10,000 timesteps) in all alloys, and the clustering behavior revealed the migration of solute atoms during the precipitation process.

Author Contributions: Conceptualization, Y.Z. (Yan Zhao); methodology, Y.Z. (Yan Zhao) and X.-G.L.; writing—original draft preparation, Z.L. and X.Z.; writing—review and editing, Y.Z. (Yan Zhao); X.-G.L., C.W., and Y.Z. (Yu Zhang). All authors have read and agreed to the published version of the manuscript.

Funding: This research received no external funding.

Institutional Review Board Statement: Not applicable.

Informed Consent Statement: Not applicable.

Data Availability Statement: Not applicable.

Conflicts of Interest: The authors declare no conflict of interest.

References

1. Soga, W.; Kaneno, Y.; Takasugi, T. Phase relation and microstructure in multi-phase intermetallic alloys based on Ni_3Si–Ni_3Ti–Ni_3Nb pseudo-ternary alloy system. *Intermetallics* **2004**, *12*, 317–325.
2. Wang, Y.; Banerjee, D.; Su, C.C.; Khachaturyan, A.G. Field kinetic model and computer simulation of precipitation of $L1_2$ ordered intermetallics from fcc solid solution. *Acta Mater.* **1998**, *46*, 2983–3001. [CrossRef]
3. Sheu, H.H.; Hsiung, L.C.; Sheu, J.R. Synthesis of multiphase intermetallic compounds by mechanical alloying in Ni–Al–Ti system. *J. Alloys Compd.* **2009**, *469*, 483–487. [CrossRef]
4. Savin, O.V.; Stepanova, N.N.; Akshentsev, Y.N.; Rodionov, D.P. Ordering kinetics in ternary Ni_3Al–X alloys. *Scr. Mater.* **2001**, *45*, 883–888. [CrossRef]
5. Chen, L.Q. A computer simulation technique for spinodal decomposition and ordering in ternary systems. *Scr. Metall. Mater.* **1993**, *29*, 683–688. [CrossRef]
6. Bendersky, L.A.; Biancaniello, F.S.; Williams, M.E. Evolution of the two-phase microstructure $L1_2$ + DO_{22} in near-eutectoid Ni_3(Al,V) alloy. *J. Mater. Res.* **1994**, *9*, 3068–3082. [CrossRef]
7. Wu, R.; Zhao, Y.; Yin, Q.; Wang, J.; Wen, Z. Atomistic simulation studies of Ni-based superalloys. *J. Alloys Compd.* **2021**, *855*, 157355. [CrossRef]

8. Wu, R.; Yin, Q.; Wang, J.; Mao, Q.; Wen, Z. Effect of Re on mechanical properties of single crystal Ni-based superalloys: Insights from first-principle and molecular dynamics. *J. Alloys Compd.* **2021**, *862*, 158643. [CrossRef]
9. Wu, R.; Zhao, Y.; Liu, Y.; Ai, X. High temperature creep mechanisms of a single crystal superalloy: A phase-field simulation and microstructure characterization. *Prog. Nat. Sci.* **2020**, *30*, 366–370. [CrossRef]
10. Cermak, J.; Rothova, V. Concentration dependence of ternary interdiffusion coefficients in Ni_3Al/Ni_3Al–X couples with X= Cr, Fe, Nb and Ti. *Acta Mater.* **2003**, *51*, 4411–4421. [CrossRef]
11. Khachaturyan, A.G. Theory of structural transformations in solids. *Mat. Res. Bull.* **1984**, *99*, 125–127.
12. Zhao, Y.; Zheng, C.; Li, X. Computer simulation of strain-induced morphological transformation of coherent precipitates. *Int. J. Miner. Metall. Mater.* **2003**, *10*, 55–60.
13. Chen, L.Q. Computer simulation of structural transformations during precipitation of an ordered intermetallic phase. *Acta Metall. Mater.* **1991**, *39*, 2533–2551. [CrossRef]
14. Li, X.L. Computer simulation for early precipitation of $\delta'(Al_3Li)$. *Prog. Nat. Sci.* **2002**, *12*, 74.
15. Poduri, R.; Chen, L.Q. Computer simulation of atomic ordering and compositional clustering in the pseudobinary Ni_3Al–Ni_3V system. *Acta Mater.* **1998**, *46*, 1719–1729. [CrossRef]
16. Lu, X.G.; Wang, Z.; Cui, Y.; Jin, Z. Computational thermodynamics, computational kinetics, and materials design. *Sci. Bull.* **2014**, *59*, 1662–1671. [CrossRef]
17. Mishin, Y.; Lozovoi, A.Y. Angular-dependent interatomic potential for tantalum. *Acta Mater.* **2006**, *54*, 5013–5026. [CrossRef]
18. Kim, H.K.; Jung, W.S.; Lee, B.J. Modified embedded-atom method interatomic potentials for the Nb-C, Nb-N, Fe-Nb-C, and Fe-Nb-N system. *J. Mater. Res.* **2010**, *25*, 1288–1297. [CrossRef]
19. Chen, L.Q.; Khachaturyan, A.G. Computer simulation of decomposition reactions accompanied by a congruent ordering of the second kind. *Scr. Metall. Mater.* **1991**, *25*, 61–66. [CrossRef]
20. Khachaturyan, A.G. Nonlinear integral equations and their application to the problem of orderable alloys. *Sov. Phys. Solid State.* **1963**, *5*, 16–22.
21. Khachaturyan, A.G. The problem of symmetry in statistical thermodynamics of substitutional and interstitial ordered solid solutions. *Phys. Status Solidi-B* **1973**, *60*, 9–37. [CrossRef]
22. Andersson, J.O.; Helander, T.; Hglund, L. Thermo-Calc & DICTRA, computational tools for materials science. *Calphad* **2002**, *26*, 273–312.
23. Wang, Y.; Chen, L.Q.; Khachaturyan, A.G. Kinetics of strain-induced morphological transformation in cubic alloys with a miscibility gap. *Acta Metall. Mater.* **1993**, *41*, 279–296. [CrossRef]
24. Chen, L.Q.; Simmons, J.A. Microscopic master equation approach to diffusion transformations in inhomogeneous systems-single-site approximation and direct exchange mechanism. *Acta Metall. Mater.* **1994**, *42*, 2943–2954. [CrossRef]

crystals

MDPI

Article

Study of the Creep Behavior of Nickel-Based Single Crystal Superalloy Micro Specimens with Dimensional Effects

Wangjiao Xiong, Xing Ai *, Jianfang Wang, Quanzhong Wang, Yanyun Zhao, Haiyan Zhu, Hao Cheng and Sheng Zhang

Aecc Hunan Aviation Powerplant Research Institute, Zhuzhou 412002, China; hqp@mail.nwpu.edu.cn (W.X.); wangjianfang_aecc@outlook.com (J.W.); quanzhongwang_aecc@outlook.com (Q.W.); yanyun_zhao@outlook.com (Y.Z.); haiyanzhu_aecc@outlook.com (H.Z.); chenghao_aecc@outlook.com (H.C.); sheng_zhang_aecc@outlook.com (S.Z.)

* Correspondence: aixing_aecc@outlook.com

Abstract: Nickel-based single-crystal superalloys are widely used in aeroengine hot-end components, owing to their unique crystal structure and outstanding high-temperature mechanical properties. In the present study, round rod specimens of different sizes were subjected to high temperature creep tests at 980 °C/300 MPa of a second-generation nickel-based single crystal superalloy. The effect of size on the creep behavior of nickel-based single-crystal superalloys was studied with reference to the creep curves and microstructure morphologies. Creep interruption tests of 3-mm micro-round rod specimens were performed for 30, 60, and 90 h until creep fracture occurred. It was found that for nickel-based single crystal superalloys, the smaller the diameter of the specimen, the longer its creep life. Furthermore, the creep fracture morphology showed obvious creep cavitation in the fracture region. The law of organization evolution was used to analyze the rafting phenomena during the creep process. A typical "N"-type drifting strip structure was found during the creep process. Meanwhile, the width of the γ-phase channel increases continuously with creep, and the rate of change of the width of the matrix phase was fastest at the earliest stage of creep, slowing significantly during the middle and late stages of creep with the completion and appearance the rafting phenomenon.

Keywords: nickel based; creep fracture; single crystal; superalloy; high temperature; low cycle fatigue

1. Introduction

The breakthrough of Ni-based single-crystal alloy turbine blade technology has been crucial for the development of aero-engines. This has resulted in great advancements in the temperature-bearing capacity of blade materials and engine performance [1–3]. After decades of development, many milestones have been achieved in the study of the mechanical properties of Ni-based single-crystal high-temperature alloy materials [4–6]. The microstructure of these single crystals exhibits unique morphological characteristics and positional relationships between the γ phase and the γ matrix. The composition of the reinforcing γ phase is the metal compound Ni_3Al, which is stable at high temperatures and has a strengthening effect on the mechanical properties of the material [7,8]. Compared with conventional high-temperature alloys, Ni-based single crystals show eliminated grain boundaries, reduced regions of crack initiation, and good resistance to high temperatures, corrosion, fatigue, and oxidation. These properties enable them to be used in large quantities in the manufacture of aero-engine blades [9]. Ni-based single crystals are anisotropic materials that exhibit a sensitive crystal orientation dependence [10]. Under unidirectional stress, they form interesting relationships between crystal orientation, temperature, tensile state, and strain rate. These properties are different from those of conventional materials; therefore, new mechanical characterization and modeling methods must be investigated. To improve the overall performance of aero-engines, it is necessary to increase the reserve of mechanical properties of materials and improve their production and processing levels. In addition, size effects, including sample size [6], grain size [11], contact size [12], and microstructure characteristic length [13], on the mechanical properties of materials are also a topic of interest for researchers at present. In terms of mechanics, research to date has largely focused on creep and fatigue properties. Prastiti [4] and Karamitros [5] studied the fatigue crack nucleation and crack propagation mechanism of nickel-based single crystal based on crystal plasticity theory. The model proposed in the literature can accurately identify the crack nucleation position and predict the crack growth rate and path.

Because aero-engines, especially their hot-end components, are exposed to high temperatures for long periods of time, creep deformation of the material occurs. In a simple analysis, the accumulation of time at constant temperature and load conditions slowly leads to the complete deformation of the material [14]. The extraordinary creep properties of Ni-based single crystals significantly impact the safety index and driving reliability of aero-engines and are an important reason for their use as engine materials. The properties of these materials must be studied separately because their mechanical behavior differs from that of conventional materials.

The creep process of Ni-based single crystals is divided into three main phases [15]: a short deceleration phase, a steady-state phase, and an accelerated creep phase. The first and second stages are prolonged when the temperature is lowered or the stress is reduced, but the three phases of the creep curve remain [16]. There is a close causal relationship between the creep behavior of Ni-based single crystals and the morphology of their microstructures. Under prolonged temperature stress, the γ' phase undergoes directional coarsening and selectively grows in a given direction according to a certain pattern, which is a phenomenon specific to the creep of Ni-based single crystals known as rafting [17]. The rafting phenomenon is an important factor affecting the creep–fatigue life of nickel-based single crystals. Pollock et al. experimentally investigated the high-temperature creep properties of CMSX-4 characterized by the directional coarsening of the γ' phase, proposed fine-scale factors affecting rafting, and established a relevant rafting model [18]. Numerous studies have shown that rafting in Ni-based single crystals is closely related to the magnitude of the test temperature and stress value [19].

Another study noted that the microstructural evolution of Ni-based single crystals is closely related to both the dislocation structure and dislocation motion of the γ' phase, where the edge portion of the γ' phase grows preferentially and expands slowly to connect with the surrounding phases, forming a raft-like structure [20]. By observing the kinematic evolution of a Ni-based single-crystal structure, Pearson et al. found that the directional diffusion of alloy elements accompanied the raft structure process and that the stress gradient influenced the alloy creep. It was also noted that the elements within the matrix and reinforced phases diffused in opposite directions [21]. According to the currently accepted model, the motion of dislocations during the creep process causes a nonuniform stress distribution accompanied by a decrease in the energy of the system, and this driving force is responsible for the directional coarsening of the γ' phase [22]. Changes in the structure and morphology of the γ phase strongly influence the creep properties of the material and determine the macroscopic properties of single-crystal blades in the service environment [23]. Pearson et al. [21] considered rafting as a hardening process that favors the properties of Ni-based single crystals and inhibits dislocation. It has also been suggested that the change in the structure of the γ phase during rafting is softening behavior [24].

Several factors affect the creep properties of Ni-based single-crystal materials. Numerous studies have found that temperature and stress of different magnitudes, crystal orientation in the principal stress direction, and lattice mismatch play important roles in the microstructural evolution of Ni-based single crystals [25,26]. Reed et al. conducted creep tests with different temperature stresses, finding that the γ phase underwent directional coarsening and rafting only at low-stress states at temperatures greater than 900 °C [27]. It was concluded that Ni-based single crystals are more prone to raft deformation at high temperatures and low stresses, which reduces the critical stress for atomic diffusion. There is also a correlation between the crystal orientation and rafting, with significant differences in the form of creep rafting for the three orientations of Ni-based single crystals [001], [011], and [111] under uniaxial stress conditions [28–30].

At this stage, most studies on the mechanical behavior and characterization of Ni-based single crystals, and creep mechanisms in particular, are based on tests conducted on standard-size specimens. This experimental method outlined in this study provides an effective analysis route to study the evolution of the creep–fatigue microstructure of Ni-based single-crystal materials and their creep–fatigue damage life. Unfortunately, experimenting with standard parts is not economical due to the high cost of Ni-based single-crystal materials. Nevertheless, it is necessary to develop a creep–fatigue study method for Ni-based single crystals based on miniature specimens. The reason for this is that in the strength assessment of some engine blades, specimens need to be cut directly from the turbine blades, and there are significant dimensional differences between the cut samples and standard parts. When the Ni-based single-crystal turbine blades are sampled again, the specimens obtained are often very small. In this study, a small specimen creep technique was developed based on a domestic single-crystal superalloy. By conducting high-temperature creep tests, the microstructure of Ni-based single-crystal materials and its evolution under creep loading were investigated, and the effect of specimen size on creep performance was analyzed. Furthermore, the creep failure mechanism of differently sized specimens was revealed from a microscopic perspective. The overarching aim of this study was to prevent the occurrence of catastrophic events by promoting the development and application of Ni-based single-crystal materials in China by studying their mechanical properties and service life at a reduced test cost.

2. Experimental Materials and Methods

2.1. Test Material

The test material used was a second-generation Ni-based single-crystal high temperature alloy commonly used in engine turbine blades. The master alloy was melted in a vacuum induction furnace, re-melted in a vacuum directional solidification furnace, and subsequently poured into a single-crystal test bar. The parent alloy was supplied in the cast state and subjected to standard heat treatment methods (1290 °C, 1 h; 1300 °C, 2 h; 1315 °C, 4 h/AC; 1120 °C, 4 h/AC; 870 °C, 32 h/AC), with the crystal orientation in the [001] direction and the deviation of the crystal orientation controlled to within 10°. The main elemental components are listed in Table 1.

Table 1. Composition of the used Ni-based single-crystal superalloy (mass %).

Element	C	Cr	Ni	Co	W	Mo	Al	Ti	Ta	Re	Nb	B	Si	Hf
Content	0.015	4.0	Excess	9.0	8.0	2.0	5.7	≤0.10	7.0	2.2	1.0	≤0.02	≤0.20	1.0

The initial composition observed by scanning electron microscopy is shown in Figure 1. The mosaic region in Figure 1a is the γ' reinforced phase of the alloy, whose main component is the metal compound Ni_3Al, which is the predominant reason for the excellent properties of the alloy. The γ' phase is sterically ordered and co-grid in the γ phase. Using Image-J image processing software, the volume fraction of the γ' phase, size of the reinforced phase, and width of the γ matrix were calculated to be approximately 66%, 0.4–0.6 μm, and 50 nm, respectively. Figure 1b shows the unit cell diagram of Ni-based single crystal superalloy. Figure 1c indicates a single crystal structure for the samples which includes a strong peak with a distinct crystalline diffraction line. Figure 1d shows the EDS composition results.

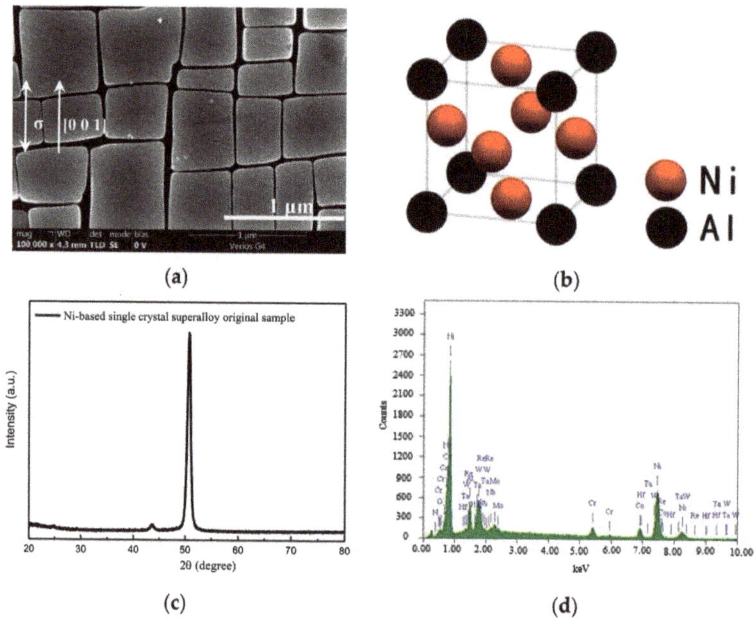

Figure 1. Nickel-based single crystal superalloy original sample. (**a**) microstructure, (**b**) unit cell, (**c**) XRD patterns, and (**d**) EDS composition results.

2.2. Test Method

A series of round bar specimens of varying sizes were used for the creep tests, which were divided into standard round bar specimens, round bar specimens, and miniature round bar specimens, with diameters of 5.0, 3.0, and 2.5 mm, respectively. The specific dimensions of the specimens are shown in Figure 2a–c, and the physical drawings of the three different round rod specimens are presented in Figure 2d.

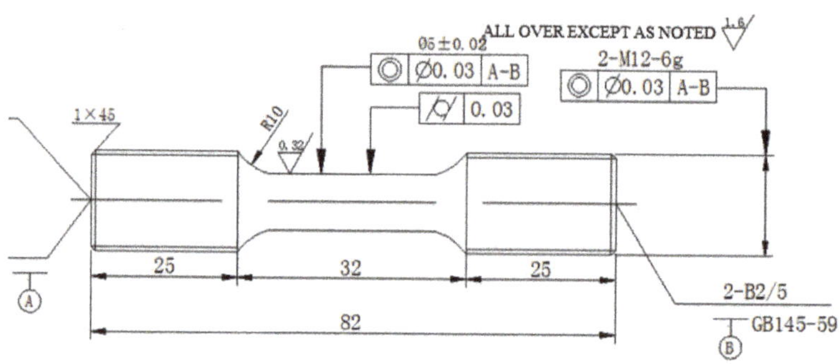

(**a**)

Figure 2. *Cont.*

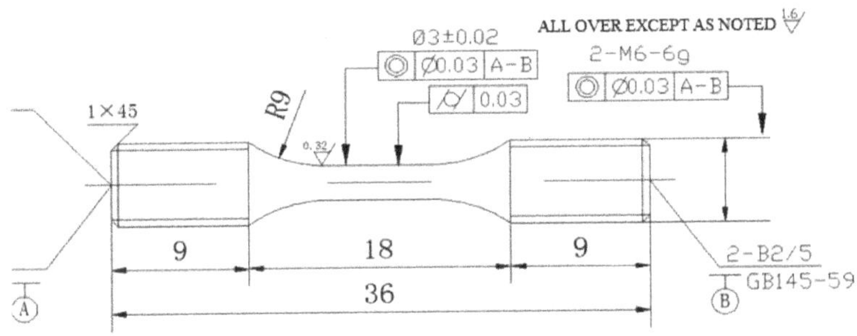

(b)

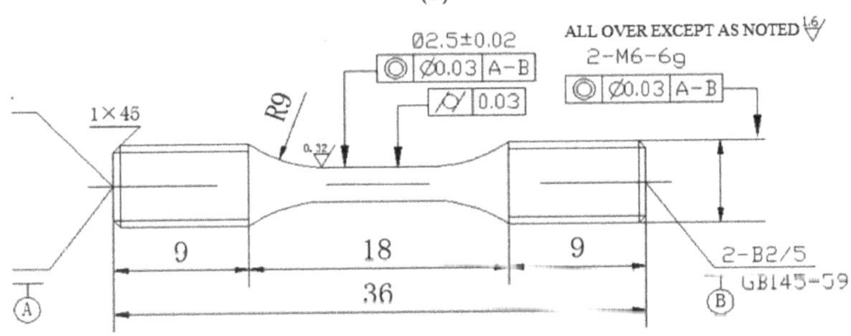

(c)

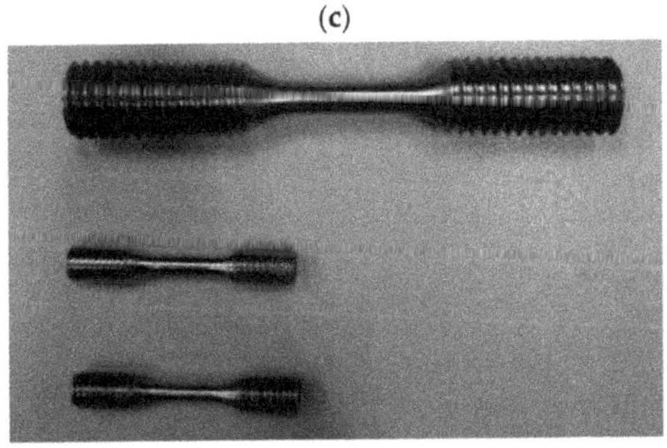

(d)

Figure 2. Test pieces of different sizes. (**a**) Standard test piece with a diameter of 5 mm, (**b**) round bar test piece with a diameter of 3 mm, (**c**) miniature test piece with a diameter of 2.5 mm, and (**d**) comparative photograph of the three kinds of test pieces.

The test was conducted in full accordance with the Metal Tensile Creep and Durability Test Method (GB/T2039-1997), and all creep tests were completed on a CSS-2910 (SINOTEST, Changchun, China) high-temperature creep machine. The entire creep test was conducted in a high-temperature furnace. The test took place in air, and thermocouples were used for temperature acquisition. The temperature difference within the specimen was controlled to within 0.5 °C to reduce the test error. Each test started 30 min after the target temperature was reached.

The test conditions were tailored for the purpose of this study. The effect of specimen size on the creep properties of Ni-based single crystals was investigated and uniaxial tensile creep tests were performed at 980 °C/300 MPa on three different sizes of specimens with diameters of 2.5 mm, 3 mm, and 5 mm, respectively, and the corresponding creep curves were plotted. In particular, the evolution of the microstructure during high-temperature creep was studied, and creep interruption tests were performed on the 3-mm specimens for periods of 30, 60, and 90 h at 980 °C. Full-life tests were also performed on 3 mm specimens at 980 °C until specimen fracture occurred.

After the test, small squares and specimen fractures were cut by wire, polished with sandpaper, and then machine-polished until smooth. Subsequently, the corrosion solution was prepared, containing a fixed ratio of concentrated HNO_3 solution, hydrofluoric acid (HF), and propanetriol. Finally, the changes in the microstructure and characteristics of the fracture morphology were observed using a Zeiss scanning electron microscope (SEM, Carl Zeiss AG, Oberkochen, Germany).

3. Experimental Results and Discussion

3.1. *Effect of Size on Creep of Ni-Based Single Crystals*

High-temperature creep tests were conducted on specimens of domestic second-generation single-crystal superalloys of different diameters (2.5, 3, and 5 mm) at 980 °C and 300 MPa. The test conditions and methods were kept the same, and only the specimen diameters were varied. The creep test results, including creep life, creep fracture strain, and cross-sectional shrinkage, are listed in Table 2.

Table 2. Creep test results of three sizes of specimens at 980 °C/300 MPa.

No.	Specimen Diameter (mm)	Creep Life (h)	Strain at Break (%)	Fracture Shrinkage (%)
A1		139.22	36.4	26.1
A2	2.5	134.19	35.2	24.8
A3		132.34	42.2	25.5
B1		122.93	43.3	25.6
B2	3.0	125.42	42.7	25.3
B3		128.66	38.9	24.4
C1		108.33	44.6	24.7
C2	5.0	111.27	43.4	26.4
C3		109.51	43.8	23.9

From the test results (Table 2 and Figure 3), it can be seen that the miniature specimen exhibits the longest creep life for constant temperature stress, i.e., 980 °C/300 MPa. All dimensions were tested in triplicate. For the specimen with a diameter of 2.5 mm, the creep life is 139.22 h, 134.19 h, and 132.34 h, respectively, with little difference. The strains at break are 36.4%, 35.2%, and 42.2%, respectively, and the strain at break of A3 is larger. The fracture shrinkage rates are 26.1%, 24.8%, and 25.5%, respectively, with a small difference; for the specimen with a diameter of 3.0 mm, the creep life is 122.93 h, 125.42 h, and 128.66 h, respectively. The strains at break are 43.3%, 42.7%, and 38.9%, respectively, and the strain at break of B3 is smaller. The fracture shrinkage rates are 25.6%, 25.3%, and 24.4%, respectively, and the difference is small; for the specimen with a diameter of 5.0 mm, the creep life is 108.33 h, 111.27 h, and 109.51 h, respectively. The strains at break are 44.6%, 43.4%, and 43.8%, respectively. The fracture shrinkage rates are 24.7%, 26.4%, and 23.9%, respectively, and the fracture shrinkage rate of C2 is larger. To sum up, in general, the difference between the test results is small and within the acceptable range.

The average creep life was found to be approximately 125.67 h, whereas the average creep life of the 5 mm specimen was approximately 109.7 h. The maximum difference in creep life between the three specimens was 25.55 h, indicating a clear correlation between the size of the specimen and its creep life under these test conditions. Overall, the smaller the specimen size, the longer its creep life. It was also observed that at this temperature stress, the average strain at fracture of the 2.5-, 3- and 5-mm specimens was approximately 37.9%, 41. 6%, and 43.9%, respectively. This result indicated that the larger the size of the specimen, the larger the creep fracture strain. In general, the size of the specimen had no significant effect on the creep fracture strain. After calculating the average shrinkage rate of each specimen after creep, it was found that there was no significant difference in the shrinkage rate of the three different sizes of round bar specimens, which were all approximately 25%, and obvious necking occurred.

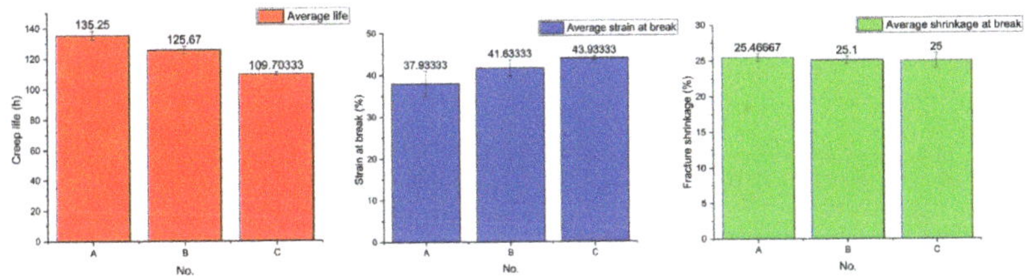

Figure 3. Creep test results of three sizes of specimens at 980 °C/300 MPa, where No. A, B, and C represent tests with specimen diameters of 2.5, 3.0, and 5.0 mm, respectively.

It can be seen from Figure 4 above that the creep curves of all three specimen sizes show exponential growth at the same temperature stress (980 °C/300 MPa). The analysis shows that the specimen with a diameter of 2.5 mm exhibits three obvious stages of creep deformation, first presenting a typical initial creep stage, also called the deceleration creep stage. In this stage, an obvious hardening of the creep process occurs, the creep strain is generated instantaneously with the loading of the stress, and the creep strain rate decreases dramatically until it reaches a minimum value. This stage was very short, lasting approximately 1.5 h, before rapidly entering the second stage of creep. The second stage is the steady-state creep stage, in which the creep rate remained stable and can be approximated as a straight line with a gradient of approximately 3.86×10^{-3}/h. This stage lasted approximately 120 h, accounting for 88% of the total creep life, but the strain only increased by ~0.18. Subsequently, the third stage of creep was entered with a higher creep rate and shorter time, also known as the accelerated creep stage.

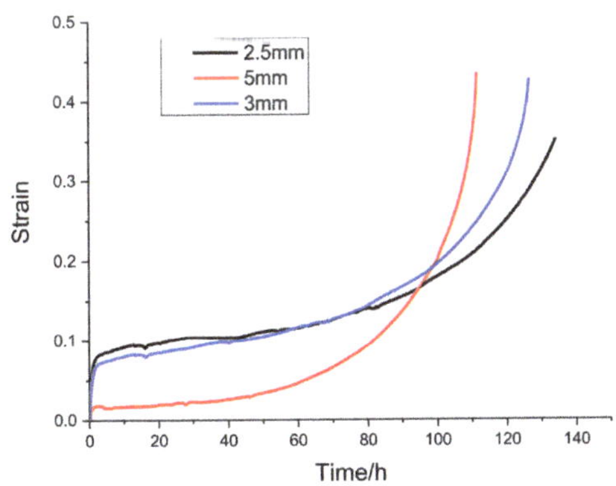

Figure 4. Creep curves of three differently sized specimens at 980 °C/300 MPa.

The creep strain rate increased monotonically, with strain increasing to a maximum value of 35.2%, at which point the specimen showed damage failure. By analyzing the creep curve for a diameter of 3 mm, it was found that the behavior was still in agreement with standard creep characteristics. The same short deceleration creep stage was observed, quickly followed by the stable second stage. This second stage involved ~115 h of slow, uniform growth, accounting for 90% of the total creep time. In the very short third stage, the creep strain rate was found to change dramatically in a sharp upward trend and finally increased to 42.7% at the point of fracture. Analysis of the 5-mm creep curve diameter shows that the creep strain in the first 5 mm of the third stage is significantly smaller than the other two sizes tested. Moreover, there is no obvious first stage, meaning direct entry into the second stage, when the creep rate is very slow and smooth, with a rate of approximately 2.41×10^{-3}/h. The total time spent in this stage was ~99 h, accounting for 89% of the total creep time. When entering the third stage, the creep strain increased significantly from 18% in the second stage to 43.4%, i.e., by a factor of almost 2.4. The creep strain rate also showed a sharp increase, which finally led to the fracture of the specimen.

Figure 5 shows the microstructural morphology of round bar specimens with diameters of 2.5, 3, and 5 mm near the point of high-temperature creep fracture at 980 °C/300 MPa. Figure 5a shows the microstructural morphology of the 2.5-mm diameter specimen, where the initial cubic γ phase evolves into a slender strip-like raft structure in the horizontal direction after creep (i.e., the classical "N" type raft structure). At this point, the γ matrix phase channels in the vertical direction were found to almost completely disappear and those in the horizontal direction fused, forming a single piece with increasing width. The two adjacent γ phases in the horizontal direction were further elongated and thickened in the horizontal direction owing to the disappearance of the matrix phase between them, and the γ' phases fused on meeting. After approximately 134 h of creep, a small part of the raft-like structure fractured into fragments. The creeping raft-like structure gradually lost its ability to resist deformation and appeared to be delaminated, which finally manifested as macroscopic damage and destruction of the alloy material.

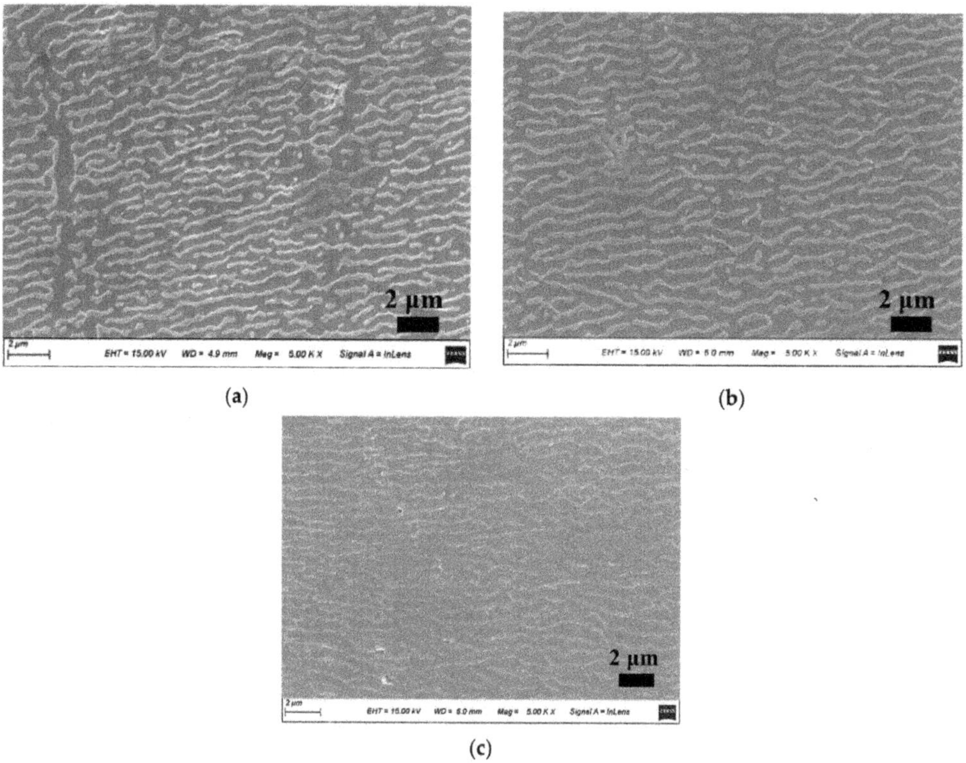

Figure 5. Creep fracture microstructure of specimens with different diameters (**a**) 2.5 mm, (**b**) 3 mm and (**c**) 5 mm.

Figure 5b shows the SEM images of the 3-mm creep specimen, from which it can be seen that a creep rafting phenomenon is also evident; however, the coarsening length of the γ phase in the horizontal direction is larger than that of the former. Although the changes in microstructure were similar, the creep time of the specimen was approximately 125 h. The occurrence of the raft shape also accompanies creep fracture, but the degree is much weaker than that of the former, and there are only a few scattered raft disintegration structures. Figure 5c shows the microstructure of a standard specimen with a diameter of 5 mm under the same test conditions. The creep life of this specimen was approximately 111 h. Compared with the first two microstructure images, the extension size of the γ phase along the horizontal direction increased. Furthermore, the connection formed a complete raft-shaped strip structure with almost no interruption, and the reinforced phases were connected in bunches and strips. There was no fragmented structure observed, indicating that the raft shape had not yet formed. Other defects are also visible, such as inclusion cracks, which are often responsible for creep damage and lead to a significantly shorter creep life and faster damage.

Figure 5 shows that, for specimens of different sizes, the microscopic morphology after creep rupture is the key to dominating the creep behavior. For the sample with a diameter of 2.5 mm (Figure 5a), the strengthening phase γ' did not completely connect into a plate shape, and the degree of rafting is small. The channel of the matrix phase γ is narrow, and its life is longer. For the sample with a diameter of 5.0 mm (Figure 5c), the strengthening phase has a high degree of rafting, which has been approximately completely connected into a plate shape. The width of the matrix phase γ channel is wider and there are obvious holes, which accelerate the creeping, Therefore, larger size specimens have shorter creep life.

These results indicate that under the given conditions at 980 °C, the creep life of Ni-based single crystal alloys decreases with increasing specimen size. This, in turn, leads to the difference in the presence and shape of rafts for each size specimen. Thus, it can be concluded that the size of the specimen is closely related to the morphology and microstructure of the alloy, and more closely related to the creep persistence performance.

SEM was used to observe the microstructural morphology around the creep fracture of the superalloy at 980 °C/300 MPa, where a large number of crack sources could be seen. A large, elliptical hole defect can be seen in Figure 6a, and the γ phase near this region has been oriented and coarsened to form a thinly striped raft-like structure, i.e., an "N"-shaped raft. The presence of the hole defect interrupts the continuity of the γ phase, resulting in the raft-like γ phase around the hole being significantly distorted. The hole was identified as a casting defect in the material that severely disrupted the continuity of the tissue and thus affected the creep life of the Ni-based superalloy. Similarly, many defects can be seen in Figure 6b, including cracks, inclusions, and holes. Casting defects are one of the most important influencers of creep life. Microdefects gradually expand and extend with creep, leading to a decrease in the effective bearing area of the specimen and an increase in the actual stress in the cross-section, which eventually leads to creep fracture.

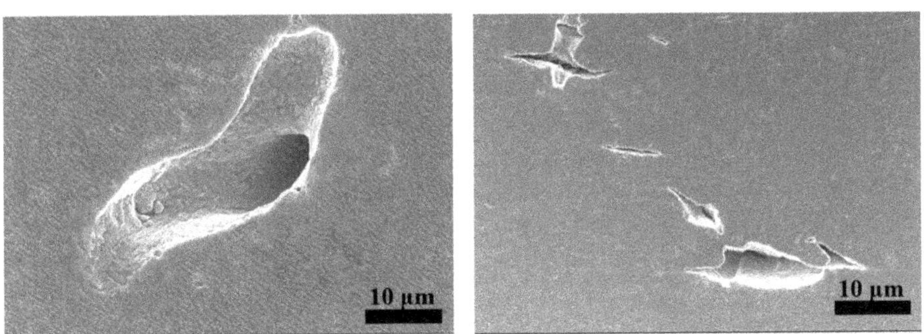

(a) (b)

Figure 6. Defect morphology of creep fracture. (**a**) holes and (**b**) cracks.

Figure 7 shows that after a long period of high-temperature creep testing, the surface of the Ni-based alloy underwent severe oxidation, and a thick oxide layer with bright white color was formed on the surface of the specimen. A large number of pores and cracks were observed near the oxide layer, causing a reduction in the finite cross-sectional area. However, the deformation resistance of the oxides (for example, Al_2O_3) in the oxide layer is not equal to that of the base alloy, and the deformation rate of the oxide layer is smaller. The uncoordinated deformation during creep causes cracks in the oxide layer, which in turn results in the fracture of the Ni-based single crystal and leads to a reduction in creep life.

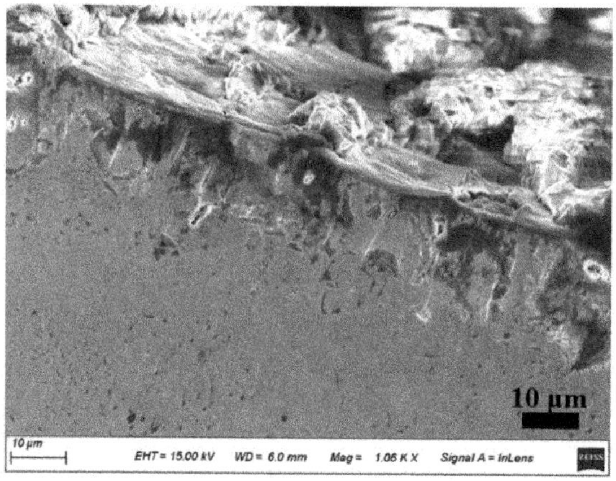

Figure 7. Creep fracture oxidation morphology.

In summary, it can be concluded that under the same test conditions, the smaller the size of the specimen, the longer its creep life. In addition to the errors caused by the test process, such as the error of the testing machine, test operation, dispersion of test data, dimension processing, and the analysis of the causes of such differences in test results from the perspective of creep damage, there are two main influencing factors. First, the casting defects of the material itself, including cracks, holes, and inclusions, cause a reduction in the effective bearing area during creep and eventually lead to specimen fracture. The 2.5-mm specimen, owing to its smaller volume and surface area, benefits from a reduced effective bearing area caused by the volume of the high-stress area. The possibility of defects or weak points is reduced, which in turn leads to the creep life of this specimen being extended. The second is the loss of the effective cross-sectional area due to oxidative corrosion on the specimen surface, leading to creep fracture due to the incompatible deformation of the oxide layer and the base alloy. Compared to standard specimens, miniature specimens are smaller in size, volume, and surface area, and have a smaller area for oxidation loss defects; therefore, in general, the smaller the specimen size, the longer the creep life.

3.2. Creep Process of Ni-Based Single Crystals at 980 °C/300 MPa

Creep interruption tests for periods of 30, 60, and 90 h and complete tests up to the point of fracture were carried out on Ni-based single-crystal superalloy specimens at 980 °C/300 MPa. These specimens were [001] oriented round bars with a diameter of 3 mm, whose full creep life curves are shown in Figure 8. The creep deformation is characteristically divided into three stages. In the first stage, the creep deformation rate decreased rapidly for a short time, typical of the creep deceleration stage. Contrast analysis of this creep process showed that this stage, the process of hardening and recovery of softening in a smooth state, accounts for a large percentage of the overall creep life. This is followed by a rapid transition to the second stage of creep. During the second stage, the creep strain grew smoothly and slowly, and the creep rate remained almost constant. At a creep time of 60 h, the creep strain was only 0.12. Finally, the third stage of creep was entered, which is the accelerated creep stage. At this point, the creep rate and creep strain suddenly and rapidly increased. The fracture occurred at approximately 125 h, at which point the strain reached 0.43. This additional value was relatively large, which finally led to the failure and destruction of the specimen.

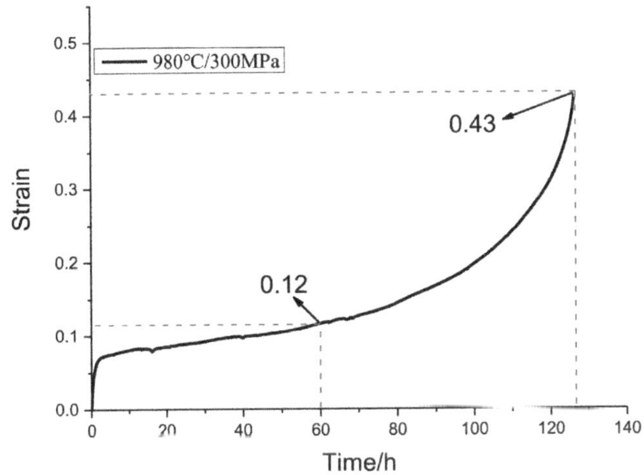

Figure 8. Creep curve of 3-mm specimen at 980 °C/300 MPa.

Numerous studies have shown that the excellent properties of Ni-based single crystal high-temperature alloys arise from their unique crystal structure, which changes during the creep process. To study the evolution of the microstructure during creep, the morphology of the specimens was observed and analyzed by scanning electron microscopy (SEM) for different periods of creep: 30, 60, and 90 h, and the final fracture moment.

Figure 9 shows the microstructure morphology of the Ni-based single-crystal superalloy at different time points during creep at 980 °C/300 MPa test conditions. Figure 9a shows the microstructure morphology at the beginning of the second stage of creep—that is, the steady-state creep stage. It can be seen that the γ phase starts to change shape at this time; it is no longer the original uniform co-grid of the γ phase, and the initial raft shape occurs. The two γ-reinforced phases that are partially adjacent to each other are interconnected and show a trend of directional coarsening along the horizontal axis. Although the reinforced phase γ maintains a block-like structure, its grain size gradually increases, and the matrix phase passages start to widen. At this time, the size of the reinforced phase γ was approximately 0.5–0.6 μm. Figure 9b shows the microstructure of the superalloy during the middle stage of steady-state creep at 60 h. The two-phase structure is clearly deformed, the matrix phase channel in the horizontal direction slowly thicker, and the matrix channel in the vertical direction gradually became thinner or disappeared completely. The grain size of the γ' phase has grown to 1.2–1.4 μm, and the surrounding cubic γ' phase is passivated and has become round and elliptical. The position of the γ phase is disordered, and a raft-like structure was observed.

When the creep enters the end of the steady-state phase at 90 h, as shown in Figure 9c, the degree of deformation of the two γ/γ' phases intensifies and significant rafting can be seen to have occurred. The two γ' phases fuse together, join to form a strip, and continue to grow in the horizontal direction. The matrix channels in the vertical direction have completely disappeared, and the coarsening of the matrix phase channels in the horizontal direction has continued to expand severely, forming a typical "N"-type raft structure. From the above analysis, it can be seen that when the specimen was in the steady-state creep stage, the creep strain and creep rate were very low, and the microstructure indicated that the initial rafting phenomenon was not very obvious. Only the outcrop and γ phase morphology did not change significantly, meaning that good creep performance can be maintained for a long period of time. While rafting was observed in the middle of the steady-state creep stage, the width of the reinforced phase morphology and the matrix phase changed significantly; at the end of the steady-state stage, the γ phase coarsened to form a plate, the rafting phenomenon was complete, and the third stage of creep was about to be entered. As shown in Figure 9d, the microstructure of the specimen at the point of fracture was a partially fractured γ phase raft-like strip structure, in which there were many scattered points. The matrix phase channel almost entirely disappeared.

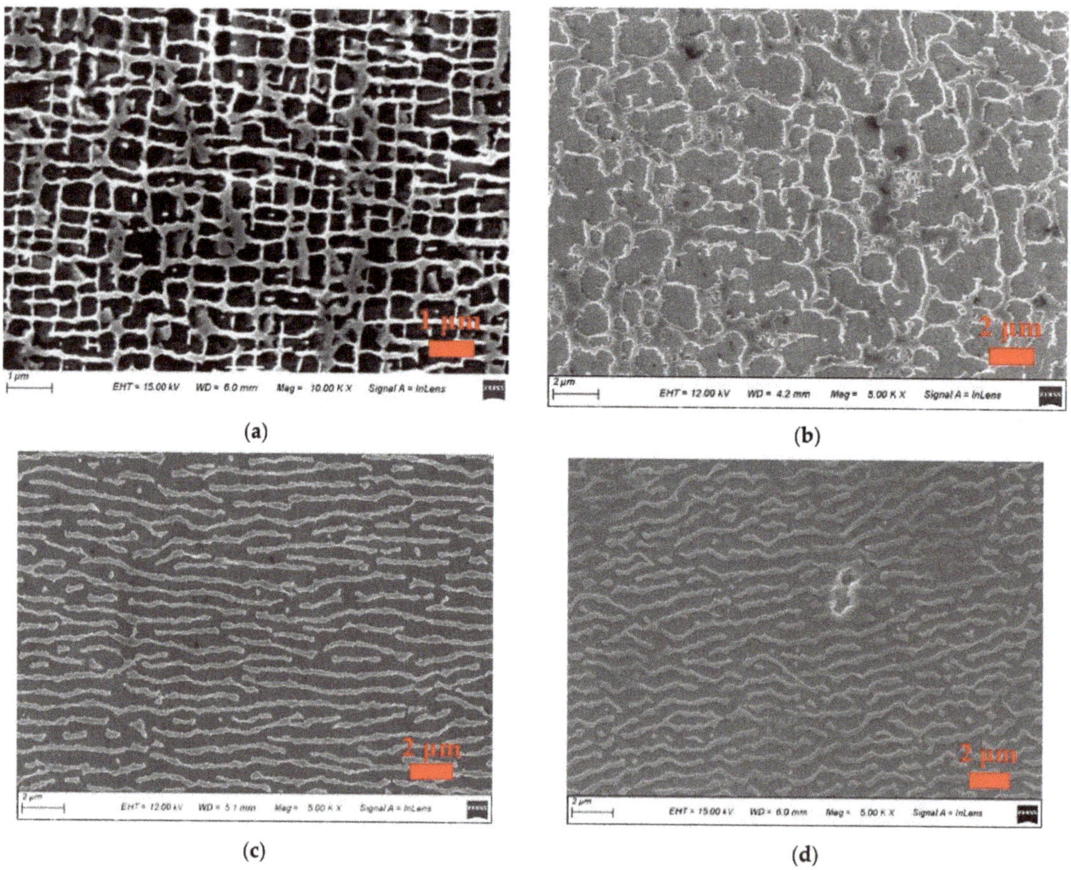

Figure 9. Tensile creep microstructure morphology at 980 °C/300 MPa. (**a**) 30 h, (**b**) 60 h, (**c**) 90 h and (**d**) 125 h.

The above analysis shows that the width of the γ-phase channel continuously increases with the extent of creep during the high-temperature creep process. The γ-phase channel widths in the microstructural diagrams of the specimens for each process were statistically calculated using ImageJ image processing software. The statistical results showed that the sample values of the γ-phase channel widths at different creep moments obeyed a log-normal distribution. The γ-phase channel widths under tensile creep at 980 °C/300 MPa were fitted according to the mean value combined with the data processing software results, as shown in Figure 10. It can be observed that the rate of change of matrix phase width is fastest at the early creep stage, and this rate of increase slows down significantly in the middle and late creep stages with the appearance and completion of rafting. The analysis of the curves shows that the width of the matrix phase channel during creep exhibits a fast and then slow overall evolution.

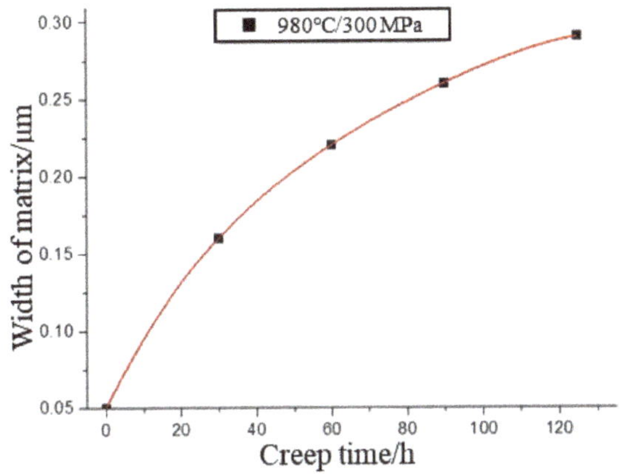

Figure 10. Variation of matrix phase channel width at 980 °C/300 MPa.

The creep fracture of the specimen at 980 °C/300 MPa is shown in Figure 11. The low-magnification morphology of the creep fracture of the material is shown in Figure 11a, where the fracture surface is relatively rough and oxidation is more severe. The deformation mechanism is mainly a diffusion creep mechanism with the directional diffusion of atoms and vacancies. This can be seen more clearly in the high-magnification image in Figure 11b: there is obvious creep cavitation in the fracture area with a large number of tough nests of different sizes. The center of these tough nests is often accompanied by many small holes, which are generally thought to be the source of crack budding, leading to creeping damage. Cracks sprout from the defect at the hole and expand radially, sometimes also causing the appearance of secondary cracks. The material collapses from the inside and finally shows the fracture pattern of holes and tough nests.

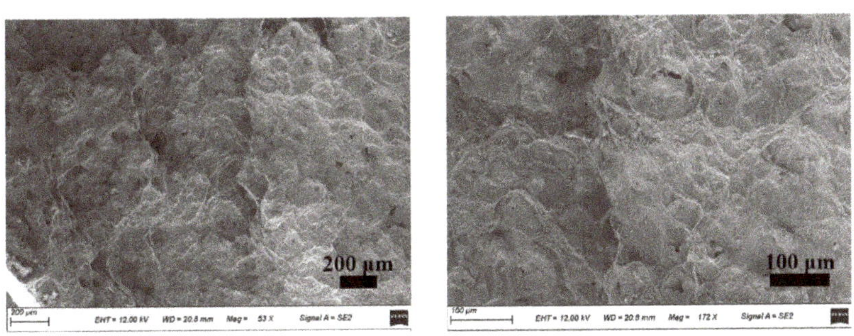

(a) (b)

Figure 11. Creep fracture of the 'micro' specimen. (**a**) Low-magnification creep fracture and (**b**) High-magnification creep fracture.

During high-temperature creep, a large number of dislocations slip or climb up the alloy matrix. Some dislocations shear into the reinforced phase, resulting in many holes near the interface between the matrix and reinforcing phases. This causes cracks to sprout and extend to form tough nests. Oxygen is able to enter from the holes and tough nests and subsequently react with Ni, Al, and other elements during oxidation, destroying the microstructure of the alloy and thus reducing its creep resistance. The cracks connect and extend towards each other, gradually forming tearing ribs in the direction of maximum shear stress, and finally, macroscopic fracture occurs in the late creep stage.

The microstructure morphology near the point of creep fracture of the Ni-based single-crystal superalloy was observed using SEM, and a large number of crack sources were found in the creep fracture region of the specimen. As shown in Figure 12a, the cracks were formed by the expansion of the original casting defects or initial microcracks during creep. Their expansion direction was perpendicular to the direction of the tensile axis, and the crack length was approximately 11.3 µm. At this point, the γ/γ phase exhibited an "N"-type raft structure. The γ phase striped raft structure was partially fractured, with many scattered points, and the matrix phase passages almost entirely disappeared. The rafting phenomenon was clearly present. Figure 12b shows the local enlargement of the crack tip, which is small in size and has a large stress concentration. The raft-like γ phase in this region is violently deformed with a large degree of tilting, the orientation of the raft-like γ phase is more disordered, and some small cracks exist in the region surrounding the crack.

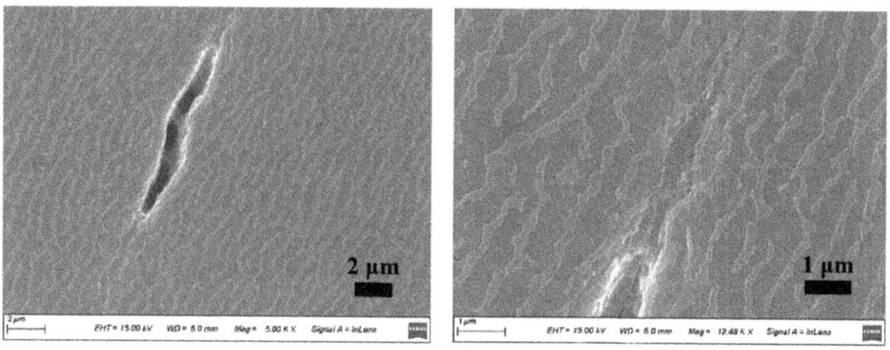

(a) (b)

Figure 12. Creep crack shape at 980 °C/300 MPa. (**a**) Full view of the crack and (**b**) Crack tip.

4. Conclusions

In this study, creep tests were performed on three different sizes of Ni-based single-crystal specimens under the same test conditions of 980 °C/300 MPa. The effect of size on the creep properties of specimens was analyzed based on the test results and microstructure morphology observed by SEM. Finally, creep interruption tests were performed at different time points as well as full-life tests to the point of fracture on another round bar specimen with a diameter of 3 mm to investigate the evolution of the microstructure during high-temperature creep. The main conclusions are as follows.

1. Under the same test conditions, the effect of different specimen diameters on the creep life of Ni-based single crystals followed a clear trend. The smaller the diameter of the specimen, the longer its creep life. From the perspective of creep damage, the reason for this difference is that a reduction in specimen size equates to a smaller volume and surface area, and thus a smaller number and lesser extent of casting and oxidation loss defects are present. This results in a longer creep life.
2. Microstructure analysis of Ni-based single crystals at different time points during high-temperature creep shows that the γ phase thickens in the direction perpendicular to the stress axis, forming a typical "N"-type rafting strip structure. Meanwhile, the width of the γ-phase channel increases continuously with creep, and the rate of change of the width of the matrix phase was fastest at the earliest stage of creep, slowing

significantly during the middle and late stages of creep with the completion and appearance the rafting phenomenon.
3. The creep fracture morphology showed obvious creep cavitation in the fracture region of the Ni-based single crystal, and the material started to fail from the inside, eventually showing holes and a tough-nest fracture morphology.

Author Contributions: Conceptualization, W.X.; Data curation, X.A.; Formal analysis, X.A. and Q.W.; Funding acquisition, X.A.; Methodology, J.W. and Y.Z.; Project administration, Y.Z. and H.Z.; Resources, H.Z.; Software, H.C.; Supervision, J.W.; Writing—original draft, W.X.; Writing—review & editing, S.Z. All authors have read and agreed to the published version of the manuscript.

Funding: This research was funded by Hunan Provincial Natural Science Foundation of China (NO.2019JJ50700) and Innovation Foundation of Aero Engine Corporation of China (NO.CXPT-2019-002).

Institutional Review Board Statement: Not applicable.

Informed Consent Statement: Not applicable.

Data Availability Statement: Not applicable.

Conflicts of Interest: The authors declare no conflict of interest.

References

1. Pei, H.; Wen, Z.; Wang, Z.; Gan, W.; Lu, G.X.; Yue, Z. Transient thermal fatigue crack propagation behavior of a nickel-based single-crystal superalloy. *Int. J. Fatigue* **2020**, *131*, 105303. [CrossRef]
2. Zhang, Y.; Wen, Z.; Pei, H.; Gan, W.; Yue, Z. Equivalent and Simplification of Nickel-Based Superalloy Plates with Close-Packed Film Cooling Holes. *J. Mech.* **2019**, *35*, 359–372. [CrossRef]
3. Sun, X.F.; Jin, T.; Zhou, Y.Z.; Hu, Z.Q. Research Progress of Nickel-Base Single Crystal Superalloys. *Mater. China* **2012**, *31*, 1–11.
4. Prastiti, N.G.; Xu, Y.; Balint, D.S.; Dunne, F.P.E. Discrete dislocation, crystal plasticity and experimental studies of fatigue crack nucleation in single-crystal nickel. *Int. J. Plast.* **2020**, *126*, 102615. [CrossRef]
5. Karamitros, V.; Maclachlan, D.W.; Dunne, F.P.E. Mechanistic fatigue in Ni-based superalloy single crystals: A study of crack paths and growth rates. *J. Mech. Phys. Solids* **2022**, *158*, 104663. [CrossRef]
6. Gao, P.; Sun, S.; Li, H.; Niu, R.; Han, S.; Zong, H.; Wang, H.; Lian, J.; Liao, X. Ultra-strong and thermally stable nanocrystalline CrCoNi alloy. *J. Mater. Sci. Technol.* **2022**, *106*, 1–9. [CrossRef]
7. Lu, L.; Chen, X.; Huang, X.; Lu, K. Revealing the Maximum Strength in Nanotwinned Copper. *Science* **2009**, *323*, 607–610. [CrossRef]
8. Yang, F.M.; Sun, X.F.; Guan, H.R.; Hu, Z.Q. Low cycle fatigue behavior of K40s cobalt-base superalloy at elevated temperature. *Acta Metall. Sin.* **2002**, *38*, 1047–1105.
9. Hou, N.X.; Yu, Q.M.; Wen, Z.X.; Yue, Z.F. Low cycle fatigue behavior of single crystal superalloy with temperature gradient. *Eur. J. Mech. A/Solids* **2010**, *29*, 611–618. [CrossRef]
10. Gu, Y.; Wen, W.; Cui, H. Prediction of fretting fatigue life of dovetail joint under high-cycle and low-cycle load. *J. Propuls. Technol.* **2008**, *29*, 240–243.
11. Balint, D.S.; Deshpande, V.S.; Needleman, A.; Giessen, E.V.D. Size effects in uniaxial deformation of single and polycrystals: A discrete dislocation plasticity analysis. *Model. Simul. Mater. Sci. Eng.* **2006**, *14*, 409–422. [CrossRef]
12. Ruebeling, F.; Xu, Y.; Richter, G.; Dini, D.; Gumbsch, P.; Greiner, C. Normal Load and Counter Body Size Influence the Initiation of Microstructural Discontinuities in Copper during Sliding. *ACS Appl. Mater. Interfaces* **2021**, *13*, 4750–4760. [CrossRef] [PubMed]
13. Xu, Y.; Gu, T.; Xian, J.; Giuliani, F.; Ben Britton, T.; Gourlay, C.M.; Dunne, F.P.E. Intermetallic size and morphology effects on creep rate of Sn-3Ag-0.5Cu solder. *Int. J. Plast.* **2021**, *137*, 102904. [CrossRef]
14. Shi, H.; Ma, X.; Yu, T. Some new progresses on the research of creep and fatigue behaviors of high temperature structural materials. *Chin. J. Solid Mech.* **2010**, *31*, 696–715.
15. Rao, S. Analysis of High-Temperature Creep of Aeroengines. *Aircr. Engine* **2004**, *30*, 10–13.
16. Yue, Q.; Liu, L.; Yang, W.; Huang, T.; Sun, D.; Huo, M.; Zhang, J.; Fu, H. Research Progress of Creep Behaviors in Advanced Ni-based Single Crystal Superalloys. *Mater. Rep.* **2019**, *33*, 479–489.
17. Cao, J.; Wang, Y.; Shi, D. A rafting model for creep of Ni base single crystal at high temperature based on microstructure cell. *J. Aerosp. Power* **2009**, *24*, 1691–1698.
18. Pollock, T.M.; Argon, A.S. Directional coarsening in nickel-base single crystals with high volume fractions of coherent precipitates. *Acta Metall. Mater.* **1994**, *42*, 1859–1874. [CrossRef]
19. Zhao, B.; Liu, G.; Hong, X. Study on high-temperature creep behavior of nickel-base single crystal supper alloy. *Die Mould. Technol.* **2017**, *2*, 9–12.

20. Peng, Z. Direction coarsening of γ' precipitates in a single crystal nickel base superalloy. *Acta Metall. Sin.* **1995**, *31*, 531–536.
21. Pearson, D.D.; Lemkey, F.D.; Kear, B.H. Stress Coarsening of γ' and Its Influence on Creep Properties of a Single Crystal Superalloy. *Superalloys* **1980**, 513–520.
22. Wu, W.; Guo, Y.; Wang, Y. Research progress on the directional coarsening behavior and high temperature creep mechanical properties in Ni-base superalloys. *Adv. Mech.* **2011**, *41*, 172–186.
23. Wang, K.; Li, J.; Cao, C. Present Situation of Study on Creep Behavior of Single Crystal Superalloys. *Mater. Eng.* **2004**, *1*, 3–7.
24. Henderson, P.J.; Mclean, M. Microstructural contributions to friction stress and recovery kinetics during creep of the nickel-base superalloy IN738LC. *Acta Metall.* **1983**, *31*, 1203–1219. [CrossRef]
25. Matan, N.; Cox, D.C.; Carter, P.; Rist, M.A.; Rae, C.M.F.; Reed, R.C. Creep of CMSX-4 superalloy single crystals: Effects of misorientation and temperature. *Acta Mater.* **1999**, *47*, 1549–1563. [CrossRef]
26. Wu, R.; Sandfeld, S. A dislocation dynamics-assisted phase field model for Nickel-based superalloys: The role of initial dislocation density and external stress during creep. *J. Alloys Compd.* **2017**, *703*, 389–395. [CrossRef]
27. Sass, V.; Glatzel, U.; Feller-Kniepmeier, M. Creep Anisotropy in the Monocrystalline Nickel-Base Superalloy CMSX-4. *Superalloys* **1996**, *96*, 283–290.
28. Han, G.M.; Yu, J.J.; Hu, Z.Q.; Sun, X.F. Creep property and microstructure evolution of a nickel-base single crystal superalloy in [011] orientation. *Mater. Charact.* **2013**, *86*, 177–184. [CrossRef]
29. Jacome, L.A.; Nörtershäuser, P.; Somsen, C.; Dlouhý, A.; Eggeler, G. On the nature of γ' phase cutting and its effect on high temperature and low stress creep anisotropy of Ni-base single crystal superalloys. *Acta Mater.* **2014**, *69*, 246–264. [CrossRef]
30. Yu, H.; Su, Y.; Tian, N.; Tian, S.; Li, Y.; Yu, X.; Yu, L. Microstructure evolution and creep behavior of a [111] oriented single crystal nickel-based superalloy during tensile creep. *Mater. Sci. Eng. A* **2013**, *565*, 292–300. [CrossRef]

MDPI AG
Grosspeteranlage 5
4052 Basel
Switzerland
Tel.: +41 61 683 77 34

Crystals Editorial Office
E-mail: crystals@mdpi.com
www.mdpi.com/journal/crystals

www.ingramcontent.com/pod-product-compliance
Lightning Source LLC
Chambersburg PA
CBHW062047220926
51850CB00010B/2691

* 9 7 8 3 7 2 5 8 5 2 0 7 9 *